Contents

Introduction

GCSE Science: Single Award for CCEA Foundation and Higher Tier has been specially written to cover the CCEA specification GCSE Science: Single Award.

It provides the essential information and develops the understanding and skills required for students to fulfil their potential and successfully complete the course.

This book includes recent changes to the specification and fully reflects the revised specification.

It is presented in the order: biology, chemistry and physics and closely follows the order of the specification. Higher Tier content is colour coded with a red tint to make it easy for teachers and students to identify the content only required for the Higher Tier examinations.

The book is written in a style particularly suitable for students entered for CCEA Science: Single Award and includes photographs and diagrams to aid understanding.

- *Definition* boxes and text box style *Notes* accompany the text at regular intervals to clarify key concepts and highlight key points
- *Test yourself* questions appear throughout each chapter to encourage reflection and reinforce learning.

The 'end of chapter' *Exam questions* are taken mainly from recent revised specification CCEA GCSE Science: Single Award examinations, making them appropriately contemporary. Many are of a data handling nature, ensuring that the questions included in this book fully reflect the style of questions used in the current examinations.

Answers to the 'Test yourself' questions and past paper Exam questions can be found at www.hodderplus.co.uk/cceagcsescienceSingleAward

Food and energy

LEARNING OBJECTIVES

By the end of this chapter you should know and understand:

- **the different food types in the human diet**
- **how to carry out a food test**
- **respiration – using food to make energy**
- **energy needs and ways of comparing amounts of energy in different foods**
- **the link between diet and health**
- **photosynthesis and photosynthesis experiments**
- **energy flow through food chains and food webs.**

Definition

A food **type** is a food group or class – do not confuse with example.

▶ Food types

We all know that we need food to keep us alive. But do we know about all the important things that we need from food?

Table 1.1 shows the main food types that we need to keep us healthy.

Table 1.1 Food types

Food type	Role in body	Examples
carbohydrate – starch	to provide slow-release energy	potato bread
carbohydrate – sugars	to provide fast-release energy	cake biscuits
protein	for growth and repair of body cells	fish beans
fat	to provide a lot of energy, can be used as an energy store	sausages butter
vitamin C	to keep the body in good working order, particularly teeth and gums	oranges lemons
vitamin D	important for normal growth of bones and teeth	fish milk
calcium (mineral)	important for normal growth of bones and teeth	milk cheese
iron (mineral)	to help the red blood cells carry oxygen	red meat spinach
water	needed as: • a solvent and for reactions that cannot take place without water • a transport medium, e.g. blood	
fibre	needed to prevent constipation and help protect against bowel cancer	wholemeal bread green vegetables

▶ Food tests

There are various tests that you can use to identify food types that are present.

The tests you need to know about are described in Table 1.2.

Table 1.2 Food tests

Food type	Name of test	Method	Positive result (what happens if the food type is present)
starch	starch test	add iodine	iodine turns from yellow-brown to blue-black
sugar	Benedict's test	add Benedict's solution and heat carefully in a water bath (Figure 1.1)	• the solution changes from a blue colour to a brick-red colour • a green or orange final colour shows that only a small amount of sugar is present
protein	Biuret test	add sodium hydroxide, add a few drops of copper sulfate, then shake	the solution turns from a blue colour to a purple, mauve or lilac colour
fat	emulsion test	shake the fat with alcohol in a boiling tube then add an equal volume of water	a cloudy white precipitate is formed

Note

These food tests show which food types are present but they do not really show how much is present. The Benedict's test is an exception.

Notes

• Oxygen is needed to help convert the sugar (glucose) into energy.
• Carbon dioxide and water are produced as waste products.
• Starch and fat must be converted into glucose before they can be used as an energy source – this is why they are slow-release energy sources.

Test yourself 1

Suggest why a shortage of iron in the diet can lead to a shortage of energy. (You will need to refer to both Table 1.1 and the section on respiration.)

You should be able to carry out a food test on a food sample to find out which food types are present. To do this you need to carry out each food test on a small piece of the sample. It is possible that the unknown food could contain more than one food type. For example, a piece of bacon will contain both protein and fat.

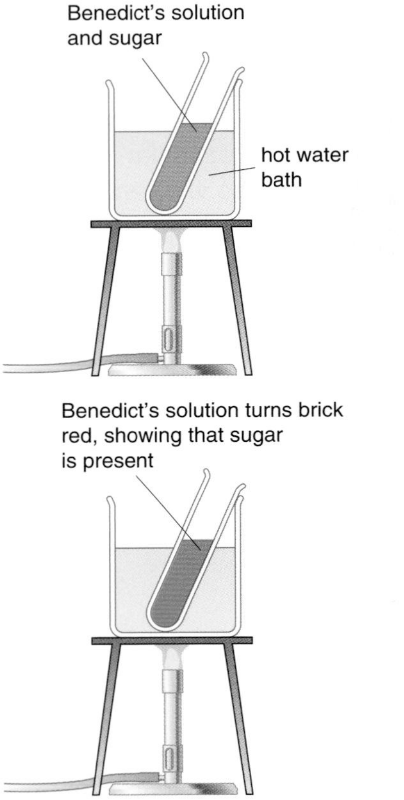

▶ Respiration – using food to make energy

Table 1.1 shows that carbohydrate and fat provide (chemical) energy. But how does the body use the food to make energy? The process of **respiration** does this.

Word equation for respiration:

glucose + oxygen → carbon dioxide + water + energy

▶ Comparing the energy content in different foods

The food tests mentioned in Table 1.2 show the food types that are present. It is also possible to compare the energy content of different foods.

Benedict's solution and sugar

hot water bath

Benedict's solution turns brick red, showing that sugar is present

Figure 1.1 Testing with Benedict's solution

Set up the apparatus as shown in Figure 1.2 and use a range of food types such as crisps, dried pasta and so on. Ignite each type in turn and measure the increase in temperature of the water for each food used.

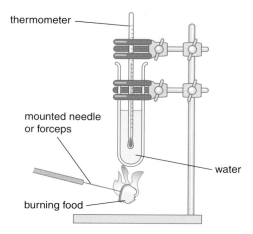

Figure 1.2 Measuring the energy content of food

To make sure the results are **valid**, and to give a fair test, always:

- use the same amount or size of each food
- hold the burning food the same distance from the boiling tube
- use the same amount of water.

Some energy will be:

- lost to the air
- used in heating the glass
- left in the remains of the food.

▶ How much energy do we need?

Different people need different amounts of energy.

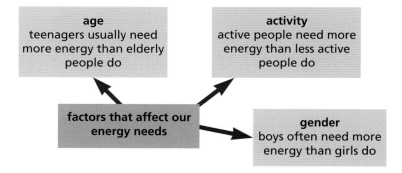

You should understand that the factors are often interlinked. For example, teenagers usually need more energy than elderly people do because they are more active.

There are exceptions, for example, some girls may be more active than some of the boys in the same class and therefore they need more energy.

▶ Diet and health

A poor diet can lead to ill health. Coronary heart disease (CHD), which kills many people in Northern Ireland, is often linked to a poor diet.

How heart attacks happen

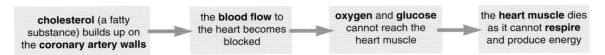

| cholesterol (a fatty substance) builds up on the **coronary artery walls** | → | the **blood flow** to the heart becomes blocked | → | **oxygen** and **glucose** cannot reach the heart muscle | → | the **heart muscle** dies as it cannot **respire** and produce energy |

> **Definition**
>
> In **coronary heart disease** it is the coronary arteries (the arteries that bring blood to the heart) that are damaged.

There are many factors that contribute to heart disease. There are therefore many things we can do to reduce our chances of getting heart disease. These factors can be grouped into **lifestyle** factors and **dietary** factors.

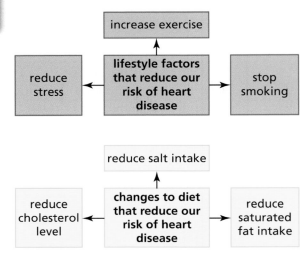

Figure 1.3 The link between lifestyle, dietary factors and heart disease

However, it is very hard to convince some people that there is a link between lifestyle and heart disease.

Strokes affect the **brain**. People who have strokes may become partially paralysed as parts of the brain stop working. There is an association between CHD and poor diet. This is also an important factor in the development of strokes. In general, the lifestyle changes and dietary changes listed in the diagram above also protect against strokes.

The costs of circulatory diseases

Strokes and heart disease are both **circulatory diseases**. They affect much more than just the patient involved.

> **Definition**
>
> **Circulatory diseases** affect the heart or the blood vessels.

Whole families are affected as patients are often very ill and need a lot of care. Heart disease and stroke patients are often unable to work for a long time.

Heart disease and strokes are very expensive to treat because:

* patients are often in hospital for a long time
* expensive drugs and medicines are often needed
* many highly-trained staff are needed to care for the patients.

The effect of exercise on heart rate and recovery rate

We can help our heart by taking regular exercise. The graph in Figure 1.4 shows the effect of exercise on heart rate and **recovery rate**.

The recovery rate is the time it takes for the pulse or heart rate to return to normal. This will usually be shorter for people who exercise regularly or play a lot of sport.

You should also know why exercise causes the heart rate to rise. When we exercise we need more energy. The heart has to pump more blood to our muscles so that they get more oxygen and glucose for respiration.

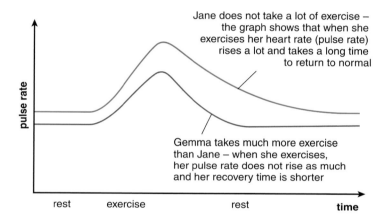

Jane does not take a lot of exercise – the graph shows that when she exercises her heart rate (pulse rate) rises a lot and takes a long time to return to normal

Gemma takes much more exercise than Jane – when she exercises, her pulse rate does not rise as much and her recovery time is shorter

Figure 1.4 The effect of exercise on heart rate

> **Definition**
>
> The heart's **output** is the volume of blood pumped over a certain period of time (e.g. one minute).

Regular exercise also strengthens the heart muscle (as it does any muscle). A stronger heart muscle can increase the heart's output, even when not exercising. The stronger muscle increases output by allowing the heart to pump more blood during each heart beat. An advantage of this is that the heart has to beat less often to pump the same amount of blood. If the heart pumps less often it will suffer less wear and tear.

Other health problems

Apart from circulatory disease, there are some other health problems associated with food. These are summarised in Table 1.3.

Table 1.3 Health problems associated with food

Condition	Description
anorexia	• reducing the amount of food eaten
	• people affected are usually young females and they lose a lot of weight
bulimia	• binge eating followed by self-induced vomiting or taking laxatives
	• again, this mainly affects young females and can lead to weight loss

Each of the eating disorders listed in the table has a strong psychological component. Treatment usually involves addressing the underlying issues that cause the eating disorders in the first place.

▶ Photosynthesis

Animals obtain their food by eating but plants make food by a different method.

Plants make food, in the form of glucose, by the process of **photosynthesis**. This process can be summarised in a word equation.

Word equation for photosynthesis:

carbon dioxide + water → glucose + oxygen

One way of showing that photosynthesis is taking place is to show that starch is being produced. The glucose that is produced during photosynthesis is usually converted to starch in the leaf for short-term storage. You can show that photosynthesis is taking place by carrying out the **starch test** on a leaf, as shown in Figure 1.5 and described in Table 1.4.

Table 1.4 The starch test

Step	What happens
1 remove a leaf from a plant and place it in boiling water	this will kill the leaf and stop any further reactions
2 boil the leaf in alcohol. (Do this in a water bath with the Bunsen burner turned off, because alcohol is flammable. Figure 1.5 shows how this is done.)	this removes the green chlorophyll from the leaf
3 dip the leaf in boiling water again	this makes the leaf soft and less brittle
4 spread the leaf on a white tile and add iodine solution	if starch is present the iodine will turn from yellow-brown to blue-black

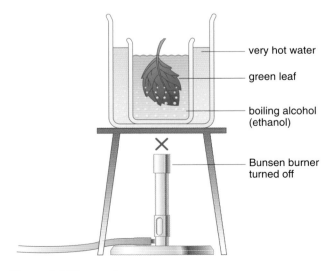

very hot water

green leaf

boiling alcohol (ethanol)

Bunsen burner turned off

Figure 1.5 The starch test

Notes

- Carbon dioxide and water are needed as raw materials for photosynthesis.
- Oxygen is produced as a waste product.
- The product glucose is often converted by plants into starch for storage.
- Light energy is needed for photosynthesis.
- **Chlorophyll**, the substance that makes plants green, is needed to trap the light energy in the plant's leaves.
- Photosynthesis is essential for life as it provides both food and oxygen for animals.

Showing that light is necessary for photosynthesis

Before carrying out experiments on photosynthesis it is important to destarch the plant. This means removing any starch that is already there before the experiment. To do this, place the plant in the dark for two days.

A leaf is then partially covered with foil as shown in Figure 1.6. The plant is kept in bright light and after a period of time is tested for starch as described on page 6.

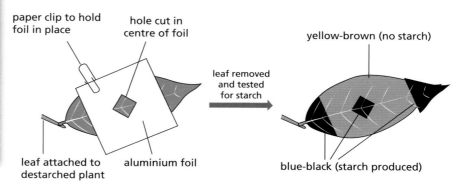

Figure 1.6 Experiment to show that light is required for photosynthesis to occur

The results show that starch is only produced in the parts of the leaf that received light. There was no starch produced in the parts of the leaf that did not receive light. This shows that light is needed for photosynthesis.

Showing that oxygen is produced

The apparatus in Figure 1.7 can be used to show that oxygen is produced during photosynthesis.

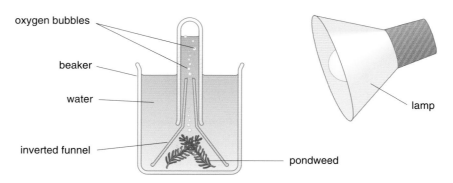

Figure 1.7 Experiment to show that oxygen is produced during photosynthesis

The rate of photosynthesis can be compared in different conditions by counting the number of bubbles produced in a set time.

The adaptations of palisade cells

Palisade cells are specialised cells found in a zone called the palisade layer, which is near the upper surface of a leaf. As most photosynthesis takes place in these cells, they are very well adapted for photosynthesis, as shown in Figure 1.8.

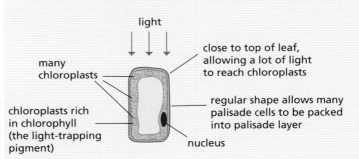

Figure 1.8 Adaptations of palisade cells

Test yourself 2

Use Figure 1.8 to describe **three** ways in which palisade cells are adapted to achieve maximum rates of photosynthesis.

► Food chains and food webs (the interdependence of living organisms)

Figure 1.9 shows a sequence of living organisms through which energy passes. It is an example of a **food chain**. Food chains show the feeding relationships and energy transfers between a number of organisms. The diagram also shows that the **Sun** is the primary (original) source of energy.

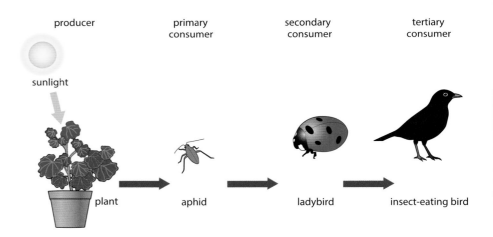

Figure 1.9 Energy and feeding relationships

Definition

Consumers are animals that feed on other living things.

This example shows that in a food chain the first organism is the **producer**. The producer provides the food and energy for the primary consumer (and other animals in the food chain). The **primary consumer** is the animal that feeds on producers. A **secondary consumer** then feeds on primary consumers, and so on.

Give **one** reason why it is an advantage for animals to have more than one source of food.

State **two** ways in which the process of photosynthesis is necessary for animals to survive.

Food chains are very simplistic in that they do not show the range of different feeding relationships that usually exist. For example, very few animals have only one food source. **Food webs** show how a number of food chains are interlinked. Figure 1.10 shows a grassland food web.

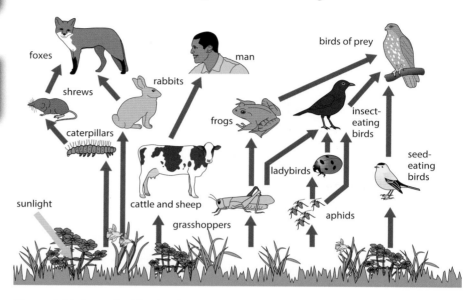

Figure 1.10 A grassland food web

▶ Exam questions

1 Shown below is Doreen who is investigating the amount of energy in different foods.

a State two things that have to be done to make this investigation valid (a fair test). *(2 marks)*

Doreen is given three foods labelled A, B and C to test. Her results are given below.

Food	Starting temperature/°C	Final temperature/°C	Temperature rise/°C
A	18	25	7
B	19	51	32
C	17	30	13

The three foods tested were: deep fried potato (chips); baked potato; boiled cabbage.

b Use the list to state which of the three foods was labelled B and explain your choice. *(2 marks)*

CCEA Science: Single Award, Unit 1, Foundation Tier, November 2012, Q4

2 a Given below are some eating disorders and the effect they have.

i Copy the text and use lines to link each disorder with one effect it has on sufferers. *(2 marks)*

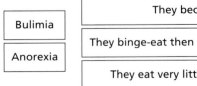

Eating disorder

Bulimia

Anorexia

Effect on sufferers

They become obese

They binge-eat then make themselves vomit

They eat very little and become thin

ii Modelling is a job that has a higher than average number of people who suffer from eating disorders. Suggest a reason for this. *(1 mark)*

iii Apart from modelling suggest another job that may have a high number of people with eating disorders. *(1 mark)*

b The table below shows the amount of fat in four types of fish.

Type	Fat/g
haddock	8
sardines	14
kippers	11
cod	1

i On a copy of the grid below:
1 complete the scaling for the *y* axis.
2 draw a bar chart for the information. *(3 marks)*

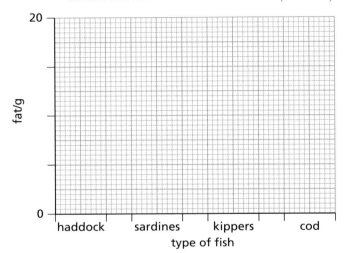

ii Name the type of fish someone should eat if they are trying to lose weight. Explain your choice. *(2 marks)*

CCEA Science: Single Award, Unit 1, Foundation Tier, March 2012, Q2

3 a The following graph shows the effect of exercise on Tracey's heart rate.

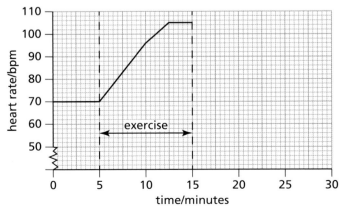

i Tracey stopped exercising at 15 minutes and her heart rate steadily returned to her resting rate in 5 minutes.

Copy and complete the graph to show Tracey's heart rate between 15 and 30 minutes. *(2 marks)*

ii Calculate the increase in Tracey's heart rate during exercise (in bpm). *(1 mark)*

iii Calculate the percentage increase in Tracey's heart rate during exercise. *(1 mark)*

iv Explain fully why Tracey's heart rate increased during exercise. *(3 marks)*

b The following table shows the average cholesterol levels for men and women in various age groups.

Age	Average cholesterol level/arbitrary units	
	Men	Women
15–24	4.2	4.1
25–34	5.2	4.8
35–44	5.5	5.1
45–54	5.9	5.8
55–64	6.5	6.3

Give two trends shown by the information in the table. *(2 marks)*

c Give two lifestyle changes that can help reduce heart disease. *(2 marks)*

CCEA Science: Single Award, Unit 1, Foundation Tier, March 2013, Q6

4 Shown below is a food chain but it is not complete because the arrows are missing.

| grass | rabbit | fox |

a **i** Copy and complete the food chain by adding the arrows. *(1 mark)*

ii What do the arrows in a food chain show? *(1 mark)*

iii Name the producer in this food chain. *(1 mark)*

iv What is the source of energy for all food chains? *(1 mark)*

b The table below shows the number of rabbits and foxes in a forest over a period of three years.

	Year		
	1st	2nd	3rd
rabbits	200	300	600
foxes	4	2	0

Explain how the drop in the number of foxes may have caused the rise in the number of rabbits. *(2 marks)*

CCEA Science: Single Award, Unit 1, Foundation Tier, March 2012, Q1

5 **a** Below is a picture of bread and popcorn.

Describe an experiment to find which of these foods contains the most energy. All common laboratory equipment including thermometers and boiling tubes is available. Your answer should include how you make your results valid (fair test) and also reliable.

In this question you will be assessed on your written communication skills including the use of scientific terms. *(6 marks)*

b A doctor has to decide which of three different brands of iron supplements (A, B or C) to prescribe to his patients. He collected facts about each brand and the table below shows his findings.

Key: High = 3; Low = 1

Brand	Number of side effects	Swallowing problems	Cost per unit
A	3	3	2
B	3	2	3
C	2	1	3

i Analyse the facts for each brand and state which one he should prescribe. Referring to each brand, fully explain your choice. *(3 marks)*

ii Suggest one other fact about each brand that he should consider before making his decision. *(1 mark)*

CCEA Science: Single Award, Unit 1, Foundation Tier, March 2012, Q7

2 Chromosomes and genes

LEARNING OBJECTIVES

By the end of this chapter you should know and understand:

- about chromosomes, genes and **DNA**
- the link between **DNA**, amino acids and protein
- about the discovery of **DNA**
- how to carry out genetic crosses
- about inherited diseases and the ethical issues they raise
- about sexual and asexual reproduction
- about **GM crops**.

▶ Chromosomes, genes and DNA

Most living cells contain a **nucleus** or control centre. The nucleus is the control centre because it contains **chromosomes** that are subdivided into smaller sections called **genes** (Figure 2.1).

The genes in your body control characteristics such as eye and hair colour. In fact, they control all the features that make us what we are.

> **Definition**
>
> A **cell** is the basic unit of a living organism. All living organisms are made up of cells – similar to bricks in a house.

> _Note_
>
> It might be easier to remember the diagram of DNA if you think of a ladder with interlinking rungs that is twisted along its length.

cell

chromosome

nucleus

each chromosome is divided into many genes

Figure 2.1 Structure of a cell

Chromosomes and genes are made of **deoxyribonucleic acid**, commonly called **DNA**. This is a very important chemical with special properties. The DNA molecule is formed in a **double helix** with the two strands being linked, as shown in Figure 2.2.

Figure 2.2 A section of the DNA double helix

DNA consists of three sub-units that are regularly repeated throughout the length of the molecule. These sub-units are **deoxyribose sugar**, **phosphate** and **bases**. There are four different types of base: **adenine**, **guanine**, **cytosine** and **thymine**. In the double helix the rungs of the 'ladder' are the bases and the sides are alternating units of deoxyribose sugar and phosphate.

Each repeating unit of DNA, consisting of a **phosphate**, a **sugar** and a **base**, is called a **nucleotide**. Figure 2.3 shows that bases link the two sides of the molecule together in such a way that adenine only pairs with thymine and guanine only pairs with cytosine. This arrangement is known as **base pairing**. The arrangement of the bases along the length of the DNA is what determines how a gene works.

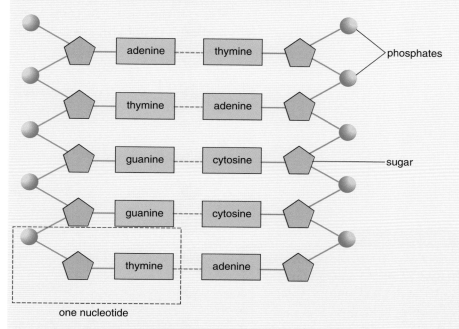

Figure 2.3 Base pairing in DNA

It is possible to map the arrangement of bases along an individual's chromosomes. We then find that, while there are similarities among different individuals, no two people have the same sequence of bases along the entire length of all their chromosomes (except for identical twins!).

How does DNA work?

DNA works by providing a code to allow the cell to make the proteins it needs. The DNA determines which proteins and, in particular, which enzymes are made. Enzymes are extremely important proteins that control the cell's reactions. Therefore, by controlling the enzymes, DNA controls the development of the cell and in turn the entire organism.

The bases along one side of the DNA molecule – the coding strand – form the genetic code. Each sequence of three bases (a triplet) along this coding strand codes for a particular amino acid – the building blocks of proteins. The sequence of three bases that codes for an amino acid is called a **base triplet**. As a protein consists of many amino acids linked together, it is important that the correct base triplets are arranged in the correct sequence along the coding strand. Figure 2.4 shows how base triplets code for particular amino acids. In Figure 2.4 the first and fourth base triplets have the same code and this means that the first and fourth amino acids are also the same. The model only shows a small section of a gene and a small section of the protein that it codes for.

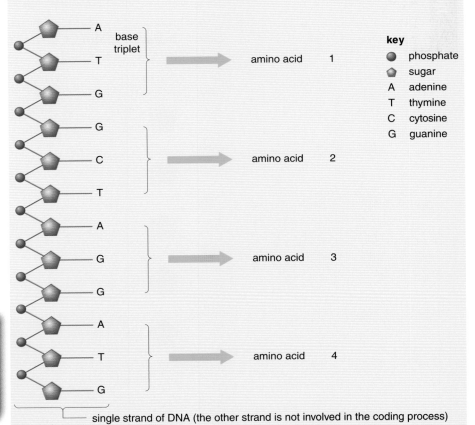

key
- ● phosphate
- ⬠ sugar
- A adenine
- T thymine
- C cytosine
- G guanine

single strand of DNA (the other strand is not involved in the coding process)

Figure 2.4 How base triplets code for amino acids

Test yourself 1

Use Figure 2.4 to work out the length of DNA required (in number of bases on the coding strand) to code for a protein consisting of 177 amino acids.

Building the theory – working out the structure of DNA

As you can see from the earlier figures, DNA is a very complex molecule. A lot of expertise and hard work was required in working out its structure. By the early 1950s scientists had worked out that DNA was the molecule that determined how organisms developed – they just didn't know its structure!

In 1950 Erwin Chargaff discovered that although the arrangement of bases in DNA varied, there was always an equal amount of adenine and thymine. Similarly there was always an equal amount of guanine and cytosine.

Test yourself 2

Explain Chargaff's observations.

The next part of the DNA jigsaw was put in place by Rosalind Franklin and Maurice Wilkins, who were research scientists working at

King's College, London. They used a process called X-ray diffraction (crystallography). In X-ray diffraction, beams of X-rays are fired into molecules of DNA. The way in which the DNA scatters the X-rays provides information about its three-dimensional structure. Franklin and Wilkins were able to work out the overall shape of DNA but they were not able to confirm exactly how the sub-units were linked together.

The last part of the puzzle was solved by James Watson and Francis Crick at Cambridge University in 1953. They were able to build on the work of the previous scientists to deduce how the bases were arranged and also to conclude that the DNA molecule is arranged as a double helix. They did this through the process of modelling.

> **Modelling** is using models – in this case standard scientific equipment (see photograph) – to represent a structure.
>
> *Definition*

Figure 2.5 Watson and Crick with their model of DNA

Figure 2.6 Model of DNA

The discovery of the structure of DNA is typical of many scientific discoveries in that theories are often built up in stages, with many scientists laying the foundations before the final details are worked out. This demonstrates the **collaborative nature of science** and also **how scientific knowledge is built up in stages**. New scientific discoveries must be validated by other scientists or experts in the field before they can be accepted by the scientific community. This is the process of **peer review** and is an important part of the scientific process.

▶ Genetics

The science of **genetics** explains how characteristics pass from parents to offspring. Figure 2.7 shows that:

- chromosomes are arranged in **pairs** – humans have 23 pairs, which is 46 chromosomes in total
- **genes** are sections of the chromosome that carry the code for particular characteristics such as eye colour
- **similar genes occupy the same position** on both chromosomes in a pair

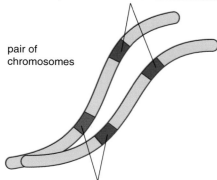

the form of gene (allele), e.g. for the presence of ear lobes, is the same in both chromosomes

pair of chromosomes

the alleles of the gene are different, e.g. one for brown eyes and one for blue eyes

Figure 2.7 Chromosomes and genes

- genes exist in different forms, called **alleles**, and the alleles may be **homozygous** (the same) or **heterozygous** (different) on the two chromosomes of a pair.

Some key genetic terms are summarised in Table 2.1.

Table 2.1 Key genetic terms I

Term	Definition	Example
gene	short section of chromosome that carries code for a particular characteristic	gene for eye colour
allele	a particular form of a gene	brown eyes and blue eyes are due to different alleles of the eye-colour gene
homozygous	both alleles of a gene are the same	both alleles are for brown eyes
heterozygous	the alleles of a gene are different	one allele is for brown eyes and the other is for blue eyes – see Figure 2.7

Questions about genetics normally ask you to work out which offspring or children would result from particular parents. Sometimes you may be asked to work backwards and work out the parents.

Note

It is common practice to use the same letter for both the dominant and recessive alleles, with the dominant allele shown as the capital and the recessive allele written in lower case.

Genetic diagrams (cross diagrams)

When you are asked to work out the offspring produced from, for example, two heterozygous parents, it is useful to set out a diagram called a **genetic diagram** or **cross**. Figure 2.8 shows a cross using the example of height in peas. Peas can be either tall or short and this is controlled by a single gene that has a tall allele and a short allele. In this example, the gene is for height and tall and short are the two alleles of the height gene.

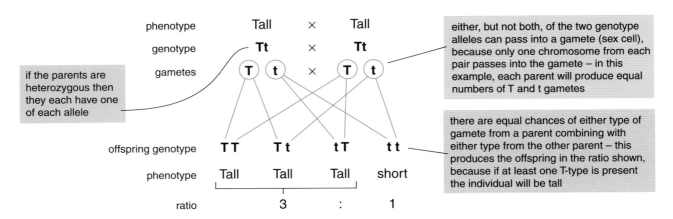

Figure 2.8 Tall and short peas

Table 2.2 explains some new terms that you will need to know. Some of these important terms are used in the genetic diagram (Figure 2.8).

Table 2.2 Key genetic terms 2

Term	Definition	Example
gamete	sex cell that contains only one chromosome from each pair	sperm or egg
genotype	the paired symbols showing the allele arrangement in an individual	the parents in the cross in Figure 2.8 both have the genotype Tt
phenotype	the outward appearance of an individual	the parents in the example have a tall phenotype
dominant	in the heterozygous condition the dominant allele will override the non-dominant (recessive) allele	the parents in the example are both tall even though they are heterozygous and have a short allele
recessive	the recessive allele will be dominated by the dominant allele – it will only show itself in the phenotype if there are two recessive alleles	only ¼ of the offspring in the cross are short, as only ¼ have no dominant T allele present (Figure 2.8)

The cross in Figure 2.9 shows how to use a **Punnett square**. This is a way of setting out a genetic cross in table format. In this example, using height in peas as before, a heterozygous pea (Tt) is crossed with a homozygous recessive pea (tt).

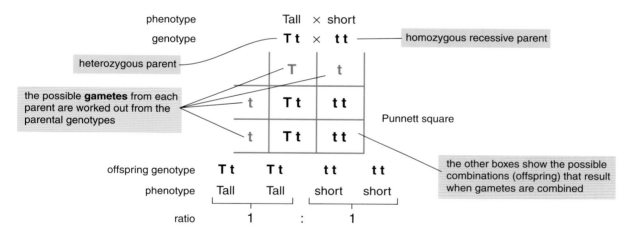

Figure 2.9 A Punnett square for tall and short peas

Pedigree diagrams

A pedigree diagram shows the way in which a genetic condition is inherited in a family or group of biologically related people. Figure 2.10 is an example of a pedigree diagram showing how the condition albinism is inherited. Albinism is a condition caused by a recessive allele.

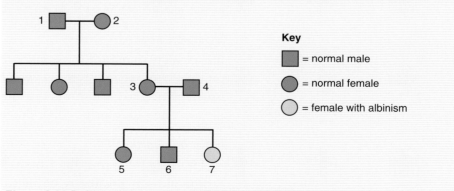

Figure 2.10 Pedigree diagram showing inheritance of albinism

In Figure 2.10 one of the grandchildren (7) has albinism. It is possible to use the information provided to work out the probability of other children having the condition. Genetic counsellors often construct pedigree diagrams and use them to advise parents who have a genetic condition or who may be carriers (heterozygous).

Pedigree diagrams can be used in any type of genetic cross but they are obviously very valuable in tracing and predicting harmful genetic conditions.

▶ Inherited diseases

Some medical conditions and diseases can be **inherited**, e.g. albinism, the inheritance of which we have just investigated. This means they are passed on genetically from parents to offspring. Another example is **cystic fibrosis**.

Cystic fibrosis

Cystic fibrosis is a condition that causes problems with breathing and with the digestion of food. The **cystic fibrosis allele** is **recessive** so children born with the condition must have received two recessive alleles (Figure 2.11). Normally, the parents of a child with cystic fibrosis do not have the condition themselves but each carries one allele for it – they are heterozygous. The parents are referred to as **carriers**.

Test yourself 3

Use Figure 2.10 and your knowledge to answer the following questions. Let A = normal allele; a = albinism allele.

(a) What is the genotype of the child (7) with albinism?

(b) What are the genotypes of the parents of child 7 (3 and 4)?

(c) What are the possible genotypes for the brother and sister of the child with albinism (5 and 6)? Explain your answer.

(d) What is the probability that the next child of these parents will be a child with albinism?

(e) What can you say about the genotypes of the grandparents of child 7?

Definition

Inherited diseases are caused by having particular alleles that are passed down from parents.

Definition

Carriers have a normal phenotype but a heterozygous genotype.

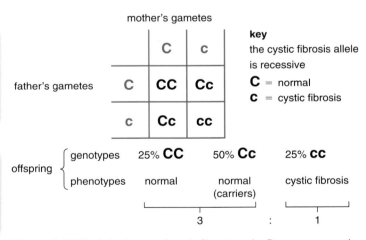

Figure 2.11 The inheritance of cystic fibrosis – the Punnett square shows a cross between parents who do not have cystic fibrosis but who carry the allele

Some ethical issues

It is possible to test for some inherited conditions by carrying out tests on the foetus when it is in the womb. This type of test raises many ethical issues, particularly if it shows that the baby will be born with an inherited disease. The issues surrounding the test include the arguments below.

Have an abortion?

- This may be against the parents' religion or principles.
- It denies the possibility of life to an unborn child who has no choice in the decision.

If no abortion?

- A child may be born who will have a poor quality of life.
- The child may require so much attention that there is less time to care for others in the family.

Genetic screening

Genetic screening may be used to reduce the incidence of diseases or conditions caused by problems with our chromosomes or genes. It involves testing people for the presence of a particular allele or genetic condition. Whole populations can be tested, or targeted groups where the probability of having (or passing on) a particular condition is high. Genetic screening can be a particular issue for pregnant mothers and their partners.

Genetic screening has been available for a long time for **Down syndrome**. In screening for Down syndrome, cells can be taken from the amniotic fluid surrounding the baby in the womb and allowed to multiply in laboratory conditions. The chromosomes in the cells can then be examined to see if the developing foetus has the condition (an **amniocentesis test**). This genetic screening is offered to pregnant women in Britain but it is probably more important for older mothers. Genetic screening is also available for cystic fibrosis. Clearly mothers who know that they and/or their partners are carriers for cystic fibrosis also have to consider the potential implications before becoming pregnant.

> **Definition**
>
> **Down syndrome** is a relatively common condition caused by having 47 (rather than 46) chromosomes.

> **Definition**
>
> **Amniocentesis** is testing the fluid (amniotic fluid) surrounding the foetus. This will normally contain foetal cells that can be examined for abnormalities.

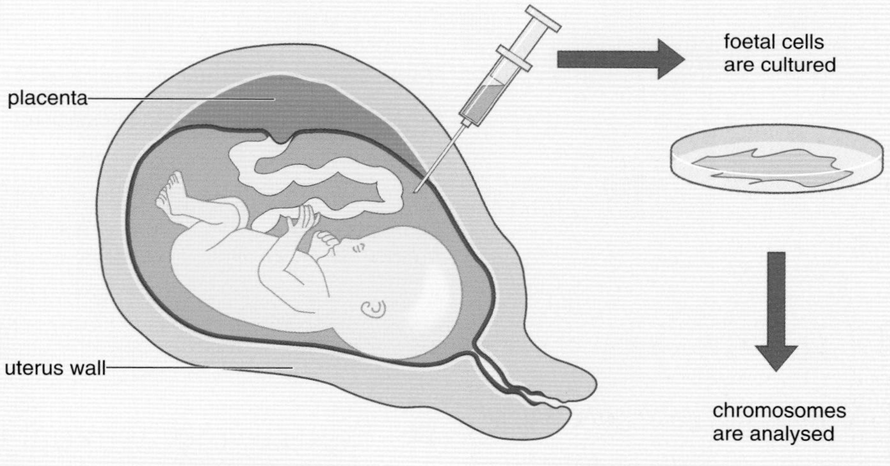

placenta

foetal cells are cultured

uterus wall

chromosomes are analysed

Figure 2.12 An amniocentesis test

Genetic screening – the ethical issues

What are the options if genetic screening shows that a foetus has a condition such as Down syndrome? Should the mother have an abortion? The results of genetic screening and even being a carrier of a genetic condition can create considerable dilemmas for the individuals involved.

This is a good topic to discuss in a class debate. Some of the issues are:

- The ethics of abortion for medical reasons.
- Is there an acceptable risk associated with genetic screening? For example, amniocentesis for Down syndrome screening has a small risk of miscarriage.

- Should parents be allowed free choice whether to screen or not?
- Should you be allowed to screen for the sex of a child? What if it is not the sex you want?

It will soon be possible to screen everyone (whether before birth, in childhood or as an adult) for many different alleles. The information obtained is referred to as a **genetic profile**. Should this information be available to life insurance companies and employers? If insurers had this information they may not provide insurance, or they may make it more expensive for someone with a genetic condition.

- Costs of screening compared to costs of treating individuals with a genetic condition – should cost be a factor?
- Should genetic screening be extended to more than just serious genetic conditions? What if it can predict life expectancy?

Gene therapy is a technique that can be used to try to treat some inherited diseases. The general idea is that the 'normal' genes can be added to parts of the body affected by the inherited disease. These genes will then make the body function normally.

Gene therapy has been used to treat cystic fibrosis with some success. The 'normal' genes can be sprayed into the lungs of patients with cystic fibrosis (the lungs are one of the areas most affected). The advantages and disadvantages of using gene therapy to treat cystic fibrosis are summarised in Table 2.3.

Table 2.3 Advantages and disadvantages of gene therapy for treating cystic fibrosis

Advantages	Disadvantages
improves lung function	only affects the parts of the body that the introduced genes can reach
patients can have a better quality of life	lung cells are rapidly replaced so the gene therapy process must be repeated regularly
	the harmful allele that causes cystic fibrosis is still passed on to the next generation

▶ Sexual and asexual reproduction

Sexual reproduction

Sexual reproduction occurs when the gametes from male and female parents combine to produce a new individual. Gametes have half the number of chromosomes that the other body cells have.

> **Definition**
>
> **Variation** is the difference between individuals.

| mother's gamete provides half the chromosomes (23 in humans) | new individual has a combination of mother's and father's chromosomes to make up the normal number (46 in humans)

as the number of possible chromosome combinations in the new individual is very large we can see that sexual reproduction produces **variation** – check this by observing the variation that exists between most siblings | father's gamete provides half the chromosomes (23 in humans) |

Definition

Not surprisingly, **asexual reproduction** is reproduction without sex. Examples include plants forming daughter bulbs, e.g. daffodils, or new plants from runners, e.g. strawberries.

Note

There are disadvantages with cloning and asexual reproduction. For example, if one individual is prone to a particular disease or has a genetic weakness then all the clones will be equally at risk.

Definition

Maize is another name for corn.

Definition

Bacteria are very simple, single-celled, microscopic organisms.

Definition

Vitamin A is a vitamin required for proper functioning of the eye.

Definition

Allergies are reactions to particular chemicals in the environment.

Test yourself 4

Suggest **two** reasons why some GM crops may be more expensive than normal varieties.

Asexual reproduction

In **asexual reproduction** only **one parent** is involved and the offspring are **genetically identical** to the parent. The offspring are called **clones**.

Genetically modified crops as an example of genetic engineering

Genetic engineering is the transfer of genes (DNA) from one type of organism (species) to another. GM crops are so called because genes from another organism have been incorporated into the plant's DNA for a particular purpose. For example, in GM **maize**, a gene from a type of **bacterium** has been added to the maize DNA. This transferred gene causes the maize to produce a type of protein that is harmful to any insect pests feeding on the maize. In effect, this makes the maize resistant to insect pests and the use of GM maize saves farmers a lot of money that would otherwise be spent on pesticides (chemicals sprayed to kill insects).

Some **advantages** of GM crops include:

- As explained in the example of GM maize, GM crops can **save money spent on pesticides** and **reduce pollution** (caused by excess pesticides entering the soil and waterways).
- GM crops can be produced that are **nutritionally enhanced**. For example, a form of GM rice ('golden rice') is being produced that is rich in a chemical needed to make **vitamin A**. Many people go blind in the developing world due to a shortage of vitamin A in their diets.
- GM crops can be produced that have a **greater ecological range** than the normal varieties. For example, some GM crops can grow on drier soils than the normal varieties can. This can lead to more food being produced – very important in many developing countries where there are often food shortages.

Arguments against GM crops include:

- They are not 'natural' (though one could argue that the domestication of animals for human use is not natural either).
- The GM genes could escape and affect non-targeted crops to produce 'super-weeds' (though very resistant weeds are capable of evolving irrespective of the use of GM crops).
- GM food could be more expensive.
- GM food can cause **allergies** (though non-GM food can already cause a wide range of allergies).

On balance, most scientists accept that GM crops offer huge benefits. GM crops are widely grown in the USA and many other countries, although they are banned in most of Europe. It is probably only a matter of time before their benefits are accepted in Europe and they become much more common.

▶ Exam questions

1 a The diagram shows how DNA codes for protein. Copy and complete the diagram by providing labels for layers 2 and 3.   *(2 marks)*

```
(1) DNA
(2)
(3)
(4) Protein
```

b State the name of the hypothesis which explains how DNA codes for proteins.   *(1 mark)*

CCEA Science: Single Award, Unit 1, Higher Tier, March 2012, Q9

2 a Rosalind Franklin and Maurice Wilkins collaborated to gain knowledge about the structure of DNA.

  i Explain the term 'collaborated'.   *(1 mark)*

  ii State what Franklin and Wilkins discovered about the structure of DNA and name the practical process they used.   *(2 marks)*

b i Name the two scientists who used modelling to investigate the structure of DNA. *(1 mark)*

  ii Erwin Chargaff also worked on the structure of DNA. Describe fully what he discovered.   *(2 marks)*

CCEA Science: Single Award, Unit 1, Higher Tier, November 2012, Q9

3 The flowers of a particular plant can be either red or white. When two plants with red flowers were crossed the following colours were produced.

	Red flowers	White flowers
number	150	50

a What is the ratio of red to white flowers?   *(1 mark)*

b i Copy and complete the genetic diagram below to explain the outcome of the cross above.   *(2 marks)*

		r
	Rr	

  ii Copy and complete the offspring genotypes and phenotypes for the cross above.

Genotypes: _____ Rr _____ _____ *(1 mark)*

Phenotypes: _____ red _____ _____

(1 mark)

CCEA Science: Single Award, Unit 1, Foundation Tier, March 2013, Q7

4 a The amniocentesis test shown below is an example of genetic screening.

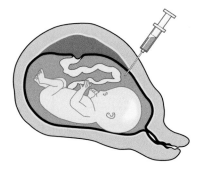

Some of the amniotic fluid is drawn up into the syringe and analysed in a laboratory.

  i Suggest what is in the amniotic fluid that is analysed during genetic screening.   *(2 marks)*

  ii Explain why amniocentesis testing may cause an increase in the number of people seeking abortions.   *(2 marks)*

b Life insurance companies have a financial interest in an individual's general health. Fully explain how and why someone with an inherited disease might be disadvantaged by these companies.   *(3 marks)*

CCEA Science: Single Award, Unit 1, Higher Tier, March 2012, Q5

5 a The following diagram shows part of a DNA molecule.

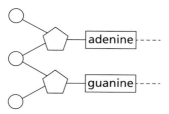

   i Copy and complete the diagram to show both strands of DNA. *(2 marks)*

   ii State what is meant by the unique nature of an individual's DNA. *(1 mark)*

b Cystic fibrosis (CF) is a condition caused by a mutation of a single gene that affects about 1 in 2500 babies. The foetus can be screened for CF but as the test has a small (2%) risk of miscarriage (loss of baby) it is usually only done when the condition is suspected. All newborn babies in the UK are tested for CF.

   i Use the information provided to explain fully why all foetuses are not screened for cystic fibrosis. *(2 marks)*

   ii Suggest one advantage of testing for cystic fibrosis in all newborn babies. *(1 mark)*

c Cystic fibrosis damages the lungs and the digestive system of those affected and can be treated by gene therapy. This involves spraying the normal alleles into the lungs using aerosols. The normal allele can pass into the lung cells that the spray reaches to give normal functioning in these cells. Use this information and your knowledge to explain fully why gene therapy is only partially successful in the long-term treatment of cystic fibrosis. *(3 marks)*

d Give one reason why most governments are not in favour of making genetic information available to insurance companies. *(1 mark)*

CCEA Science: Single Award, Unit 1, Higher Tier, March 2013, Q6

3 Nervous system and hormones

LEARNING OBJECTIVES

By the end of this chapter you should know and understand:

- the main features of the nervous system
- hormones
- phototropism
- the male and female reproductive systems and contraception
- diabetes.

▶ The nervous system

We are able to respond to the environment around us. Anything that we respond to is called a **stimulus**.

In animals, each type of stimulus affects a **receptor** in the body. There are many types of receptor, each responding to a particular type of stimulus. If a receptor is stimulated, it may cause an **effector** such as a muscle to produce a **response**.

| stimulus | → | receptor | → | effector | → | response |

Receptors are often found in sense organs. The main senses and their sense organs are listed in Table 3.1.

The flow chart above is a simplification as it suggests that any stimulation will automatically produce a response. In reality, if we hear a sound (the stimulus), we might respond or not, depending on what the sound is.

Table 3.1 Senses and sense organs

Sense	Sense organ
smell	nose
touch	skin
sight	eye
sound	ear
taste	tongue

Co-ordination

In reality the receptors and effectors (muscles) are linked by a co-ordinator. This is usually the **brain** but may also be the **spinal cord**. Together, these two structures make up the **central nervous system** (**CNS**).

> **Definition**
>
> The **CNS** (brain and spinal cord) ensures that nerve impulses (electrical signals) get from the right receptor (e.g. sense organ) to the right effector (e.g. muscle).

Nerve cells or **neurones** link the receptors and effectors to the co-ordinator. A neurone carries information in the form of small electrical charges called **nerve impulses**.

The CNS acts as a filter and determines which receptors link up with which effectors, and even whether or not a particular stimulus brings about a response.

A more complete flow diagram than the previous one looks like this.

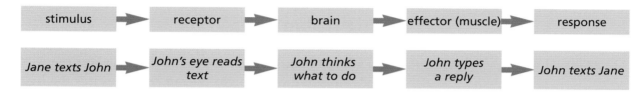

Voluntary and reflex actions

> **Definition**
>
> **Reflexes** are automatic and protective reactions that do not involve thinking time.

When the brain is involved in thinking about an action, as in the example above, this is called a **voluntary action**. Occasionally, we need to make very fast responses without thinking. This type of very rapid response is called a **reflex action**. It does not involve a conscious response from the brain.

Generally, nervous actions work rapidly and bring about reasonably rapid responses to a range of **stimuli**.

▶ Hormones

> **Definition**
>
> **Hormones** are chemical messengers that travel in the blood to a target organ where they act.

Another type of messenger system used by the body to bring about responses involves the use of special chemicals called **hormones**.

Hormones are produced by glands that release them into the blood. Although the hormones travel all round the body in the blood, they only affect certain organs, called **target organs**. The target organs differ for each hormone, although some hormones affect many organs.

Hormones usually act more **slowly** than the nervous system and act over a **longer period of time**.

Summarising the differences between the nervous system and hormones

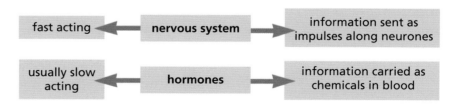

▶ Sensitivity in plants

Plants, like animals, respond to changes in the environment. However, they respond to fewer different types of stimuli and in general the response is slower. Plants respond to the environmental stimuli that have the greatest effect on their growth. Roots grow towards water when a moisture gradient exists. Shoots tend to grow away from the effects of gravity, i.e. they grow upwards. Reasons for these responses are fairly obvious as they ensure that plants react in such a way that they receive the best conditions for growth.

The response of a plant shoot to light is called **phototropism** and this response has been investigated in detail to establish how it occurs.

Phototropism – responding to light

Most of you will have observed that plants grow in the direction of a light source. Plants left on a windowsill or against the wall of a house usually do not grow straight up, but bend towards the light source. You can probably also guess that this response ensures that the plant stem and leaves receive *more* light than they otherwise would. This means that *more* photosynthesis takes place and there will be *more* growth.

It is easy to observe the effect of phototropism, but what causes it to occur? Figure 3.1 shows the growth of young seedlings in unilateral light (light coming from one side or source only). It highlights some of the features of phototropism. Can you use the diagram to identify what part of the plant perceives (is sensitive to) the light source?

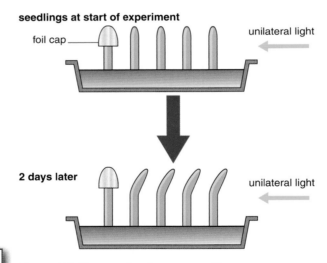

Figure 3.1 Phototropism in young seedlings

Figure 3.1 shows that it is the shoot tip that is sensitive to light, as when it is covered the phototropic response does not occur. Plant stems produce a hormone called **auxin** in the tip. When a stem is illuminated from one side this hormone tends to accumulate more on the non-illuminated side.

As the effect of auxin is increased growth, this leads to the non-illuminated side growing more rapidly than the side that is receiving more light. The non-illuminated side therefore grows more than the other side, leading to the stem bending in the direction of the light.

Test yourself 1

Using your knowledge of phototropism, explain the following:

(a) How is it possible to keep plants that are in uneven light, for example on a windowsill, growing straight?

(b) Why do plants that have had their tips removed often stop growing?

▶ The male and female reproductive systems

Mammals, including humans, produce young by means of **sexual reproduction**, which involves the joining together of two **gametes** – the egg and sperm. Figures 3.2 and 3.3 show the human reproductive systems.

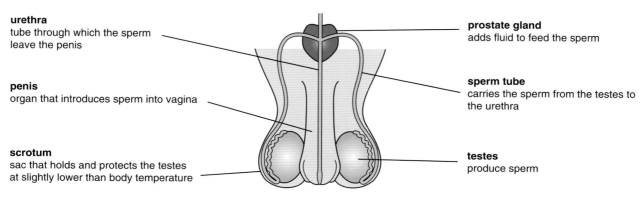

urethra
tube through which the sperm leave the penis

penis
organ that introduces sperm into vagina

scrotum
sac that holds and protects the testes at slightly lower than body temperature

prostate gland
adds fluid to feed the sperm

sperm tube
carries the sperm from the testes to the urethra

testes
produce sperm

Figure 3.2 The male reproductive system

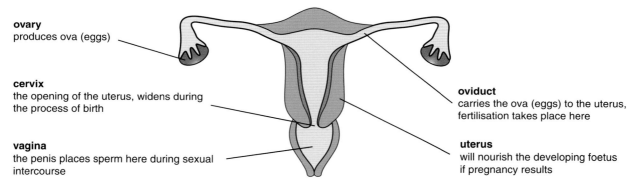

ovary
produces ova (eggs)

cervix
the opening of the uterus, widens during the process of birth

vagina
the penis places sperm here during sexual intercourse

oviduct
carries the ova (eggs) to the uterus, fertilisation takes place here

uterus
will nourish the developing foetus if pregnancy results

Figure 3.3 The female reproductive system

Hormones and the menstrual cycle

The process of **menstruation** (having periods) starts in girls at puberty and continues until the end of a woman's reproductive life. Each menstrual cycle lasts about 28 days. It is a cyclical event with the release of an ovum, the development of a thick lining on the uterus wall, and the breakdown of this lining (menstruation) occurring in each cycle. The menstrual cycle is controlled by a number of female hormones.

One of the most important female hormones is **oestrogen**. At the start of each menstrual cycle (the onset of bleeding, which we call day 1), the level of oestrogen is low. As the cycle progresses the level of oestrogen rises. It peaks mid-cycle, causing the release of the ovum (ovulation).

> **Definition**
>
> **Oestrogen** and **progesterone** are female reproductive hormones that prepare the body for pregnancy.

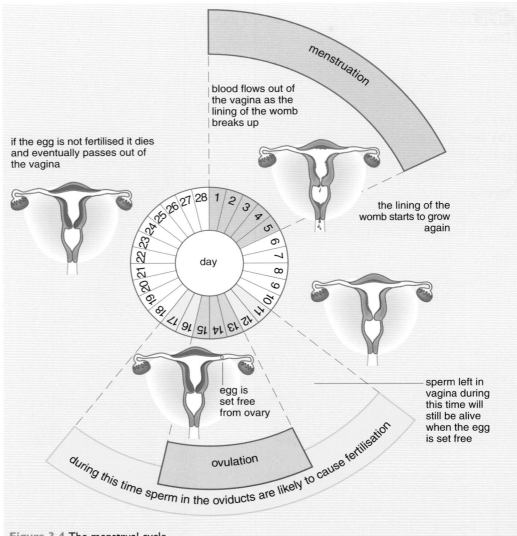

Figure 3.4 The menstrual cycle

Another very important hormone is **progesterone**. The level of progesterone is also low at the start of the menstrual cycle and peaks in the days following ovulation. The role of progesterone is to build up and maintain the thick uterine lining (and the subsequent development of the placenta and other structures associated with pregnancy), should pregnancy occur. Oestrogen is also important in ensuring that the uterine lining is built up again.

If pregnancy does not occur, the levels of oestrogen and progesterone drop towards the end of the cycle and this causes menstruation to occur. Then the cycle begins again.

Contraception – preventing pregnancy

Many people want to have sex but do not want to have children at that particular time. Pregnancy may be prevented by **contraception**. For some people, contraception is a moral dilemma, for religious or other reasons.

> **Test yourself 2**
>
> **(a)** Suggest why it is important to have a thick lining in the uterus at the time of pregnancy.
>
> **(b)** Suggest what happens to the menstrual cycle if pregnancy occurs. Explain your answer.

Test yourself 3

Draw a diagram of the female reproductive system. On it label the ovaries, oviducts, uterus, cervix and vagina, and show where:

(a) ova are released
(b) fertilisation will take place
(c) surgical contraception can take place.

Methods of contraception

Some people who are opposed to contraception may want to **reduce** their chances of having children, perhaps because they already have a large family. They can do this by avoiding having sex around the time when the female releases an ovum each month. This has been called the **rhythm** or **natural method** of contraception.

The three main types of contraception, as described in Table 3.2, are:

- physical
- chemical
- surgical.

Table 3.2 Methods of contraception

Type	Example	Method	Advantages	Disadvantages
physical	condom	acts as a barrier to prevent the sperm entering the female	easily obtained and also protects against sexually transmitted diseases such as AIDS and gonorrhoea	unreliable if not used properly
chemical	contraceptive pill	when taken regularly by the female, it changes her hormone levels and prevents the ovaries from releasing eggs	very reliable	can cause some side-effects such as weight gain
surgical	vasectomy	cutting sperm tubes, preventing sperm from entering the penis	virtually 100% reliable	very difficult or impossible to reverse
surgical	female sterilisation	cutting oviducts, preventing ova from reaching the uterus and being fertilised	virtually 100% reliable	very difficult or impossible to reverse

Insulin

Definition

Insulin is the hormone that reduces blood glucose levels.

A very important hormone you need to know about is **insulin**.

It is vital to keep the amount of glucose (sugar) in the blood at just the right level. If it gets too high it can cause the body harm.

Figure 3.5 shows how insulin stops blood glucose levels from rising too high.

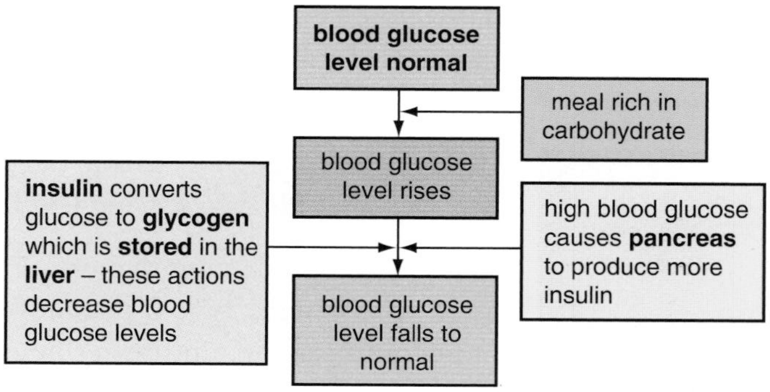

Figure 3.5 The action of insulin

Definition

Diabetes is the inability to control blood glucose levels.

Definition

A **symptom** is a sign that shows something is wrong.

Test yourself 4

(a) Suggest why people with diabetes often take extra glucose (a biscuit or a glucose drink) before they take part in strenuous exercise.

(b) People with diabetes check their blood glucose levels regularly. Suggest what they could do if their blood glucose level is too high when tested.

Definition

Long-term complications are medical effects that can result after having conditions like diabetes for many years.

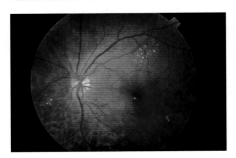

Figure 3.6 The retina of a diabetes sufferer – the areas of small yellow dots, caused by leakage from damaged blood vessels, can cause permanent loss of vision.

Diabetes

Diabetes is a condition in which the body does not produce enough insulin. Individuals who develop diabetes are unable to control their blood glucose levels without treatment. The **symptoms** or effects of diabetes can include:

* sugar in the urine
* thirst and needing to go to the toilet often
* a coma, if diagnosis and treatment are delayed too long.

Diabetes is becoming more common in young people. It is usually **treated** by the **injection of insulin** and a **carefully controlled diet**, where the intake of carbohydrate is accurately monitored.

If the blood sugar level drops too far a **hypoglycaemic attack** or **hypo** may occur, resulting in unconsciousness.

Types of diabetes

The type of diabetes normally developed in childhood, and discussed above, is referred to as **Type 1 diabetes**.

Generally, **Type 2 diabetes** only develops in older people. It has a slightly different cause in that insulin is produced but it stops working effectively.

Type 2 diabetes is often linked to a poor diet, obesity and lack of exercise. With more people being obese and fewer people taking exercise, Type 2 diabetes is becoming more common. Many people with Type 2 diabetes are able to regulate their blood sugar levels by diet alone, without the need for insulin injections.

Long-term effects and future trends

People who have had diabetes for a long time and whose blood sugar level is not tightly controlled may develop serious **long-term complications** (effects). These include **eye damage** (Figure 3.6) or even **blindness**, **heart disease** and **strokes**, and **kidney damage**. These complications are usually the result of high blood-sugar levels damaging the **capillaries**, which are the fine blood vessels that supply the part of the body involved.

As the number of people with diabetes is steadily increasing, the **cost of treatment is becoming very high**. It amounts to around 10% of the National Health Service (NHS) budget. This is largely due to:

* many people having diabetes – the large increase in the number of people with Type 2 diabetes is mainly due to more people becoming obese and fewer people taking exercise
* diabetes being a lifelong condition
* equipment to treat complications such as eye and kidney disease being very expensive.

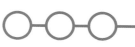

▶ Exam questions

1 a Copy and complete the table to show the differences between a voluntary and a reflex action. *(2 marks)*
Choose from: varies; fast; always the same; slow

Differences	Voluntary	Reflex
speed of response		
response to stimuli		

b Describe the pathway taken when we respond to the stimulus of a loud noise by covering our ears with our hands. Include three structures of the nervous system in your answer. *(3 marks)*
CCEA Science: Single Award, Unit 1, Foundation Tier, November 2012, Q9

2 The picture below shows cress plant seedlings.

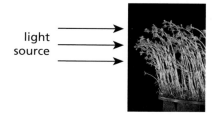

light source

Name and fully explain the process that causes the seedlings to bend to one side. *(3 marks)*
CCEA Science: Single Award, Unit 1, Foundation Tier, March 2012, Q6

3 a The diagram shows the female reproductive system.

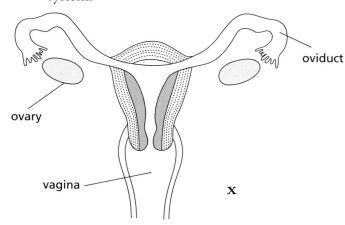

oviduct

ovary

vagina

x

i On a copy of the diagram draw a line from **X** to the cervix. *(1 mark)*
ii Name the part where a sperm fertilises an ovum (egg). *(1 mark)*
iii What is the function of the ovaries? *(1 mark)*

b The table below shows some methods of contraception used by 20 and 40 year olds.

Method	Percentage	
	20 year olds	40 year olds
contraceptive pill	27	22
male condom	22	18
vasectomy	8	20
female sterilisation	6	14

i On a copy of the grid below draw a bar chart showing the contraceptive methods used by 40 year olds. *(2 marks)*

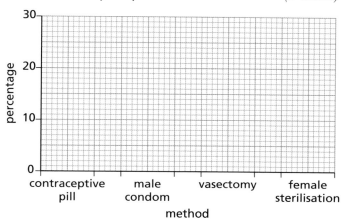

ii State the method least used by 20 year olds and suggest a reason for this. *(2 marks)*
CCEA Science: Single Award, Unit 1, Foundation Tier, November 2012, Q3

4 a The table below shows information about some methods of contraception. Using a tick (✔) copy and complete the table to give one statement for each method. The first is done for you. *(2 marks)*

Method of contraception	Permanent	Prevents sexually transmitted diseases	Changes hormone levels
female sterilisation	✔		
condoms			
contraceptive pill			

b i Copy and complete the sentences below. *(3 marks)*
Choose from: cervix; oviduct; sperm; testes; fertilisation; prostate
Female sterilisation is permanent because the _____ is cut. Therefore an ovum (egg) and a _____ do not meet and _____ cannot happen.

 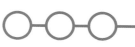

ii Give two reasons why some people do not approve of contraception. *(2 marks)*

CCEA Science: Single Award, Unit 1, Foundation Tier, March 2012, Q3

5 **a** Given below are two named parts of the female reproductive system and some functions. Copy the text and use lines to link each named part to its correct function.

(2 marks)

Name	Function
Ovary	Where the foetus (baby) develops
Uterus	Produces eggs (ova)
	Where fertilisation occurs

b Copy and complete the sentence below.

(2 marks)

Choose from: antibody; hormone; egg; sperm
Females can take a contraceptive pill which changes their _____ level and stops the development of an _____.

c Connor and Anne are 20 year olds with no children and have just got married. The diagram below shows the discussion they had about contraception.

Why don't you get sterilised? It's less hassle!

I think condoms are the best for us for now.

Connor   Anne

Explain fully why most people would agree with Anne. *(2 marks)*

CCEA Science: Single Award, Unit 1, Foundation Tier, March 2013, Q2

6 **a** The graph shows the levels of insulin and glucose in the blood.

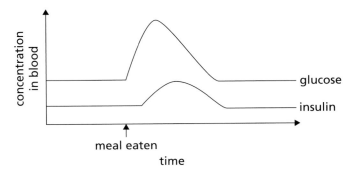

i Use the graph to describe one difference between the concentration of glucose and the concentration of insulin in the blood. *(1 mark)*

ii Explain how the graph suggests that insulin is released into the blood because of an increase in glucose. *(1 mark)*

b Insulin is a chemical messenger carried in the blood to the liver. What general name is given to chemical messengers? *(1 mark)*

Choose from: antibodies; phagocytes; hormones

c Diabetes Type 1 is caused when the body does not produce enough insulin.

i State two symptoms of diabetes. *(2 marks)*

ii Diabetes Type 1 is treated with injections of insulin. Suggest what might happen to glucose levels if too much insulin is taken.

(1 mark)

d Suggest one reason why the number of teenagers with diabetes Type 2 is rising. *(1 mark)*

CCEA Science: Single Award, Unit 1, Foundation Tier, November 2012, Q5

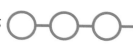

7 a The following graph shows the number of patients with diabetes attending a hospital over a ten-year period.

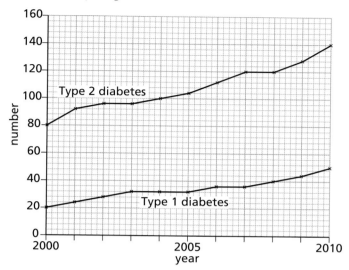

   i Calculate the difference in the number of people being treated for Type 2 and Type 1 diabetes in 2010. (Show your working out.) *(2 marks)*

  ii Why has Type 2 diabetes increased over the ten-year period? *(1 mark)*
Choose from: more obesity; increased exercise; increased stress

b Type 1 diabetes usually develops in childhood and is managed by self-injection of insulin. Type 2 usually develops in adults and is managed by a change in diet without injecting insulin. Both types can produce long-term effects including kidney failure if the condition is poorly managed. Use the information provided and your knowledge to answer the following questions.

   i The cost of treating diabetes is increasing. Suggest two reasons why the treatment of diabetes is very expensive. *(2 marks)*

  ii Describe one way in which diabetes could be 'poorly managed' by the patient. *(1 mark)*

c Apart from kidney failure, give one other long-term effect of diabetes. *(1 mark)*

CCEA Science: Single Award, Unit 1, Foundation Tier, March 2013, Q5

 Adaptation and variation

LEARNING OBJECTIVES

By the end of this chapter you should know and understand:

- **about types of variation**
- **mutations and their effects**
- **about natural selection and evolution**
- **about endangered species and extinction**
- **classification of living organisms.**

▶ Variation

If you look at the other members of your class, you will notice that they all look different – this is called **variation**. Most of this variation in appearance is controlled by our **genes** – it is **genetic**.

The **environment** can also play a part in variation. This can be seen if we grow cuttings of a geranium plant in different environmental conditions, for example, one in very bright conditions and one in the shade. If they are cuttings from the same plant, they must be genetically the same. However, the one grown in the light will be much bigger and healthier than the one grown in the shade. The difference can only be due to environmental conditions.

Continuous and discontinuous variation

Continuous variation

Continuous variation is a gradual change in a characteristic across a population. This means that there are no clear boundaries between groups (categories) and it may be difficult to decide where one group ends and another starts. A good example is height in humans (Figure 4.1). There is no clear cut-off between being tall or not.

Note

Height in humans is an example of variation affected by both genetics and the environment but our blood group is purely genetic.

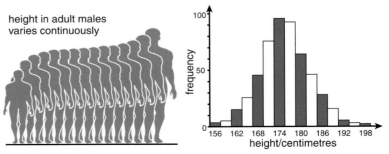

Figure 4.1 Height – an example of continuous variation in humans

Definition

If you can clearly allocate an individual to a particular group – there is no debate – then it is **discontinuous variation**.

Test yourself 1

Draw a table with two columns. Use continuous variation and discontinuous variation as the two headings. Place the following examples of variation in the correct column: eye colour; blood group; hand span; hair length; shoe size; foot size.

Discontinuous variation

Discontinuous variation occurs when all the individuals can be clearly divided into two or more groups and there are no intermediate states, i.e. individuals can be easily allocated to a particular group.

A good example is tongue-rolling in humans – everyone either can or cannot roll their tongue (Figure 4.2).

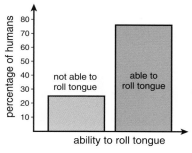

Figure 4.2 Tongue-rolling – an example of discontinuous variation in humans

▶ Mutations

Mutations are random changes in the structure or numbers of **chromosomes** or **genes**.

Although variation is a normal feature of living organisms the change caused by some mutations can be harmful.

Ultraviolet light and skin cancer

Environmental factors, such as the amount of **ultraviolet** (**UV**) light coming from the Sun, can trigger mutations. Particular mutations caused by UV light can lead to **skin cancer**. Cancer is **uncontrolled cell division** caused by damage to the genes or chromosomes in the cells affected so that many more cells than normal are produced, leading to a growth or **tumour**.

There has been an increase in the number of skin cancer cases diagnosed in Northern Ireland in recent years. This is probably due to an increase in the number of continental holidays taken in sunny resorts and to people using tanning studios.

Although getting a tan can make us feel better and increases the amount of vitamin D we have, it is important that we are careful when exposed to UV light. Things we can do to **reduce the damage** UV light causes include:

- avoiding the mid-day and early afternoon sun
- using sunscreen
- wearing a hat to protect the face and eyes
- limiting the length of time spent in UV light by limiting time in the sun or in tanning studios (or avoiding them altogether).

Down syndrome

Down syndrome is also caused by a mutation. However, it is caused by a change to the number of chromosomes, not their structure. Individuals with Down syndrome have 47 chromosomes instead of the normal 46.

Note

Body cells do divide under normal circumstances but in a controlled way. With cancer the rate of division is out of control.

Note

There is a clear link between getting too much UV light and skin cancer. The UV light causes mutations in the chromosomes in the skin cells.

Figure 4.3 Karyotypes of a normal individual (left) and an individual with Down syndrome (right) – note that with Down syndrome there is an extra chromosome 21

> **Definition**
>
> **Natural selection** favours the best-adapted individuals – they are more likely to survive and pass their favourable characteristics (genes) on.

Test yourself 2

Polar bears feed on seals in the Arctic. The Arctic is extremely cold and the bears are covered with thick white fur. Suggest why natural selection favours the development of the thick white fur in polar bears.

Figure 4.4 Charles Darwin

It is possible to tell if someone has Down syndrome by studying a **karyotype**. This is a diagram or photograph of someone's chromosomes, laid out so they can be counted (Figure 4.3).

▶ Natural selection and evolution

Natural selection

In nature, adaptations in living organisms are essential for survival and success in all habitats. It is not difficult to work out some of the main adaptations in polar bears, for example. These adaptations are even more important when organisms compete with each other for resources. This competition ensures that the best-adapted individuals will survive. For example, the larger seedlings growing in a clump of plants will be able to obtain vital resources such as light, nutrients and water more easily than the smaller seedlings. As a result of this competition, the stronger individuals will survive, possibly at the expense of the weaker ones. This competition for survival, with the result that the better-equipped individuals survive, is the cornerstone of Charles Darwin's theory of **natural selection**.

Charles Darwin and the theory of natural selection

Charles Darwin (1809–1882) was a naturalist who devoted much of his life to scientific research. As part of his research he spent 5 years as a ship's naturalist on the *HMS Beagle* as it travelled to South America. Darwin was greatly influenced by the variety of life he observed on his travels and, in particular, by the animals of the Galapagos Islands. Darwin's famous account of natural selection, *On the Origin of Species*, was published in 1859.

Darwin's main conclusions about natural selection can be summarised as:

- There is variation among the individuals in a population.
- If there is competition for resources there will be a struggle for existence.
- The better-adapted individuals survive this struggle or competition. This leads to survival of the fittest and these individuals are more likely to pass their genes on to the next generation.

It is useful to look at an example of natural selection in action to highlight the key features of Darwin's theory.

Antibiotic resistance in bacteria

When bacteria are treated with an antibiotic such as penicillin, most of them are destroyed. However, a small number (the fittest) may survive, probably because they have an allele (caused by a mutation) that provides resistance. Very soon the resistant bacteria are the only ones remaining, as they are the only ones surviving and passing their beneficial mutations on to their offspring.

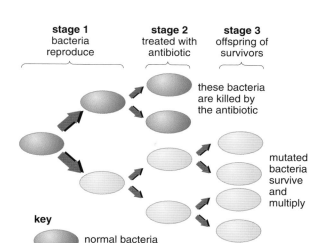

stage 1
bacteria
reproduce

stage 2
treated with
antibiotic

stage 3
offspring of
survivors

these bacteria
are killed by
the antibiotic

mutated
bacteria
survive
and
multiply

key

normal bacteria

bacteria with a mutation
that gives resistance to
the antibiotics used in stage 2

Figure 4.5 Antibiotic resistance in bacteria

The link between natural selection and evolution

Darwin used the theory of natural selection to explain the process of evolution. He suggested that *species have changed gradually through time* in response to changes in the environment and that evolution is a *continuing process*. He was not the first to propose that organisms could evolve, but he was the first to propose a plausible theory to explain the mechanism and support it with extensive evidence.

There are a number of reasons why not everyone accepts the theory of evolution. These include:

- It contradicts some religious beliefs.
- The very long time scales involved mean that it is difficult to see evolution actually happening.

Test yourself 3

Using the example of antibiotic resistance in bacteria, explain the difference between natural selection and evolution.

▶ Extinction

Each type of living organism is called a **species**. For example, every human on Earth belongs to the same species.

Definition

For many (but not all) species, being **endangered** is the stage before becoming extinct. Some endangered species do make a successful recovery in numbers.

Species are **extinct** if there are no living examples left. Many species have become extinct and often we only know they did exist in the past due to the discovery of fossils. Examples of extinct species include the dodo, dinosaurs and the woolly mammoth (Figure 4.6).

Figure 4.6 Woolly mammoths

Species that are not quite extinct but are at risk are called **endangered species**. For example, pandas still exist but are endangered.

Reasons why some species become endangered or extinct

- **Climate change or natural disasters**, for example, the dinosaurs probably became extinct when a meteor hit the Earth and caused the climate to change.
- **Loss of habitat** is what is causing a lot of species to become extinct today. The loss of habitat is often caused by human activities.
- **Hunting by humans**, for example, the dodo was hunted until it became extinct.
- **Hunting by animals** introduced by humans to areas where they are not normally found.

What we can do to help endangered species and prevent them becoming extinct

- **Legislation** preventing the hunting of endangered species and laws to reduce climate change.
- **Special programmes** such as creating nature reserves to protect habitats.
- **Education** to encourage people to do their part in protecting the environment.

> **Definition**
>
> The **habitat** is the area where an organism lives, e.g. a woodland.

> **Definition**
>
> **Legislation** means setting laws.

> **Test yourself 4**
>
> Do some research on a species at risk of extinction, e.g. the panda. Try to find out the factor(s) making it endangered and at risk of extinction. Find out what is being done to save it.

► Classification of living organisms

There are millions of different types of living organisms (species) in the world today. Scientists traditionally give each type a name in Latin. For example, humans are *Homo sapiens*. In the science of classification, very closely related species are grouped together within a larger group and so on. For example, hedgehogs form a relatively small group that includes only the different types of hedgehog. However, mammals form a larger group that includes all the different types of mammal (including hedgehogs).

Organisms are classified using a range of features including physical appearance, e.g. presence or absence of wings, number of limbs, presence or absence of a backbone, and so on.

There are many reasons why it is very important to group (classify) living organisms, including:

- Experts can allocate any previously unknown animal or plant to a related group.
- It helps in studying the relationships between different groups of organisms.
- It is possible to work out evolutionary pathways using both fossils and living organisms.
- By classifying the different types of disease-causing microorganisms it is possible to target treatment more accurately.

> **Definition**
>
> **Classification** is the naming of organisms and their allocation to particular groups.

> **Note**
>
> You should be able to use keys to group living organisms – see the question examples at the end of the chapter.

▶ Exam questions

1 a The picture below shows cows feeding in a field.

The picture shows the food chain: grass → cow.

i What term is used to describe the grass in the food chain above? *(1 mark)*
Choose from: primary consumer; secondary consumer; producer

ii State the source of energy for all food chains. *(1 mark)*

b The photograph above shows that the pattern of skin colours on each cow is different. What type of variation is shown by this difference in skin colour?
Choose from: uniform; discontinuous; continuous *(1 mark)*

c Variation in living organisms can be caused by mutations in cells.

i Describe fully what is meant by the term 'mutation'. *(2 marks)*

ii Name one disease caused by a mutation.
(1 mark)

CCEA Science: Single Award, Unit 1, Foundation Tier, March 2013, Q3

2 The peppered moth exists in two genetically distinct forms, the light and dark variety, as shown in the following diagram.

Both types of moth spend a lot of time resting on tree trunks where they are prone to being eaten by birds. The table below shows the percentage of moths of each variety in two regions of England in 1950.

Region	% moths	
	Light variety	**Dark variety**
Dorset	96	4
Manchester	9	91

In highly industrialised Manchester the trees were blackened due to smoke (soot) pollution in 1950 whereas there was little pollution in the more rural Dorset.

a Describe and explain the results in the table. *(3 marks)*

b Since 1950 Government legislation has reduced the amount of soot pollution throughout the UK. Suggest how this may have changed the numbers of peppered moths in each region. Explain your answer. *(2 marks)*

c i Explain fully what is meant by the term 'evolution'. *(2 marks)*

ii Suggest why the theory of evolution is not universally accepted. *(1 mark)*

CCEA Science: Single Award, Unit 1, Higher Tier, March 2013, Q7

3 a The fen violet is a plant that is nearly extinct.

What word is used to describe plants that are nearly extinct?
Choose from: discontinuing; non-active; endangered *(1 mark)*

b Copy and complete the sentence below.
Choose from: water; oxygen; carbon dioxide; food; colour
It is important to save plants from extinction as they provide us with _____ and _____. *(2 marks)*

CCEA Science: Single Award, Unit 1, Foundation Tier, November 2012, Q1

4 Shown below are pictures of whales and dolphins.

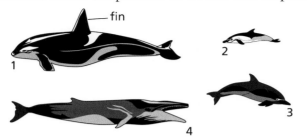

a Identify the animals 1, 2, 3 and 4 using the classification key below. *(3 marks)*

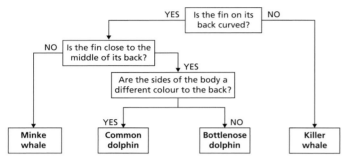

b i Copy and complete the sentence below. Choose from: boxes; features; diet; groups; areas

Classification means putting species into different _____ according to their _____. *(2 marks)*

ii State one reason why scientists classify organisms. *(1 mark)*

CCEA Science: Single Award, Unit 1, Foundation Tier, March 2012, Q4

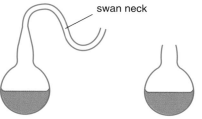

sterilised meat broth was placed into a number of sterilised flasks – some had 'swan-neck' openings and others had the neck removed (as a control)

↓ the broth was left for a few weeks

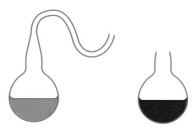

the broth in the swan-necked flasks did not become contaminated but the broth in the open flasks did

Figure 5.1 Pasteur's swan-neck experiment

> **Definition**
>
> If an experiment is **valid** this really means it is a '**fair test**'.

5 Disease and body defences

> **LEARNING OBJECTIVES**
>
> **By the end of this chapter you should know and understand:**
>
> - **about types of microorganisms (microbes)**
> - **about defence against disease including antibodies, phagocytosis, active and passive immunity**
> - **about vaccines and antibiotics**
> - **the development of medicines**
> - **the use and misuse of drugs.**

▶ Microbes

Many years ago, people did not know what caused disease or even what made food go bad. The French scientist Louis Pasteur showed that microorganisms (microbes) caused food to go bad when it became contaminated. He carried out a very famous experiment to show this (Figure 5.1).

Pasteur concluded that microorganisms were trapped in the swan neck and could not reach the broth but could gain entry to the broth in the open flasks.

He proposed that it was the presence of microbes that caused the broth to go bad.

To get **valid results** Pasteur had to:

- make sure the flasks and the broth were sterilised at the start of the experiment
- keep the flasks at the same temperature
- use the same type of broth.

You should be able to work out why it was important for him to do this.

Types of microorganism

There are different types of microorganism that can make food go bad or cause human disease. The main types of microorganism that cause disease are shown in Table 5.1.

Table 5.1 Microorganisms that cause disease

Type of microorganism	Examples of disease
bacteria	chlamydia, gonorrhoea, salmonella, tuberculosis
viruses	HIV leading to AIDS, colds and flu, polio, chickenpox, rubella
fungi	athlete's foot, thrush

Definition

The **mucous membranes** trap microorganisms as they have a fine lining of sticky mucus that microbes stick to.

Definition

Antigens are 'marker' chemicals on the surface of microorganisms that trigger the production of antibodies.

the **lymphocytes** produce **antibodies** in response to the antigen – the antibodies produced are **complementary** in shape to the shape of the antigen – they fit together like a lock and key

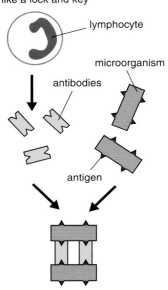

the antibodies '**latch on**' to the antigens of the microorganism causing them to **clump** together – the immobilised microorganism can then be destroyed by other white blood cells called **phagocytes**

Figure 5.2 How antibodies work

Definition

Active immunity takes time (usually several days) to become effective as the body has to make the antibodies first, but it usually lasts for many years.

▶ The body's defences

There are microorganisms all around us, yet the majority of people are not sick most of the time. This is because our bodies have their own defences.

These include:

- **The skin** – the skin provides a covering to stop microorganisms getting in.
- **Mucous membranes** – the lining of the nose and other parts of the respiratory system has a fine lining that traps microorganisms.
- **Blood clotting** – stops blood escaping and prevents microorganisms getting in through cuts.

Antibodies

Antibodies are produced by special white blood cells called **lymphocytes** to help defend us against microorganisms in the blood. Microorganisms have special marker chemicals called **antigens** that 'alert' lymphocytes and cause the body to produce the right antibodies.

Making antibodies

Figure 5.2 shows a very important feature of antibodies – they have to fit exactly with the microbe. This is why we have different antibodies for different diseases.

Once the microbes are clumped together they are destroyed by the **phagocytes** (Figure 5.3), which are the other main type of white blood cell. This process is called **phagocytosis**.

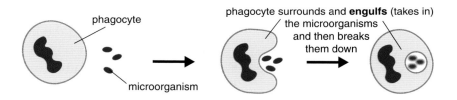

Figure 5.3 Phagocytosis

When do we make antibodies?

We make antibodies when we catch a **disease**. This provides **active immunity** (Figure 5.4).

- It is active immunity because the body makes its own antibodies.
- When we build up enough antibodies to stop the disease we are described as being **immune**.
- Immunity is freedom from disease and is produced by raised antibody levels.

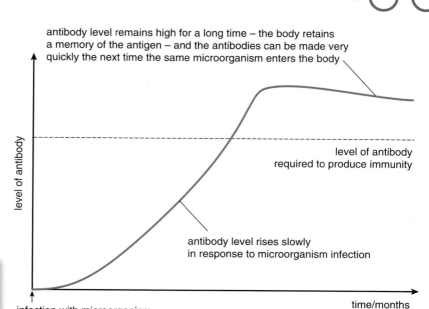

Figure 5.4 Active immunity acquired by having the disease

We also have active immunity when we have a **vaccination** (Figure 5.5).

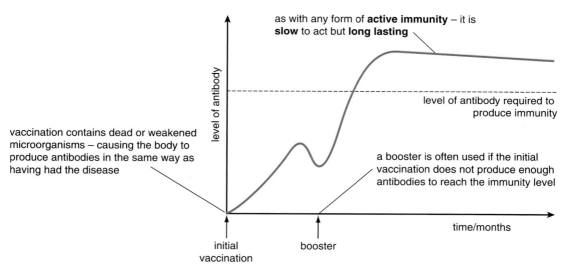

Figure 5.5 Active immunity by vaccination

Passive immunity

Passive immunity occurs when we are given ready-made antibodies (Figure 5.6). These antibodies are produced by medical companies and **not** the body of the person involved.

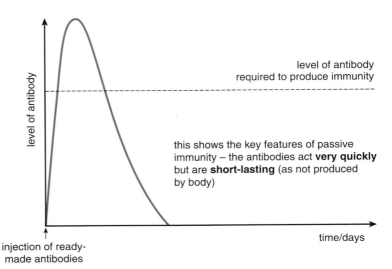

Figure 5.6 Passive immunity by the injection of ready-made antibodies

Test yourself 1

(a) Describe **two** differences between active immunity and passive immunity.
(b) Give **one** advantage of each.

before 1998 over 90% of children were vaccinated with MMR

⬇

in 1998 some research suggested that there was a link between the MMR vaccination and autism

⬇

in 1998 the percentage of children being vaccinated fell

⬇

by 2006 the numbers being vaccinated had risen again to over 90%

Definition

A **side-effect** is a harmful or unwelcome reaction to a drug.

Test yourself 2

Suggest why most vaccination programmes are targeted at young children rather than adults.

Are vaccines safe? The case of MMR

The MMR vaccine protects against three diseases – measles, mumps and rubella. In 1998 it was suggested that there might be a link between having the MMR vaccine and the development of the condition called **autism**. The flow chart shows how this affected the number of children who have been vaccinated since then.

The current position

In Northern Ireland, about 90% of children are now vaccinated and scientists agree that there is *not* a link between having the MMR vaccination and autism. However, some parents still worry about getting children vaccinated for any condition as there may be some **side-effects**, with the child feeling unwell for a short period of time. It is important to realise that the benefits of having the vaccination usually far outweigh the problems.

Parents, schools and the Government can all play their part in the vaccination programme.

- **Parents** can make sure that their children are vaccinated. The parents have to give permission for this to happen.
- **Schools** can educate young people about the importance of vaccination. When these young people eventually become parents they will know the benefits of vaccinating their children. Some vaccinations also take place in schools.
- **The Government** pays for children's vaccinations. The Government also encourages parents to have their children vaccinated.

▶ Antibiotics

Another way of defending against disease is to take **antibiotics**. These are chemicals that **kill bacteria**. When we take an antibiotic, such as penicillin, we usually take it over a number of days to make sure it kills *all* the bacteria. Unlike antibodies, antibiotics can defend us against a **range** of bacterial infections.

The discovery of penicillin – the first antibiotic

In 1928 Alexander Fleming, a Scottish scientist, was growing bacteria in his laboratory on plates containing a nutrient jelly (agar). One of his plates became infected with a fungus. Fleming noticed, to his surprise, that in the region around where the fungus was growing, bacteria did not grow. Clearly something was spreading from the fungus to kill the bacteria (Figure 5.7).

Fleming himself was unable to get a pure form of the substance that killed the bacteria. Later, this was done by other scientists and the first antibiotic, **penicillin**, was created.

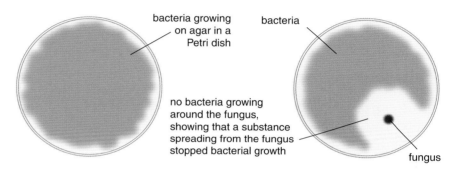

bacteria growing on agar in a Petri dish

bacteria

no bacteria growing around the fungus, showing that a substance spreading from the fungus stopped bacterial growth

fungus

Figure 5.7 Fleming's discovery

Microbe resistance to antibiotics

Sometimes bacteria can mutate and this makes them **resistant** to antibiotics. It is important to note that the mutations occur randomly – they are **not** *caused* by the antibiotics. However, in the presence of antibiotics 'normal' bacteria are killed leaving only the resistant mutated bacteria, which then spread. Superbugs such as **methicillin-resistant *Staphylococcus aureus*, or **MRSA**, are so called because they are resistant to many antibiotics. Superbugs can be a big problem in hospitals because antibiotics will not kill them.

Why are superbugs a particular problem in hospitals?

- In hospitals people are already ill and may have weak immune systems.
- Patients may have open wounds that are easily infected.
- Microbes can easily spread from patient to patient.

What can hospitals do to stop MRSA spreading?

- Apply very strict hygiene conditions such as washing hands regularly and mopping up spills of blood or body fluids immediately.
- Isolate patients who have a superbug, keeping them away from other patients.
- Do not over-use antibiotics.

Definition

Mutations are changes to the DNA that give the bacteria new properties.

Note

The terms **epidemic** and **pandemic** both refer to widespread infections and differ only in scale.

Test yourself 3

Explain why it is possible to catch the flu more than once.

▶ Epidemics and pandemics

These two terms describe widespread infections. We use the term **epidemic** when the disease, such as flu, spreads rapidly through a town or a small region like Northern Ireland. A **pandemic** is much more widespread and may affect several countries.

Epidemics and pandemics are more likely to occur if the disease can spread rapidly, as with flu, but also if the disease is more difficult to control. This can happen when the disease-causing microorganisms **mutate**. This has happened with many types of flu in the past. When the microorganism mutates, a vaccination that previously worked may fail to do so. This is because the antibodies produced as a result of the vaccination may not be complementary to (match) the antigens on the mutated microorganism.

▶ Development of medicines

We have already seen the role Alexander Fleming played in the discovery of penicillin. However, before a medicine or drug can be made available to the public there are a number of stages that must take place. These stages usually take a very long time (often many years), and cost a very large amount of money.

The stages include:

In-vitro testing

This is the testing of a very early version of the drug on living **cells** in the **laboratory**. Unless the scientists find that the drug works in living cells and that the cells are not harmed, further testing is unlikely to happen. *In-vitro* testing can be very expensive as it is very much a 'trial and error' process. Highly trained scientists and usually a lot of very expensive equipment are needed.

Animal testing

Animal testing is usually the next stage. It is an important process as it tests the drug on **whole animals** with complete immune systems. Animal testing is usually carried out on animals that have similar body systems to humans (i.e. other mammals). There are many advantages of testing on animals, including the fact that the test is on a whole animal as noted above. It also avoids testing on **humans** at this early stage of the drug's development and risking their health.

However, many people are opposed to animal testing. They argue that it is cruel to test on animals and that animals are **different to humans**, so proving that a drug is safe in animals is no guarantee that it is safe to use on humans. Although this is a complex **ethical** issue, it appears that animal testing will continue until some suitable alternative is found.

Clinical trials

Clinical trials follow animal testing. In clinical trials the drug is tested on human volunteers. Initially the drug is tested on a

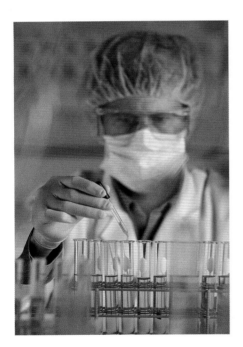

Figure 5.8 *In-vitro* testing in the laboratory

Volunteers wanted for medical research

Volunteers should be between 20 and 30 years old and currently taking no medication.

Volunteers will be asked to spend one night in a clinic and take part in a number of follow-up visits.

For further details contact …

Figure 5.9 Advert asking for clinical trial volunteers

Test yourself 4

(a) Give **one** argument for the use of animal testing and **one** argument against it.

(b) Give **three** reasons why it is so expensive to produce a new drug.

very small number of people but in due course much larger numbers are involved. The trials usually involve **patients** who have the condition the drug is targeting and **volunteers** (who are often paid a fee). Figure 5.9 shows an advert asking for volunteers to take part in a clinical trial. Would you be willing to act as a volunteer in a drug trial?

Following clinical testing, if it is clear that the drug both **works** in the way it was intended and that the patients do not suffer serious side-effects, the drug may be **licensed** for use. Some drugs may be licensed even though they do have side effects. This could happen if the benefits of the drug outweigh the harm it causes.

▶ Other drugs

There are other chemicals that some people take for reasons other than making them better when they are ill. These include alcohol, nicotine in cigarettes and so-called **recreational drugs** such as cannabis and cocaine.

Alcohol

Many people drink alcohol in moderation and are unlikely to suffer any serious harm. However, other people, including many teenagers, drink too much and cause harm to themselves and others.

Why do teenagers drink too much?

Some of the reasons include:

- peer pressure
- experimentation
- trying to escape from problems.

Harm caused by alcohol

Long-term excessive drinking can damage the **liver** as well as other parts of the body. Drinking too much can also harm those around you and society, as a result of:

- violence – many people become aggressive when drinking alcohol
- absence from college or work
- family breakup
- breakdown in relationships
- drink-driving.

Binge drinking is a particular problem. This occurs when a large amount of alcohol is taken over a short period of time, for example, on one night out (Figure 5.10).

Figure 5.10 A consequence of binge-drinking

The Government has tried to reduce the effect of binge-drinking by extending the licensing hours. It is debatable whether this is having the desired effect!

What can we do to reduce the harm caused by alcohol?

There are many things that we can do:

- Drink less each time, by taking low-alcohol drinks or by just drinking more slowly.
- Drink on fewer occasions, for example, only on special occasions or at weekends.
- Education – everyone should know how many units make up the recommended maximum weekly limit and about the problems alcohol can cause.
- Never drink and drive.
- Do not drink alcohol until you reach the legal age limit.

Smoking

Smoking remains a big problem. It is disappointing that so many young people start smoking. Cigarette smoke contains many harmful substances. Some of them are listed in Table 5.2, along with the harm they do.

Table 5.2 Harmful substances in cigarette smoke and what they do

Substance	Harmful effect
tar	causes (lung) cancer, bronchitis and emphysema
nicotine	is addictive and affects (increases) heart rate
carbon monoxide	reduces the ability of the red blood cells to carry oxygen

Illegal drugs

Cannabis and cocaine are two of the most common illegal drugs used in Northern Ireland. Cannabis has been widely used, mainly by young people, for many years but the use of cocaine has risen rapidly in recent years (Figure 5.11).

Cannabis

- It is widely used throughout the UK, due to its availability and low cost.
- When using cannabis, people may feel relaxed or 'chilled out'.
- However, it is possible that using cannabis can lead to taking other, harder drugs. There is also evidence that cannabis can lead to mental health problems in some people.

Cocaine

- Cocaine can give users a 'high', as it is a stimulant.
- It is very addictive.
- As its effects are short-lived, users often increase their dose over time.
- An overdose can result in death.

It is important to remember that cannabis and cocaine are **illegal drugs**. Cocaine is a Class A drug, which the law says is the most dangerous category. The classification of cannabis has changed twice in recent years. It is now a Class B drug. However, there is still a lot of debate about the classification of drugs for legal purposes.

> **Definition**
>
> **Bronchitis** and **emphysema** are medical conditions that reduce the ability of the lungs to supply the blood with oxygen.

> **Definition**
>
> **Red blood cells** carry oxygen from the lungs to the rest of the body.

> **Definition**
>
> **Carbon monoxide** is a gas that takes the place of oxygen in red blood cells.

Figure 5.11 Some of the illegal drugs in use in the UK

▶ Exam questions

1 a The following diagram shows the apparatus Louis Pasteur used to show that contamination of food was caused by microorganisms from the air.

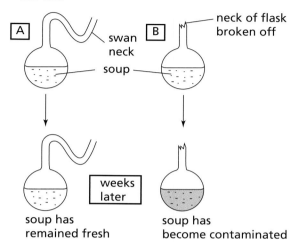

i Explain fully why the soup in A stayed fresh and the soup in B did not. *(3 marks)*

ii Suggest one reason why there were fewer deaths from open wounds after Pasteur's discovery. *(1 mark)*

b i Explain fully why diseases such as flu cannot be treated with antibiotics. *(2 marks)*

ii Give one example of a disease that can be treated by antibiotics. *(1 mark)*

CCEA Science: Single Award, Unit 1, Foundation Tier, November 2012, Q8

2 a Name two parts of the body that act as barriers to microbes (microorganisms). *(2 marks)*

b The statements below give the steps the immune system takes to defend us against microbes, but they are not in the correct order.

A – antibodies attach to the microbes' antigens

B – microbes enter blood

C – microbes clump together

D – microbes are 'eaten'

E – white blood cells produce antibodies

Using the letters A, B, C, D and E put the steps in the correct order.

The first one has been done.

B __ __ __ __ *(2 marks)*

c Jilly has rubella (German measles). Suggest a reason why her doctor has not given her antibiotics. *(1 mark)*

CCEA Science: Single Award, Unit 1, Foundation Tier, March 2012, Q5

3 a The bar chart shows the number of patients who caught MRSA in a hospital between July 1985 and October 1987. Part of their treatment involved antibiotics.

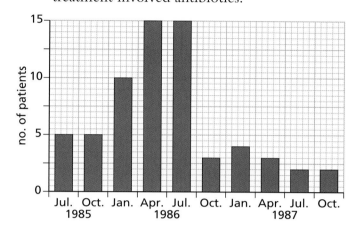

i Suggest when the hospital started to take measures to control the spread of MRSA. Explain your answer. *(2 marks)*

ii What is the evidence in the graph that suggests that MRSA bacteria are resistant to antibiotics? *(1 mark)*

b i One of the measures to control the spread of MRSA is to put infected patients into isolation wards. Suggest a reason why this method is not widely used in hospitals. *(1 mark)*

ii Apart from isolation, describe one measure that controls the spread of MRSA and suggest why it is effective. *(2 marks)*

c MRSA is caused by a type of skin bacteria becoming resistant to antibiotics. The diagram below shows how this would have happened.

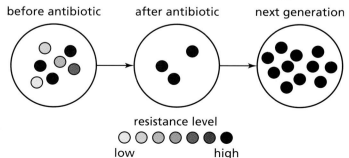

Use the diagram and your knowledge to explain how the population of skin bacteria became resistant. *(3 marks)*

CCEA Science: Single Award, Unit 1, Foundation Tier, March 2012, Q8

4 a Explain fully the main difference between active and passive immunity. Suggest an advantage and disadvantage for each type. In this question you will be assessed on your written communication skills including the use of scientific terms. *(6 marks)*

b Sometimes diseases spread rapidly in a short period of time and become epidemics. Explain fully why epidemics are more likely to happen when the disease is caused by microbes that are more likely to mutate. *(3 marks)*

CCEA Science: Single Award, Unit 1, Higher Tier, March 2012, Q7

5 a Vaccinations help us defend against disease by giving us active immunity.
Describe and explain how vaccinations protect against disease and why they provide long-term active immunity. In this question you will be assessed on your written communication skills including the use of specialist scientific terms. *(6 marks)*

b The following graph shows how the percentage of children being vaccinated against MMR has changed between 1995 and 2010.

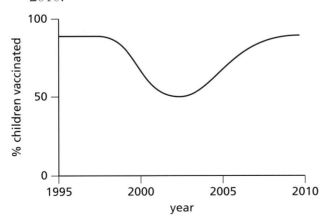

Use the graph to answer the following questions.

i In 1998 a scientist suggested that there was a link between the MMR vaccination and autism. What is the evidence that the link between autism and the MMR vaccination has been disproved? *(1 mark)*

ii Give one piece of evidence that suggests that some parents still have other concerns about the MMR vaccination. *(1 mark)*

CCEA Science: Single Award, Unit 1, Foundation Tier, March 2013, Q9

6 In a study, two methods were investigated to see which was better at reducing binge drinking. At the start one hundred men who were binge drinkers were divided into two groups of fifty.

Group one received one 5-minute session being given advice on how to reduce alcohol intake.

Group two received two 30-minute sessions being given advice on how to reduce alcohol intake.

Both groups were monitored over the following three weeks to note how many had been binge drinking.

Women were also involved in the trial. The same number were used and treated in the same way. The results are shown in the table.

		Number binge drinking				Overall decrease	
		Week				Number	Percentage
		1	2	3	4		
Men	Group 1	50	49	30	22	28	56
	Group 2	50	37	15	12	38	76
Women	Group 1	50	15	13	12	38	76
	Group 2	50	9	7	5	45	

a Copy and complete the table by calculating the overall percentage decrease for Group 2 women over the 4-week period. *(1 mark)*

b Compare the effectiveness of the two methods in reducing binge drinking in the men in the study. *(1 mark)*

c It is often said that women take better care of their health than men. Discuss the evidence from this study for and against this statement. *(3 marks)*

d State two reasons why any conclusions from this study may not be reliable. *(2 marks)*

CCEA Science: Single Award, Unit 1, Higher Tier, November 2012, Q5

6 Human activity on Earth

LEARNING OBJECTIVES

By the end of this chapter you should know and understand:

- **human population growth**
- **pollution, including global warming**
- **the history of the Earth's atmosphere**
- **the nitrogen cycle**
- **competition between living organisms**
- **monitoring environmental change**
- **conservation.**

► Population

Humans affect the world around them more than any other living thing does. The rapid rate of human population growth (Figure 6.1) makes these effects very obvious.

Why is the human population rising rapidly?

The human population is rising because advances in technology mean that fewer people are dying young than was the case in the past.

People are living longer because of:

- **medical improvements** such as new drugs and vaccinations
- improved **diet**
- improved **hygiene**.

Harmful effects of human population growth

- We are using up **resources** such as fish stocks.
- We are destroying many natural **habitats** such as the Amazon rainforest.
- We are **polluting** the environment.

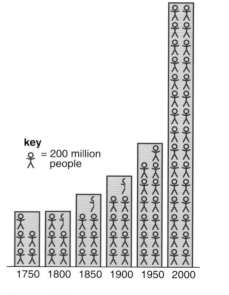

Figure 6.1 Growth of the human population since 1750

The problems caused by humans are due to both the rapid rate of population growth and also the increased industrialisation in the world.

It is important to realise that there has to be a balance between population and economic growth and the environment around us.

Definition

Hygiene includes the development of good sewage systems, disinfectants and washing powders as well as increased personal cleanliness.

> **Definition**
>
> Being **sustainable** means that we do not harm the environment or deplete our resources.

Working at the balance – conserving fish stocks

Many of our favourite fish, such as cod and herring, are becoming very rare now because of over-fishing. To stop these and other fish becoming extinct we must fish at a **sustainable level**. This means fishing at a level that does not cause the numbers to fall too much (Figure 6.2).

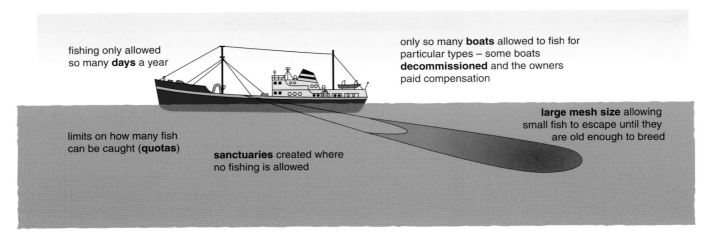

fishing only allowed so many **days** a year

only so many **boats** allowed to fish for particular types – some boats **decommissioned** and the owners paid compensation

large mesh size allowing small fish to escape until they are old enough to breed

limits on how many fish can be caught (**quotas**)

sanctuaries created where no fishing is allowed

Figure 6.2 Some methods used to conserve fish stocks

> **Definition**
>
> **Mesh sizes** refer to the size of the gaps in the nets – large gaps allow smaller fish to escape.

▶ Pollution

All living organisms produce waste and affect the environment around them. Pollution occurs when there is so much waste that the environment is harmed. Almost all pollution is due to humans and this affects the **air**, the **water** and the **land**.

Air pollution

The air is polluted by the release of excessive amounts of **carbon dioxide**. This will be discussed on pages 54–55.

Fossil fuels produce **sulfur dioxide** when they are burned. This can combine with rainwater to produce **acid rain** (Figure 6.3).

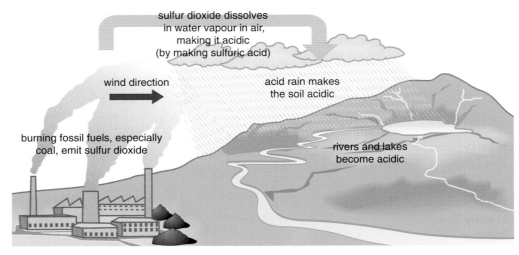

sulfur dioxide dissolves in water vapour in air, making it acidic (by making sulfuric acid)

wind direction

acid rain makes the soil acidic

burning fossil fuels, especially coal, emit sulfur dioxide

rivers and lakes become acidic

Figure 6.3 How acid rain is produced

Test yourself 1

Use Figure 6.3 to explain how power stations in the United Kingdom could help to cause acid rain in Norway (hundreds of miles away).

Acid rain kills trees. Because it makes our rivers and lakes acidic, it also kills the fish and other animals in them.

The country that produces the acid rain is not always the one that is affected by it. This makes acid rain an international problem.

We can stop acid rain by using filters in the chimneys of power stations to absorb the sulfur dioxide or we can use alternative fuels. Many countries have dramatically cut their sulfur dioxide emissions.

Land pollution

Much of our waste ends up in landfill sites (Figure 6.4). Large landfill sites can pollute surrounding land and attract vermin. They are not pleasant to look at and can produce strong smells. Would you want to live beside a landfill site? We are running out of suitable landfill sites, and this may soon become a serious problem.

Figure 6.4 A landfill site – it is estimated that between 70% and 80% of our rubbish ends up in landfill sites

We can reduce problems caused by household refuse by:

- reducing
- reusing
- recycling.

Water pollution

Sewage and slurry from farms is very rich in nutrients, particularly **nitrates**, which is why animal waste is used as a fertiliser. However, if the sewage or slurry drains from the farmland into surrounding waterways it can cause very harmful pollution.

Definition

Slurry is a mixture of manure from farm animals and water. It is often stored in underground tanks.

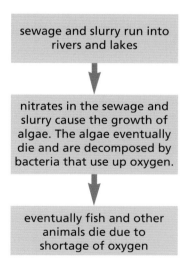

sewage and slurry run into rivers and lakes

↓

nitrates in the sewage and slurry cause the growth of algae. The algae eventually die and are decomposed by bacteria that use up oxygen.

↓

eventually fish and other animals die due to shortage of oxygen

Test yourself 2

Give **two** reasons why the spreading of nitrate-rich fertiliser in winter is more likely to cause water pollution than spreading it in early summer.

How can we stop pollution by nitrates?

Here are two important measures we can take:

1 Only spread sewage and slurry on farmland during the growing season and not when the weather is wet.
2 Make sure sewage and slurry are properly stored before use so they cannot leak into surrounding fields and waterways.

▶ Global warming

There is increasing evidence that the level of **carbon dioxide** in the atmosphere is rising. There is also evidence that humans are responsible. Figure 6.5 shows the **carbon cycle**.

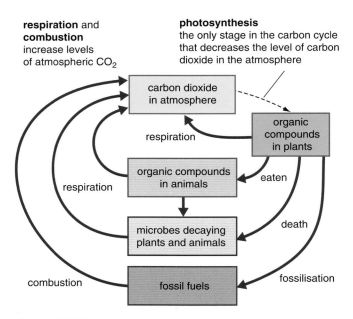

respiration and **combustion** increase levels of atmospheric CO_2

photosynthesis the only stage in the carbon cycle that decreases the level of carbon dioxide in the atmosphere

Figure 6.5 The carbon cycle

Over the last 150 years or so there have been two major changes to the way this cycle works:

1 Increased **combustion of fossil fuels** has added more carbon dioxide to the atmosphere.
2 Increased **deforestation** has removed many forests, meaning that less carbon dioxide can be taken out of the atmosphere by photosynthesis.

These changes mean that the **carbon cycle has become unbalanced**, leading to an **increase** in carbon dioxide in the atmosphere.

The link between increased carbon dioxide levels and global warming

It is known that carbon dioxide and some other gases in the atmosphere form a 'greenhouse blanket', trapping the heat from the Sun's rays within the atmosphere. This is explained in more detail in Figure 6.6. It is thought that the increase in carbon dioxide is increasing the **greenhouse effect** and this is leading to global warming.

> **Definition**
>
> **Deforestation** is the removal of trees on a large scale. It occurs for many reasons, e.g. clearing land for agriculture or housing.

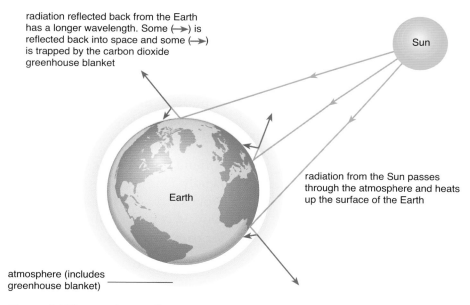

radiation reflected back from the Earth has a longer wavelength. Some (→) is reflected back into space and some (→) is trapped by the carbon dioxide greenhouse blanket

Sun

Earth

radiation from the Sun passes through the atmosphere and heats up the surface of the Earth

atmosphere (includes greenhouse blanket)

Figure 6.6 The greenhouse effect

The evidence for global warming

It is only recently that many politicians and people have accepted that it is the increase in carbon dioxide levels that causes global warming. This may be because accepting this link also means accepting that humans are responsible and therefore it is up to us to do something about it!

The effects of global warming

The warming of the atmosphere causes:

- climate change – more weather extremes such as droughts and severe storms
- polar ice-caps to melt
- increased flooding
- more land to become desert.

What can be done to reduce global warming?

- Plant more trees.
- Reduce deforestation.
- Burn less fossil fuel by using alternative fuels and/or by being more energy-efficient.

Many people believe that it is very important to act now before it is too late. We may not be able to stop global warming but we can slow it down. We can also manage it better. For example, it would be better not to build houses in areas that are likely to flood, unless we make sure there are better flood defences.

▶ The history of the Earth's atmosphere

Approximately 20% of the Earth's atmosphere consists of oxygen. There is much more nitrogen – nearly 80% – and much smaller amounts of carbon dioxide and other gases. However, the proportion of oxygen (and the other gases) has changed throughout time – it is not only the carbon dioxide that has changed.

Oxygen levels began to increase about 2.4 billion years ago (bya) as **photosynthesis** evolved in very simple 'plant-like' organisms. Eventually 'true plants' evolved around 750 million years ago (0.75 bya) and rates of photosynthesis began to increase even more.

Around this time the atmospheric oxygen levels began to increase rapidly. This increase in oxygen allowed animals to evolve, as it provided the oxygen levels needed for high rates of **respiration**. This allowed complex animals to produce the high levels of energy required for **movement** and other processes.

In recent centuries, the processes of respiration and photosynthesis have kept oxygen levels reasonably stable. Figure 6.7 summarises the main changes in oxygen levels in the Earth's atmosphere over the last 2.5 billion years.

Note

You should remember from Chapter I that **photosynthesis** uses carbon dioxide and produces oxygen. Also remember that **respiration** uses oxygen and produces carbon dioxide.

Test yourself 3

Explain why it was important that plants evolved before animals.

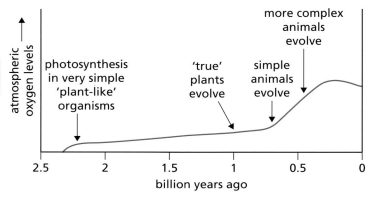

Figure 6.7 The changing levels of atmospheric oxygen

► The nitrogen cycle

In previous sections we investigated the carbon cycle. We noted how carbon was part of a cycle that included the carbon dioxide in the atmosphere and the carbon in compounds in plants and animals.

The **nitrogen cycle** is another example of a nutrient cycle. Just as all living organisms need carbon, they also need nitrogen. For example, nitrogen is needed to make amino acids and proteins and also DNA (compounds that we have come across in earlier chapters).

Plants obtain nitrogen in the form of **nitrates** from the soil. The nitrates are absorbed through the roots and converted into **protein** by the plants. Proteins are needed for **growth**. If the plants are **eaten by animals** the protein in the plants is digested and broken down into amino acids. The amino acids are then used to make new proteins in the animal, which again can be used for growth.

Definition

Excretion means removing waste containing nitrogen in the urine. Don't confuse it with the removal of undigested food from the gut.

Test yourself 4

(a) Explain why the harvesting of crops reduces the level of nitrates in the soil.
(b) Suggest what farmers can do to increase soil nitrate levels.

<u>Note</u>

Competition causes some (or all) of the organisms involved to grow less well as they are deprived of resources.

(a) when there are more plants in the pot each plant will not grow as well – they are **competing** for resources such as water, nutrients and light

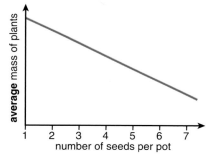

(b) when there are more plants in the pot each plant will not grow as well but because there are more plants the total mass will increase up to a limit when they become too cramped

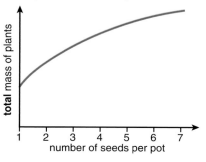

Figure 6.9 Competition in plants

When the animal produces urine (**excretion**) some of the nitrogen is returned to the ground. When the animal dies (and when plants that are not eaten die), **decomposers** (microorganisms such as bacteria and fungi) break their protein down to **ammonia** in the process of **decay**. Urine is also broken down to ammonia by decomposers.

However, to be of use to plants the ammonia needs to be converted to nitrates. Special bacteria called **nitrifying bacteria** convert the ammonia to nitrates in a process called **nitrification**.

The nitrogen cycle is summarised in Figure 6.8.

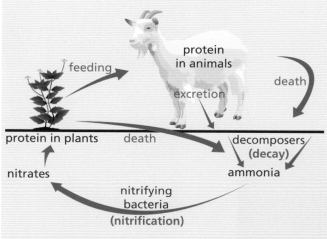

Figure 6.8 The nitrogen cycle

▶ Competition between living things

Living things compete with each other for resources. You can show this if you plant different numbers of seeds in some flowerpots and then measure the mass of the plants when they are grown. The graphs in Figure 6.9 show what usually happens.

In this type of experiment there are a number of things that need to be kept constant for all the pots to make it a 'fair test' and give valid results.

These include:

- using the same size of pot
- using the same volume and type of compost
- ensuring that each pot gets the same amount of water
- placing the pots in the same conditions, for example, light and temperature.

The effect of humans on competition

Humans affect how living organisms compete in nature. One way they do this is by the introduction of new species into areas where they are not naturally found. This can be particularly harmful if **competitive invasive species** are introduced into new areas. Competitive invasive species:

* out-compete similar native species, usually causing them harm
* spread rapidly when introduced into a region
* are almost always introduced to a country by humans.

Two examples are given below.

Grey squirrels

Grey squirrels are native to North America. They were introduced by humans to Ireland about 100 years ago. Now they have spread rapidly and out-compete the red squirrel because they are larger and can feed on a wider range of foods. One way to prevent the red squirrel becoming extinct in Ireland is to keep some woodland areas free of grey squirrels.

Rhododendrons

The rhododendron is not a native British tree but was introduced as an ornamental plant. It spreads rapidly and, because it has leaves all year round, casts a dense shadow that prevents other types of plants living underneath it. Its effect can be reduced by removing young rhododendron shrubs as they grow.

▶ Monitoring change in the environment

We can check how the environment is changing by observing both **biotic**, or living, factors and **abiotic**, or non-living, factors.

Abiotic (non-living) factors

We can monitor global warming by collecting information on:

* carbon dioxide levels
* size of ice fields and water levels
* climate change.

In addition:

* chemicals in water can be used to monitor water pollution levels.

Biotic (living) factors

We can monitor the environment by studying its effect on living organisms. A good example is the use of lichens as pollution monitors.

Lichens are small, plant-like organisms that can be used to monitor pollution levels. The lichens grow on trees, rocks and house roofs and grow best when there is no pollution. Heavy pollution prevents the growth of lichens.

Figure 6.10 Invasive species: rhododendrons outgrow other plants

Figure 6.11 Lichens growing on a rock

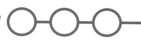

► Conservation

Conservation means looking after and managing the environment properly. Conservation does not mean keeping everything exactly as it is, but rather allowing development to take place in a **sustainable** way.

Sustainable development is development that does not harm the environment or use up resources at a greater rate than they can be replaced. An example is described below.

Growing willow for biofuel

Plantations of willow can be used to provide fuel to save the reserves of fossil fuels.

Advantages

As it grows, the willow uses up carbon dioxide in photosynthesis, helping to reduce carbon dioxide levels. (However, its use as a fuel puts the carbon dioxide back into the atmosphere.)

Willow grows quickly and following harvesting it rapidly grows back again, saving reserves of fossil fuels.

Maintaining biodiversity

Biodiversity refers to the range of species (different types of living organisms) that occur in a particular area. This means that an area with high biodiversity has many different types of living organism (species). It is important that we conserve areas that show high levels of biodiversity. One way of doing this is to develop **nature reserves**. Nature reserves help to protect and conserve the environment in many ways, including:

- **restricting public access** to certain areas that contain very rare or fragile habitats or species (even damage caused by trampling could cause the extinction of fragile and endangered species)
- **managing the habitat**, for example removing invasive shrub and tree species that threaten delicate plant species by restricting the amount of light that reaches ground level, e.g. rhododendron
- **education** – many nature reserves have educational centres that educate the public about the habitats and species that are being protected.

> **Definition**
>
> **Biofuels** are plants that are grown for the specific purpose of providing energy.

Test yourself 5

Explain why willow can be described as a carbon-neutral fuel.

Figure 6.12 A field of willow

▶ Exam questions

1 a Below are some processes in the carbon cycle and their descriptions. Copy them and link each process with its correct description.

(2 marks)

| Burning |

| Carbon released into the air from fossil fuels |

| Carbon taken in by animals from plants |

| Feeding |

| Carbon taken in by plants from animals |

Increasing carbon dioxide is causing global warming and affecting the area of ice in polar regions.

Year	1998	1999	2000	2001	2002
average area of ice/ thousands km^2	10.3	10.2	8.8	7.2	5.4

The picture shows how a polar bear uses ice to hunt for food.

b Use the information to suggest how global warming is affecting the polar bear. *(2 marks)*

The pie chart shows some sources of carbon dioxide in the UK.

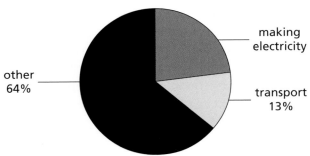

other 64%

making electricity

transport 13%

c Calculate the percentage of carbon dioxide produced when making electricity. (Show your working out.) *(2 marks)*

d To reduce the carbon dioxide in the air more trees are being planted.

Name the process by which trees remove carbon dioxide from the air. *(1 mark)*

CCEA Science: Single Award, Unit 1, Foundation Tier, November 2012, Q2

2 The graph below shows the human population from the year 1300 to the year 2000.

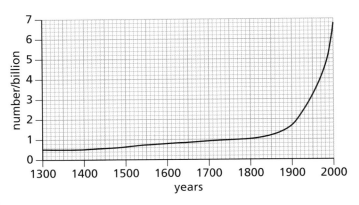

Use this graph and your knowledge to explain why there is concern that the human population size is putting planet Earth at risk.

In this question you will be assessed on your written communication skills including the use of specialist scientific terms. *(6 marks)*

CCEA Science: Single Award, Unit 1, Foundation Tier, November 2012, Q7

3 Below are three causes of pollution. For each, state which part of our environment is being polluted and give one strategy for reducing its effect. *(3 marks)*

a Household waste

b Acid rain

c Nitrate levels

CCEA Science: Single Award, Unit 1, Higher Tier, November 2012, Q7

4 a The graph below shows the changes in the volume of the ice fields in the Arctic Circle. This data was obtained by many scientists analysing many thousands of images of the Arctic Circle obtained from satellites.

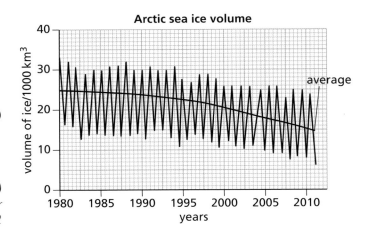

i The graph shows changes in the volume of ice over time.

Describe and explain fully the change within each year. *(2 marks)*

ii State fully the trend shown by this graph. *(2 marks)*

iii The data in this graph is considered to be evidence of global warming. Suggest three reasons why it is reliable. *(3 marks)*

b Before the data was published it was subject to peer review.

Describe the process of peer review. *(2 marks)*

CCEA Science: Single Award, Unit 1, Higher Tier, March 2012, Q8

5 a The graph below shows the percentage of oxygen in the Earth's atmosphere over the past 550 million years.

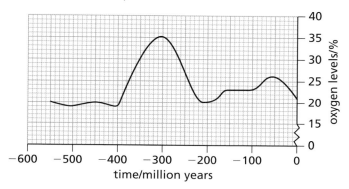

Describe and fully explain the change in oxygen levels between 400 and 200 million years ago.

In this question you will be assessed on your written communication skills including the use of specialist scientific terms. *(6 marks)*

b Suggest two reasons why the Church was opposed to Darwin's theory of evolution. *(2 marks)*

CCEA Science: Single Award, Unit 1, Higher Tier, November 2012, Q8

6 The photograph shows lichen growing on a tree.

Lichen is a biotic pollution monitor as it only grows in large numbers where there is very little pollution.

a What is meant by the term 'biotic'? *(1 mark)*

b The graph shows the relationship between the number of lichen plants on trees and their distance from Belfast in the years 1950, 1975 and 2000.

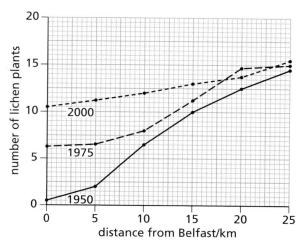

i Using the information provided, describe and explain one trend about the change in air pollution in and around Belfast. *(2 marks)*

ii When collecting the data suggest two things that must be done to make the investigation valid (a fair test). *(2 marks)*

CCEA Science: Single Award, Unit 1, Foundation Tier, March 2013, Q8

7 a The planting of willow as a biofuel is an example of sustainable development that both conserves natural resources and does not add to global warming.

Describe and explain how the use of willow as a biofuel is a positive conservation measure.

In this question you will be assessed on your written communication skills including the use of specialist scientific terms. *(6 marks)*

b In contrast to using willow, the introduction of competitive invasive species such as rhododendron creates conservation problems.

Explain why it is important to restrict the spread of rhododendron. *(3 marks)*

CCEA Science: Single Award, Unit 1, Higher Tier, March 2013, Q8

7 Acids and bases

LEARNING OBJECTIVES

By the end of this chapter you should know and understand:

- **the hazard labelling associated with some chemicals**
- **about the common acids, bases and alkalis around the home**
- **about indicators, including natural indicators and universal indicator**
- **the pH scale and neutralisation**
- **common reactions of acids, bases and alkalis**
- **the importance of acids in the home, in farming and in medicine**
- **how to write word equations for neutralisation reactions**
- **how to write balanced symbol equations for neutralisation reactions.**

▶ Hazard labelling

The common hazard labels (or symbols) shown in Table 7.1 are used to identify products that represent hazards. They have a greater visual impact than written warnings and can be recognised easily and quickly by anyone, whatever language they speak.

Table 7.1 Hazard symbols

Hazard symbols	Hazard
	Some acids and alkalis can burn your skin. Any substance that can burn skin is called **corrosive**.
	Some substances, including some acids, can poison you. Any substance that can poison you is called **toxic**.
	Some acids can be used to make substances that can cause an explosion. Any substance that can explode is called **explosive**.
	Some substances can catch fire easily. Any substance that can catch fire easily is called **flammable**.

Some substances found in industry and around the home have hazard labels on them:

- Dynamite is explosive.
- Oven cleaner is corrosive.
- Weedkiller is toxic.
- Methylated spirit is flammable.

Figure 7.1 Products that contain an acid or base

▶ Acids and bases

Acids are solutions that have a pH of less than 7 (see page 64). Soluble **bases** (**alkalis**) have a pH greater than 7. Acids react with bases in a reaction called **neutralisation**. There are many acids and bases around your home. Each of the products in Figure 7.1 contains an acid or a base.

- Oven cleaners and drain cleaners contain sodium hydroxide (a base).
- Lemon juice contains citric acid (an acid).
- Vinegar contains ethanoic acid (an acid).
- Baking soda (a base) contains sodium hydrogencarbonate (sometimes called sodium hydrogen carbonate).
- Ammonia is used in many cleaning products. Ammonia is an alkali.
- Milk of magnesia contains magnesium hydroxide (a base).

A base that dissolves in water is also called an alkali. Sodium hydroxide is a base because it can neutralise an acid, but it also dissolves in water so it is an alkali as well as a base.

Indicators

A colourless liquid may be neutral or it may be an acid or an alkali. A substance called an **indicator** can be used to distinguish between acids, alkalis and neutral solutions.

Some indicators occur naturally. Plants such as blackcurrant, beetroot and red cabbage contain a coloured substance that can act as an indicator.

> **Definition**
>
> An **indicator** is a substance that changes colour when it is placed in an acid, an alkali or a neutral solution.

Activity 1

Extracting a natural indicator from a plant

Wear safety glasses.

1 Chop some red cabbage into small pieces.
2 Place the pieces into a mortar and add a small amount of water.
3 Use the pestle to grind the cabbage in the water until the water is well coloured. The water is now a solution of the indicator.
4 Pour off the indicator solution into a small beaker.
5 Dispose of the used red cabbage.

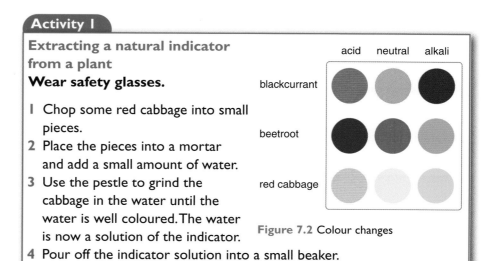

Figure 7.2 Colour changes

You can do the same thing with beetroot and blackcurrant. The juices of all these plants contain indicators that can show the difference between an acid and an alkali.

Figure 7.2 shows the colour changes that occur when a few drops of each indicator (red cabbage, beetroot or blackcurrant) are added to an acid, to water (neutral) and to an alkali.

Universal indicator and pH

Although these natural indicators can show whether a liquid is acidic, they cannot measure its strength. They do not show the difference between a strong acid, such as hydrochloric acid, and a weak acid, such as ethanoic acid in vinegar or citric acid in lemon juice. You need to use **universal indicator** to show this.

Universal indicator changes to a range of colours, depending on the strength of the acid or alkali.

The pH scale

The strength of an acid or alkali is measured on the **pH scale**, which goes from 1 to 14. Table 7.2 shows the colours of some acids and alkalis with universal indicator and the values of the pH scale they represent for strong and weak acids and alkalis.

Table 7.2 The pH scale

pH	1	2	3	4	5	6	7	8	9	10	11	12	13	14
Colour with universal indicator	red		orange		yellow		green	green/blue		blue		purple		
Strength	strong acid		weak acid				neutral	weak alkali				strong alkali		
Examples	hydrochloric acid sulfuric acid		ethanoic acid citric acid				water	ammonia				sodium hydroxide potassium hydroxide		
Common solutions	stomach juice		vinegar lemon juice				pure water	blood sea water				washing soda solution		

Test yourself 1

What colour would you see if universal indicator was added to a solution of pH 2?

To use universal indicator, you need to put some of the solution you want to test into a test tube. Then add a few drops of universal indicator to it.

Universal indicator is a solution but you can also use **pH paper**, which is paper that has been soaked in universal indicator and allowed to dry.

To test a solution, put a piece of pH paper on a white tile and then use a glass rod to put one drop of the solution onto the paper. The colour can be compared to a pH colour chart to work out the pH of the solution.

You can also use a **pH sensor** to measure pH. Attaching the sensor to a **data logger** allows the pH values to be transferred to a computer, and a graph of the change in pH value over time can be produced. A pH sensor is sometimes called a pH probe.

pH

The pH (always written with a small p and a capital H) of a solution is a number from 1 to 14.

- If the pH is **less than 7** then the solution is **acidic**.
- If the pH is **equal to 7** then the solution is **neutral**.
- If the pH is **greater than 7** then the solution is **alkaline**.

A pH meter can be used to measure pH accurately. It gives a numerical reading of pH to one or sometimes two decimal places. The one in Figure 7.3 shows a pH of 5.48.

Figure 7.3 A pH meter

▶ Neutralisation

When an acid reacts with an alkali, a neutralisation reaction occurs. If the alkali is added to the acid, the pH changes from a low value to a higher value as more alkali is added.

An acid is put in a beaker, with the pH sensor, and the alkali is added from a burette, as shown in Figure 7.4.

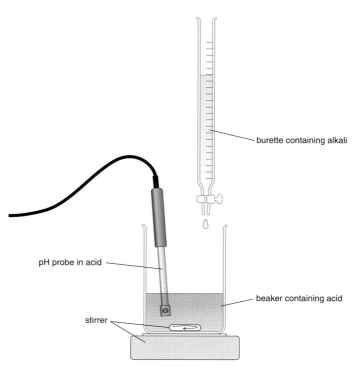

burette containing alkali

pH probe in acid

beaker containing acid

stirrer

Figure 7.4 A neutralisation reaction

A computer can draw a graph of pH against volume of alkali added. If the acid is hydrochloric acid and the alkali is sodium hydroxide, the graph may look like that in Figure 7.5.

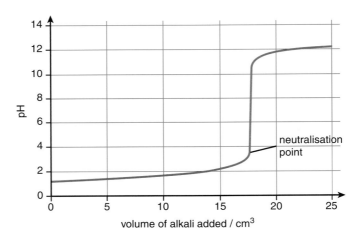

Figure 7.5 A neutralisation reaction graph

Using data logging to record the data from a pH probe is much more accurate than trying to record the colour of an indicator as the neutralisation reaction takes place.

The reaction could also be studied using a chemical indicator such as universal indicator.

Add a few drops of universal indicator to the acid in the beaker (it will be red). Add the alkali slowly from the burette. The indicator will gradually change and when the solution is neutral the indicator will be green.

A pH sensor is a more accurate way of making sure that neutralisation has occurred.

Note

Neutralisation is the reaction between an acid and a base forming water as one of the products. Bases react with acids producing a salt and water only.

▶ *EXAMPLE 1*

Neutralisation example 1

Sodium hydroxide reacts with hydrochloric acid, as in the word equation below.

sodium hydroxide + hydrochloric acid → sodium chloride + water
 ↓ ↓ ↓
 base acid salt

- Sodium hydroxide is the base and hydrochloric acid is the acid.
- Hydrochloric acid always forms salts that are chlorides.

The first part of the name of the salt comes from the metal in the base – in this example, it is sodium. The second part of the name of this salt is chloride, which comes from the hydrochloric acid.
Water is also formed as sodium hydroxide is a base.
Remember that sodium hydroxide is also an alkali as it dissolves in water.

▶ Chemical formulae

You will encounter many chemical formulae in this unit. These can represent elements and compounds. It is important that you are familiar with them and can recognise and write them accurately. The symbols for the elements are given in the Periodic Table.

A single symbol represents an atom of the element. Na represents an atom of sodium, O represents an atom of oxygen, H represents an atom of hydrogen and Cl represents an atom of chlorine.

In this example the chemical formulae are as follows:

- sodium hydroxide is NaOH
- hydrochloric acid is HCl
- sodium chloride is NaCl
- water is H_2O.

For any formula is it important that the correct symbols for the elements are used, with correct capital and lower case letters. The numbers are subscript.

- The formula for sodium hydroxide (NaOH) contains atoms of three different elements. There is one atom of sodium (Na), one atom of oxygen (O) and one atom of hydrogen (H).
- Hydrochloric acid (HCl) contains atoms of two different elements – one atom of hydrogen (H) and one atom of chlorine (Cl).
- Sodium chloride (NaCl) contains atoms of two different elements – one atom of sodium (Na) and one atom of chlorine (Cl).
- Water contains atoms of two different elements – two atoms of hydrogen (H) and one atom of oxygen. The little $_2$ after H in H_2O means there are two H atoms.

> **Test yourself 2**
>
> Write the chemical formulae for sodium hydroxide and sodium chloride.

A chemical reaction can be shown using a word equation or a balanced symbol equation. The balanced symbol equation for the reaction between sodium hydroxide and hydrochloric acid is:

$$NaOH + HCl \rightarrow NaCl + H_2O$$

This equation is balanced as there are the same numbers of each type of atom on the left-hand side of the arrow as there are on the right-hand side of the arrow:

- 1 Na atom on each side (on the left 1 in NaOH and on the right 1 in NaCl)
- 1 O atom on each side (on the left 1 in NaOH and on the right 1 in H_2O)
- 2 H atoms on each side (on the left 1 in NaOH and 1 in HCl and on the right 2 in H_2O)
- 1 Cl atom on each side (on the left 1 in HCl and on the right 1 in NaCl).

▶ EXAMPLE 2

Neutralisation example 2

Magnesium oxide reacts with sulfuric acid, as in the word equation below.

magnesium oxide + sulfuric acid → magnesium sulfate + water

   ↓   ↓   ↓

  base   acid   salt

● Magnesium oxide is the base and sulfuric acid is the acid.
● Sulfuric acid always forms salts that are sulfates.

The first part of the name of the salt comes from the metal in the base – in this case, it is magnesium. The second part of the name of this salt is sulfate, which comes from the sulfuric acid.

Water is also formed as magnesium oxide is a base.

Magnesium oxide is not an alkali as it does not dissolve in water.

The chemical formulae in this equation are as follows:

- magnesium oxide is MgO
- sulfuric acid is H_2SO_4
- magnesium sulfate is $MgSO_4$
- water was met in the previous example, H_2O.

The balanced symbol equation for this reaction is:

$$MgO + H_2SO_4 \rightarrow MgSO_4 + H_2O$$

This equation is balanced as there are the same numbers of each type of atom on the left-hand side of the arrow as there are on the right-hand side of the arrow:

- 1 Mg atom on each side (on the left 1 in MgO and on the right 1 in $MgSO_4$)
- 5 O atoms on each side (on the left 1 in MgO and 4 in H_2SO_4 and on the right 4 in $MgSO_4$ and 1 in H_2O)
- 2 H atoms on each side (on the left 2 in H_2SO_4 and on the right 2 in H_2O)
- 1 S atom on each side (on the left 1 in H_2SO_4 and on the right 1 in $MgSO_4$).

Test yourself 3

How many atoms of sulfur are there in $MgSO_4$?

Acid indigestion

A neutralisation reaction can be useful. For example, your stomach contains hydrochloric acid, which helps prevent infection and digest food. Sometimes, though, there can be too much acid in your stomach. This **excess** acid causes acid indigestion. An indigestion remedy such as baking soda can neutralise some of the stomach acid. Substances that are used to neutralise excess hydrochloric acid in the stomach are called **antacids**.

The main antacids are magnesium hydroxide, calcium carbonate and sodium hydrogencarbonate.

▶ EXAMPLE 3

The indigestion remedy called *Milk of magnesia* contains **magnesium hydroxide**. Magnesium hydroxide neutralises hydrochloric acid, producing the salt magnesium chloride and water.

The word equation for the reaction is:

magnesium hydroxide + hydrochloric acid → magnesium chloride + water

The chemical formulae in this equation are as follows:

- magnesium hydroxide is $Mg(OH)_2$
- hydrochloric acid is HCl
- magnesium chloride is $MgCl_2$
- water is H_2O.

Magnesium hydroxide is the first formula in this unit that has used brackets. The brackets mean that the little $_2$ in $Mg(OH)_2$ multiplies everything in the bracket by 2. Magnesium hydroxide therefore contains 1 Mg atom, 2 O atoms and 2 H atoms.

The balanced symbol equation for this reaction is:

$$Mg(OH)_2 + 2HCl \rightarrow MgCl_2 + 2H_2O$$

The '2' before HCl and the '2' before H_2O are balancing numbers. They are used to make sure the same number of each type of atom is on the left-hand side of the arrow as on the right-hand side of the arrow. The '2' in front of the HCl means 2 'HCl', so 2 H atoms and 2 Cl atoms are present. The '2' in front of the water means 2 'H_2O', which is 4 H atoms and 2 O atoms.

This equation is balanced as there are the same numbers of each type of atom on the left-hand side of the arrow as there are on the right-hand side of the arrow:

- 1 Mg atom on each side (on the left 1 in $Mg(OH)_2$ and on the right 1 in $MgCl_2$)
- 2 O atoms on each side (on the left 2 in $Mg(OH)_2$ and on the right 2 in $2H_2O$)
- 4 H atoms on each side (on the left 2 in $Mg(OH)_2$ and 2 in 2HCl and on the right 4 in $2H_2O$)
- 2 Cl atoms on each side (on the left 2 in 2HCl and on the right 2 in $MgCl_2$).

Test yourself 4

Explain how magnesium hydroxide can cure acid indigestion.

▶ EXAMPLE 4

Baking soda contains sodium hydrogencarbonate. Sodium hydrogencarbonate can neutralise hydrochloric acid, producing the salt sodium chloride, carbon dioxide and water.

The word equation for the reaction is:

sodium hydrogencarbonate + hydrochloric acid → sodium chloride + carbon dioxide + water

The chemical formulae in this equation are as follows:

- sodium hydrogencarbonate is $NaHCO_3$
- hydrochloric acid is HCl
- sodium chloride is NaCl
- carbon dioxide is CO_2
- water is H_2O.

The balanced symbol equation for this reaction is:

$$NaHCO_3 + HCl \rightarrow NaCl + CO_2 + H_2O$$

This equation is balanced as there are the same numbers of each type of atom on the left-hand side of the arrow as there are on the right-hand side of the arrow.

- 1 Na atom on each side (on the left 1 in $NaHCO_3$ and on the right 1 in $NaCl$)
- 3 O atoms on each side (on the left 3 in $NaHCO_3$ and on the right 2 in CO_2 and 1 in H_2O)
- 2 H atoms on each side (on the left 1 in $NaHCO_3$ and 1 in HCl and on the right 2 in H_2O)
- 1 C atom on each side (on the left 1 in $NaHCO_3$ and on the right 1 in CO_2)
- 1 Cl atom on each side (on the left 1 in HCl and on the right 1 in NaCl).

▶ EXAMPLE 5

Calcium carbonate reacts with hydrochloric acid in the stomach. The word equation for this reaction is:

calcium carbonate + hydrochloric acid → calcium chloride + carbon dioxide + water

The chemical formulae in this equation are as follows:

- calcium carbonate is $CaCO_3$
- hydrochloric acid is HCl
- calcium chloride is $CaCl_2$
- carbon dioxide is CO_2
- water is H_2O.

The balanced symbol equation for this reaction is:

$$CaCO_3 + 2HCl \rightarrow CaCl_2 + CO_2 + H_2O$$

This equation is balanced as there are the same numbers of each type of atom on the left-hand side of the arrow as there are on the right-hand side of the arrow:

- 1 Ca atom on each side (on the left 1 in $CaCO_3$ and on the right 1 in $CaCl_2$)
- 3 O atoms on each side (on the left 3 in $CaCO_3$ and on the right 2 in CO_2 and 1 in H_2O)
- 2 H atoms on each side (on the left 2 in 2HCl and on the right 2 in H_2O)
- 1 C atom on each side (on the left 1 in $CaCO_3$ and on the right 1 in CO_2)
- 2 Cl atoms on each side (on the left 2 in 2HCl and on the right 2 in $CaCl_2$).

When you use an antacid such as calcium carbonate or sodium hydrogencarbonate, the carbon dioxide produced in your stomach is often released as a burp. This does not happen with antacids such as magnesium hydroxide as they do not produce carbon dioxide when they react with the acid.

You can use limewater to identify carbon dioxide gas. Figure 7.6 shows how some sodium hydrogencarbonate, in the form of baking soda, and hydrochloric acid react together in the test tube on the left. The gas produced bubbles through a solution called limewater in the test tube on the right.

The gas produced in the reaction is carbon dioxide. The limewater will change from colourless to milky. The limewater stays colourless with other gases. The baking soda (sodium hydrogencarbonate) could be replaced with any other metal hydrogencarbonate or metal carbonate. All metal hydrogencarbonates and metal carbonates react with acids to produce carbon dioxide.

Test yourself 5

Describe how to carry out a test for carbon dioxide.

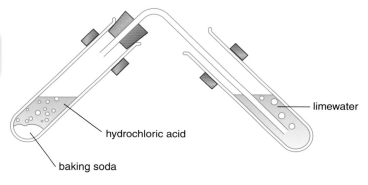

Figure 7.6 Testing for carbon dioxide gas

Neutralising acidic soil (liming soil)

The combination of artificial fertilisers with rain can make soils acidic. Most plants prefer a neutral or slightly alkaline soil to grow. Farmers can add **lime** (calcium hydroxide) to their soil (Figure 7.7). Lime is a base and neutralises the acid in the soil to make it neutral or even slightly alkaline. This is better for growing most crops. Lime is a white powder and the picture shows it being spread on a field. Limestone, which is calcium carbonate, can also be used. It is also a white powder and it is being used more and more frequently. The calcium carbonate again neutralises some of the acid in the soil.

Figure 7.7 Application of lime

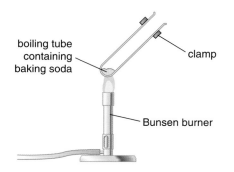

Figure 7.8 Heating baking soda

▶ Baking soda and baking powder

Baking soda

The chemical name for baking soda is sodium hydrogencarbonate. A sample in a test tube will break down when heated strongly in a Bunsen flame (Figure 7.8).

If the total mass of the baking soda and the boiling tube is measured before heating and after heating, the mass has gone down. This is because water vapour and carbon dioxide are lost from the boiling tube.

The equation for the reaction is:

$$\text{sodium hydrogen carbonate} \xrightarrow{\text{HEAT}} \text{sodium carbonate} + \text{carbon dioxide} + \text{water}$$

The chemical formulae in this equation are as follows:

- sodium hydrogencarbonate is $NaHCO_3$
- sodium carbonate is Na_2CO_3
- carbon dioxide is CO_2
- water is H_2O.

The balanced symbol equation for this reaction is:

$$2NaHCO_3 \rightarrow Na_2CO_3 + CO_2 + H_2O$$

This equation is balanced as there are the same numbers of each type of atom on the left-hand side of the arrow as there are on the right-hand side of the arrow:

- 2 Na atoms on each side (2 in $2NaHCO_3$ on the left and 2 in Na_2CO_3 on the right)
- 6 O atoms on each side (6 in $2NaHCO_3$ on the left and 3 in Na_2CO_3, 2 in CO_2 and 1 in H_2O on the right)
- 2 H atoms on each side (2 in $2NaHCO_3$ on the left and 2 in H_2O on the right)
- 2 C atoms on each side (2 in $2NaHCO_3$ on the left and 1 in Na_2CO_3 and 1 in CO_2 on the right).

Definition

Thermal decomposition is the breakdown of a compound on heating.

When sodium hydrogencarbonate is heated, some condensation is seen at the top of the boiling tube. This is the water vapour condensing on the colder surface of the boiling tube. Also, there is a crackling noise from the solid in the boiling tube.

When heat is used to break down a compound such as sodium hydrogencarbonate, the reaction is called **thermal decomposition**.

Baking soda will react with acids such as hydrochloric acid, sulfuric acid and vinegar. When acid is added to a beaker containing baking soda, bubbles can be seen and the baking soda will disappear (Figure 7.9). The bubbles are the carbon dioxide gas that the reaction produces. This is the same reaction that removes excess acid from the stomach when baking soda is used as an antacid.

Figure 7.9 Baking soda and acid

Figure 7.10 Baking powder, a cooking ingredient

Baking powder

Baking powder (Figure 7.10) is a mixture of solid sodium hydrogencarbonate, commonly known as baking soda, and solid **tartaric acid**. It is a white solid. When water is added to it, the sodium hydrogencarbonate and the tartaric acid can react.

Baking powder produces bubbles of carbon dioxide when water is added. This is useful in baking as the bubbles help the cake or bread mixture to rise, giving it a lighter texture.

The word equation for the reaction that occurs between sodium hydrogencarbonate and tartaric acid in baking powder is:

$$\text{sodium hydrogencarbonate} + \text{tartaric acid} \rightarrow \text{sodium tartrate} + \text{carbon dioxide} + \text{water}$$

Sherbet is a mixture of solid sodium hydrogencarbonate and solid citric acid. When you put the mixture in your mouth, your saliva allows the two to mix and react. Carbon dioxide gas is produced, which gives the pleasant fizzing in the mouth.

The word equation for the reaction that occurs between sodium hydrogencarbonate and citric acid in sherbet is:

$$\text{sodium hydrogencarbonate} + \text{citric acid} \rightarrow \text{sodium citrate} + \text{carbon dioxide} + \text{water}$$

▶ Exam questions

1 The table below gives some information about acids and alkalis.

a Copy and complete the table.   *(2 marks)*
Choose from: strong acid; red; strong alkali; yellow

Solution	pH	Colour with universal indicator	Type of solution
milk of magnesia	8	blue	weak alkali
oven cleaner	13	purple	
lemon juice	5		weak acid

b Copy and complete the following sentence.   *(1 mark)*
A solution with a pH value of 7 is described as _____.

c **i** Draw the hazard symbol you would expect to see on a strong acid such as hydrochloric acid.   *(1 mark)*

ii Name the hazard symbol found on a bottle of strong acid.   *(1 mark)*

d Give **one** reason why hazard symbols and not just words are put on boxes of chemicals.   *(1 mark)*

CCEA Science: Single Award, Unit 2, Foundation Tier, November 2012, Q3

2 Common household substances contain chemicals. Copy the text and use lines to link each household substance to one chemical it contains.   *(4 marks)*

Household substance	Chemical
vinegar	sodium chloride
oven cleaner	citric acid
baking soda	sodium hydroxide
lemon juice	ethanoic acid
	sodium hydrogencarbonate

CCEA Science: Single Award, Module 3, Foundation Tier, November 2012, Q1a

3 The picture below shows a farmer spraying lime on the soil.

a Copy and complete the following sentence.   *(1 mark)*
Choose from: alkaline; neutral; acidic
Farmers add lime to soil because the soil is _____.

b Universal indicator solution was shaken with four soil samples **A**, **B**, **C** and **D**.
The colour of universal indicator at different pH values is given below.

Colour	red	orange	yellow	light green	dark green	dark blue	purple
pH	1	3	5	7	9	11	13

Use this information to copy and complete the table below.   *(3 marks)*

Soil sample	Colour	pH	Acidic, alkaline or neutral
A		3	
B	dark blue		alkaline
C		7	
D	yellow		acidic

c Which soil sample (**A**, **B**, **C** or **D**) would be best for growing garlic, which needs soil with a pH of 5?   *(1 mark)*

CCEA Science: Single Award, Module 3, Foundation Tier, November 2012, Q2

4 Many sweets contain sherbet.

Copy and complete the following sentences. *(4 marks)*
Choose from: citric acid; oxygen; fizzing; hot; icing sugar; carbon dioxide; salt
Sherbet can be made by mixing together baking soda, _____ and _____. A gas called _____ is produced when sherbet mixes with water in the mouth. This gas produces a pleasant _____ sensation.

CCEA Science: Single Award, Module 3, Foundation Tier, November 2012, Q3

5 a The table below gives information about three different indicators.

Chemical	Colour of universal indicator paper	Colour of red litmus paper	Colour of red cabbage dye	pH range
hydrochloric acid	red	red	red	1–2
sodium hydroxide	dark blue	blue	yellow	12–14
water	green	red	purple	7
ethanoic acid	orange	red	red	3–6
sodium hydrogencarbonate	blue	blue	green	8–10

Use this information to answer the questions that follow.

i Explain why red litmus paper is not suitable to show that a chemical is acidic. *(2 marks)*

ii Suggest which indicator would be most useful to give a full range of pH values. Explain your answer fully. *(3 marks)*

b The pH changes during the reaction between hydrochloric acid and sodium hydroxide were measured using a pH meter. The following graph was obtained.

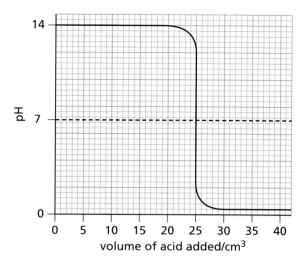

i What was the pH value of sodium hydroxide at the start of this experiment? *(1 mark)*

ii What volume of acid was needed to cause a sudden drop in the pH value? *(1 mark)*

iii Name a suitable piece of apparatus that could have been used to add the acid during this experiment. *(1 mark)*

iv Give the formula of hydrochloric acid and sodium hydroxide. *(2 marks)*

CCEA Chemistry: Unit 2, Higher Tier, February 2013, Q5

6 Acid indigestion is caused by excess hydrochloric acid in the stomach.
Calcium carbonate is present in many antacid tablets.

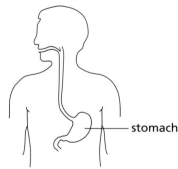

a What name is given to the type of chemical reaction which takes place in the stomach after swallowing an antacid tablet? *(1 mark)*

b Give the name of another chemical substance which could be used as an alternative to calcium carbonate. *(1 mark)*

c Copy, complete and balance the symbol equation below to show the reaction between calcium carbonate and hydrochloric acid.

$$CaCO_3 + \text{_____} \rightarrow CaCl_2 + H_2O + \text{_____}$$

(3 marks)

CCEA Science: Single Award, Module 3, Higher Tier, March 2012, Q7

8 *The world about us*

▶ The structure of the Earth

The world around us is made up of **chemical elements**. Most of these elements are combined together in the oceans and in rocks that make up the Earth.

It is very important to know about the **structure** of the Earth (Figure 8.1) in order to understand about **rocks**, **volcanoes**, **earthquakes** and **mountains**.

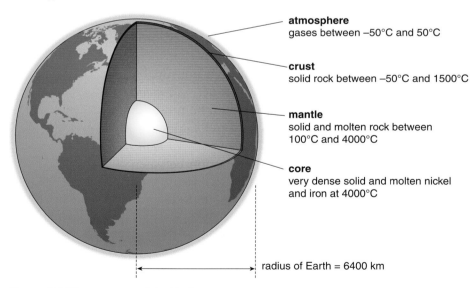

atmosphere
gases between –50°C and 50°C

crust
solid rock between –50°C and 1500°C

mantle
solid and molten rock between 100°C and 4000°C

core
very dense solid and molten nickel and iron at 4000°C

radius of Earth = 6400 km

Figure 8.1 The structure of the Earth

The surface of the Earth is called the **crust**. In the theory of **plate tectonics**, the crust is made up of plates that float on the **mantle**.

These plates are called **tectonic plates** and the study of them is called plate tectonics. These plates are less dense than the mantle so they float on it. They move about because of convection currents in the mantle. As the plates move about they collide with each other. Mountain formation is common near the boundaries of tectonic plates.

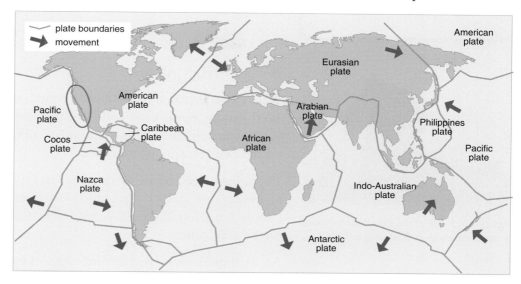

Figure 8.2 Tectonic plates of the Earth

The German scientist Alfred Wegener proposed the theory of **continental drift** in 1912. He suggested that the continents on the surface of the Earth are moving. He proposed that millions of years ago the continents were one large land mass, and that they have since drifted away from each other.

He used the following evidence to help support his theory:

- The **shape of the continents**, for example, South America would fit almost exactly into Africa (see Figure 8.3).
- The **fossils** found in continents that he thought had once been joined were very similar.
- There were **similar species of animals** still living in continents that he thought had once been joined. None of these animals had ever been able to survive in water.

Wegener's theory was not accepted by other scientists. They did not think it was possible as he could not provide a mechanism to explain how the continents moved.

In the 1950s, however, advances in science helped

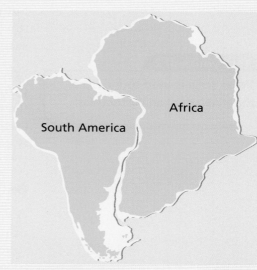

Figure 8.3 Evidence for continental drift in the shape of the continents

Test yourself 1

State two pieces of evidence that Wegener used to back up his theory of continental drift.

to show that the Earth is indeed made up of large plates (tectonic plates) that float on the mantle because they are less dense. The plates move due to convection currents in the mantle. This helped to prove that Wegener's theory of continental drift was correct, as there was now a mechanism by which the continents could move.

▶ Earthquakes

Where two tectonic plates meet on land, there may be a major **earthquake zone**. One zone like this is the San Andreas Fault in California (ringed in red on the map in Figure 8.2). A **fault** is the line where two tectonic plates meet.

There have been many earthquakes in this region of California, including one in 1906 that killed 700 people and left 250 000 people homeless. Figure 8.4 shows some of the devastation that this earthquake caused.

Figure 8.4 Some of the devastation caused by the earthquake in California in 1906

An earthquake is caused by the edges of two tectonic plates trying to move past each other. The tension builds up over time until the plates shift, releasing the stress as an earthquake. The centre of an earthquake is called the **epicentre** and the strength of the earthquake is measured on the **Richter scale**. Charles Richter devised this scale in 1935 to make it easier to describe the power of an earthquake.

Figure 8.5 shows the results of a shift in two tectonic plates after an earthquake in Tennessee in the United States.

Earthquakes release **seismic waves** of **energy**. These travel through the Earth as **body waves** and in the surface of the Earth as **surface waves**. **Seismologists** are scientists who study seismic waves. They can measure these waves on a **seismograph**, which gives the location and strength of the earthquake as measured on the Richter scale.

Figure 8.5 The result of a shift of two tectonic plates

Since earthquakes have been measured and recorded, the strongest reached 9.5 on the Richter scale. There have been no recorded earthquakes with a value of 10 or above.

Seismologists cannot predict where an earthquake will occur. Most people killed in an earthquake are killed by falling buildings, not by the earthquake itself. If possible, in populated areas near a fault line, earthquake-resistant buildings (or earthquake-safe buildings) are built to prevent as many deaths as possible.

Test yourself 2

What scale is used to measure the strength of an earthquake?

▶ Volcanoes

A **volcano** occurs where two tectonic plates are being pulled apart or pushed together, allowing the liquid in the mantle, called **magma**, to reach the surface. When the liquid magma reaches the surface it is called **lava**. Lava comes out of cracks in the Earth's crust. This may be on land or on the sea bed. Around 80% of volcanic eruptions occur on the sea bed.

Volcanoes are cone-shaped. This shape is caused by the layers of lava that have built up during volcanic eruptions over many years. Figure 8.6 shows an erupting volcano. The magma chamber has a build-up of magma and over time this erupts. People living in the area often say there are rumblings for a long time before a volcano erupts, which can give a warning, but there is no scientific way of predicting when a volcano will erupt.

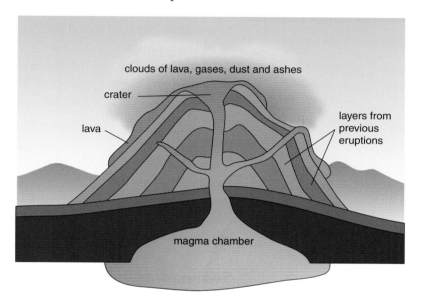

Figure 8.6 The structure of a volcano

The pressure in the magma chamber under the Earth's surface builds up until the magma forces its way up and out. The magma runs down the side of the volcano as lava and, as it cools, it forms a layer on top of the existing rocks. Eruptions that occur in icy or snowy conditions cause the lava to cool more quickly and the solid rock forms faster. The dust and ash and lava thrown into the air will settle on the volcano and form another layer on its surface. This forms the conical shape of the volcano.

Volcanic eruptions result in dust settling in the surrounding area and lava flowing down from the volcano causing destruction of trees. It can also cause loss of life and destruction of property and animals' habitats.

▶ Rocks

The surface of the Earth is made up of rocks, which have formed in different ways. The three different types of rock are:

- igneous
- sedimentary
- metamorphic.

Igneous rocks

Igneous rocks are formed by volcanic activity. An igneous rock is formed when magma cools and solidifies (becomes a solid).

Figure 8.7 Granite has large crystals

Figure 8.8 Basalt has smaller crystals

Granite

If the magma cools below the surface, it forms rocks such as **granite**. Granite has large crystals because the molten magma cools slowly, allowing large crystals to form. The Mourne Mountains in Northern Ireland are formed from granite.

Igneous rocks that form below the ground are described as **intrusive**. The two processes that can bring granite to the surface are:

- **weathering and erosion** – rocks above the granite are weathered away by rain, wind and ice
- **extrusion** – if tectonic plates move, the granite rocks can be forced to the surface by a process of folding that pushes them up and through the rocks above them.

Basalt

If the magma from volcanic eruptions cools above the surface, it forms rocks such as **basalt**. Basalt has much smaller crystals because the magma (or lava as it is above the surface) cools quickly, which only allows small crystals to form. Igneous rocks that form above the surface are described as **extrusive**.

Sedimentary rocks

Erosion by the wind, rain and ice causes rocks to break down into smaller pieces. These smaller pieces gather at the bottom of the seas and rivers and build up, forming layers. This is called **sediment**. The sediment is often mixed with the remains of plants and animals, such as leaves and shells. The pressure from the layers above compacts the sediment, forcing it together to form a solid **sedimentary rock**. Examples of sedimentary rock include **limestone** and **sandstone**.

Figure 8.9 Sandstone rocks near Scrabo Tower in Newtownards, County Down

Fossils

Definition
Fossils are the remains of dead plants and animals preserved in sedimentary rock.

Figure 8.10 An ammonite fossil – ammonites were marine creatures; their fossils have been found all over the world

Fossils are the remains of dead plants and animals preserved in sedimentary rocks. The plants and animals were buried in the rock as it formed.

Some fossils are found on beaches or mountains. Some are found buried deep in the rocks in the Earth's surface. The fact that fossils were all formed within the Earth but now some of them are on the surface tells us that there have been movements in the Earth's crust. Rocks that were buried are now on the surface.

South America and Africa both contain similar fossils at the same depth in the rock. This is because South America and Africa used to be part of one continent but have moved apart over a very long period of time.

Figure 8.11 Slate in County Kerry

Metamorphic rocks

Sedimentary rocks that are buried underground can be changed or **metamorphosed** into **metamorphic rocks**. Limestone can be changed into marble. Mudstone can be changed into slate. This change is caused by high temperature and/or pressure.

► Age and structure of the Earth

In 1648 Archbishop James Ussher calculated the age of the Earth by adding together all the generations in the Bible. He calculated that the creation of the Earth occurred in 4004BC, meaning the Earth is around 6000 years old. However, fossil records suggested that the Earth was much older than Ussher's estimate, as living creatures from millions of years ago were found preserved in rock. Scientific evidence has since suggested that the Earth is actually 4500 million years old (4.5 billion years or 4 500 000 000 years).

Radioactive isotopes decay in a certain period of time. The age of rocks can be estimated using radioactive elements such as uranium and potassium in the rocks. The proportion of daughter nuclei or elements found in these rocks allows scientists to work out how long it has taken them to decay. This is called **radiometric dating**.

The vast age of the Earth (4 500 000 000 years) has led to the concept of '**deep time**'. 4 500 000 000 years is so much longer than any of the periods of time we are familiar with that it can be hard for us to imagine. Human history takes up only a fraction of the total history of the Earth.

▶ Exam questions

1 a Below are two types of rock and some named examples. Copy and match each type of rock with one example.   *(2 marks)*

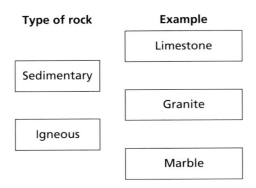

Type of rock	Example
	Limestone
Sedimentary	
	Granite
Igneous	
	Marble

b Label a copy of the structure of the Earth shown below.
Choose from: volcano; crust; core; skin; mantle   *(3 marks)*

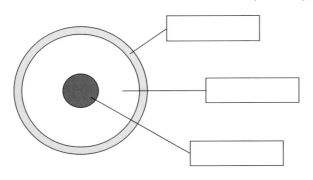

CCEA Science: Single Award, Unit 2, Foundation Tier, November 2012, Q2

2 a Explain fully how Archbishop Ussher used the Bible to estimate the age of the Earth.   *(2 marks)*

b What is the age of the Earth estimated by Ussher?   *(1 mark)*

c Some rocks contain fossils. These can help scientists in estimating the age of the Earth. Explain fully what is meant by the term fossil.   *(2 marks)*

d The modern scientific method for estimating the age of the Earth suggests that the Earth is very much older than Ussher's estimate.
Explain fully how the modern scientific method works.   *(3 marks)*

CCEA Science: Single Award, Unit 2, Higher Tier, March 2012, Q6

3 The diagram below shows the structure of the Earth.

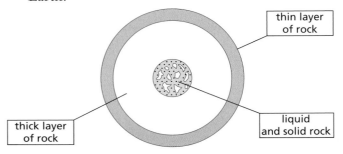

a Use the diagram to describe what the mantle is made from.   *(1 mark)*

b What name is given to the outer layer?   *(1 mark)*

c The following diagram shows a section through a volcano.

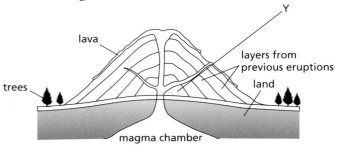

The line from Y shows the first eruption. How many eruptions has this volcano had?   *(1 mark)*

d Describe fully what happens during an eruption and give one effect this will have on the surrounding area.   *(3 marks)*

CCEA Science: Single Award, Module 3, Foundation Tier, November 2012, Q4

4 Ideas on the formation of the continents have been debated since 1597 but a full explanation wasn't developed until 1915 when Alfred Wegener put forward his theory of continental drift. However, it wasn't until 1960 that scientists accepted his theory as being correct.

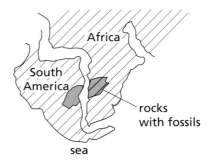

Map showing the relative positions of South America and Africa millions of years ago

Use the information given and your knowledge to explain Alfred Wegener's theory, including the evidence that supports it and reasons why other scientists rejected it.

In this question you will be assessed on your written communication skills including the use of specialist scientific terms. *(6 marks)*

CCEA Science: Single Award, Unit 2, Higher Tier, November 2012, Q8

5 Copy and complete the following sentences.
Choose from: Richter; lava; tectonic; magma

(3 marks)

The intensity of earthquakes is measured on the _____ scale.

Earthquakes are formed when _____ plates rub against each other.

Deep inside a volcano there is a liquid called

_____ .

CCEA Science: Single Award, Module 3, Foundation Tier, November 2011, Q5b

6 **a** There are different ideas about the age of the Earth. One is based on the Book of Genesis in the Bible and involves counting the generations of ancestors.

i Name the person who is known to have based his ideas on the Book of Genesis.

(1 mark)

ii What is the age of the Earth calculated from this method? *(1 mark)*

Another theory is based on radiometric dating.

b Describe how radiometric dating is used to find the age of the Earth. *(3 marks)*

CCEA Science: Single Award, Module 3, Higher Tier, November 2011, Q5

 Elements and compounds

LEARNING OBJECTIVES

By the end of this chapter you should know and understand:

- the structure of an atom in terms of protons, electrons and neutrons
- the symbols for elements and the formulae of some simple compounds
- the reactions of sodium and potassium with water
- that a more reactive metal will displace a less reactive one
- the history of development of the Periodic Table
- the formation of simple compounds from the atoms they contain
- oxidation and reduction
- how to write chemical formulae and word equations
- how to write balanced symbol equations.

▶ Atoms

All substances are **elements**, **compounds** or **mixtures**. They are made up of **particles** called **atoms**.

The atoms of any one element are all identical. For example, all carbon atoms are the same type of atom.

The atoms of different elements are different. For example, an atom of sodium is different from an atom of helium.

Atoms were once thought to be the smallest particles of matter. However, we know now that atoms are made up of three **subatomic** particles, which are **protons**, **electrons** and **neutrons**. Subatomic particles are smaller than the atom (Figure 9.1).

The protons and neutrons are found in the **nucleus** at the centre of the atom. The electrons are arranged in **shells** orbiting the nucleus.

The mass of an atom depends on the number of these subatomic particles.

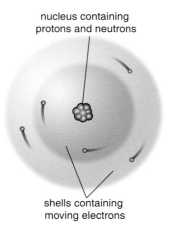

nucleus containing protons and neutrons

shells containing moving electrons

Figure 9.1 The structure of the atom

Table 9.1 Subatomic particles

Subatomic particle	Relative mass	Relative charge
proton	1	+1
neutron	1	0
electron	$\frac{1}{1840}$	−1

Protons and neutrons have the same mass. The mass of an electron is very small in comparison.

The presence of the electrons does not affect the mass of an atom by any noticeable amount. So the mass of an atom depends on the number of protons and neutrons in the nucleus.

Every atom of an element has an **atomic number**. This number is the number of protons in the nucleus of a particular atom. It is used to arrange the elements in the **Periodic Table** (see page 88).

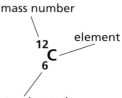

Every atom of an element has a **mass number**, which tells you the total mass of protons and neutrons in the nucleus of that particular atom. The mass number is equal to the total number of protons and neutrons in the nucleus of the atom.

The atomic number and mass number of an atom of an element are often written as shown in this example.

Other examples include $^{23}_{11}$Na, $^{24}_{12}$Mg, $^{1}_{1}$H and $^{35}_{17}$Cl.

To work out the numbers of the three subatomic particles in an atom, we need to use the atomic number and the mass number.

Rule 1   number of protons = atomic number

Rule 2   number of neutrons = mass number − atomic number

Rule 3   number of electrons = number of protons (as an atom is electrically neutral, meaning that it has no charge overall).

> **► EXAMPLE 1**
>
> For $^{23}_{11}$Na, the atomic number is 11 and the mass number is 23.
> Using rule 1: number of protons = 11
> Using rule 2: number of neutrons = 23 − 11 = 12
> Using rule 3: number of electrons = 11
> So an atom of sodium ($^{23}_{11}$Na) has 11 protons, 12 neutrons and 11 electrons.

Some more examples are shown in Table 9.2. Check each of them to see that you can work out the number of each subatomic particle.

Table 9.2 Numbers of subatomic particles

Atom	Number of protons	Number of neutrons	Number of electrons
$^{23}_{11}$Na	11	12	11
$^{12}_{6}$C	6	6	6
$^{24}_{12}$Mg	12	12	12
$^{1}_{1}$H	1	0	1
$^{35}_{17}$Cl	17	18	17

The atomic number is the number of protons in the nucleus of an atom.

Test yourself 1

State the number of protons, electrons and neutrons present in an atom of aluminium (atomic number = 13; mass number = 27).

The arrangement of electrons

Around the nucleus there are several shells or orbits that hold the electrons. Electrons have a negative charge. The nucleus has protons in it so it has a positive charge. The negative electrons are attracted to the positive protons in the nucleus. This attraction means that electrons will try to get into a shell as close to the nucleus as they can.

The maximum numbers of electrons that each shell can hold are given in Table 9.3.

Table 9.3 Numbers of electrons in the atomic shells

Shell	Maximum number of electrons
first	2
second	8
third	8

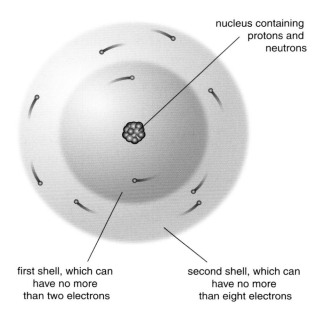

Figure 9.2 The arrangement of shells round a nucleus

This means that if an atom has 11 electrons, then two electrons go in the first shell, eight electrons go in the second shell and there is one electron on its own in the third shell.

This is often written as 2, 8, 1. This is the arrangement of electrons for a sodium atom (Na).

Figure 9.3 is a diagram of an atom of sodium, showing the numbers of particles and the arrangement of the electrons. In each shell, electrons will pair up only when they have to. So in a second shell with five electrons, there will be one pair and the three electrons not paired.

For 2, 8, 1, the electrons in the first shell are paired, all the electrons in the second shell are paired and the one electron in the third shell is on its own. Electrons are usually shown as crosses (×).

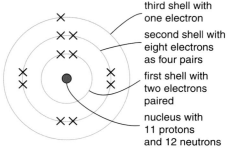

third shell with one electron

second shell with eight electrons as four pairs

first shell with two electrons paired

nucleus with 11 protons and 12 neutrons

Figure 9.3 The arrangement of electrons for a sodium atom

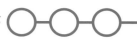

Elements 1 to 20

Figure 9.4 shows the arrangement of the electrons in the atoms of elements with atomic numbers from 1 to 20. When you are drawing a complete atom, you should label the nucleus to show the numbers of protons and neutrons.

The last shell that has electrons is called the outer shell. The electrons in the outer shell are transferred or shared when chemical reactions happen. The movement of these outer shell electrons is the cause of all chemical reactions.

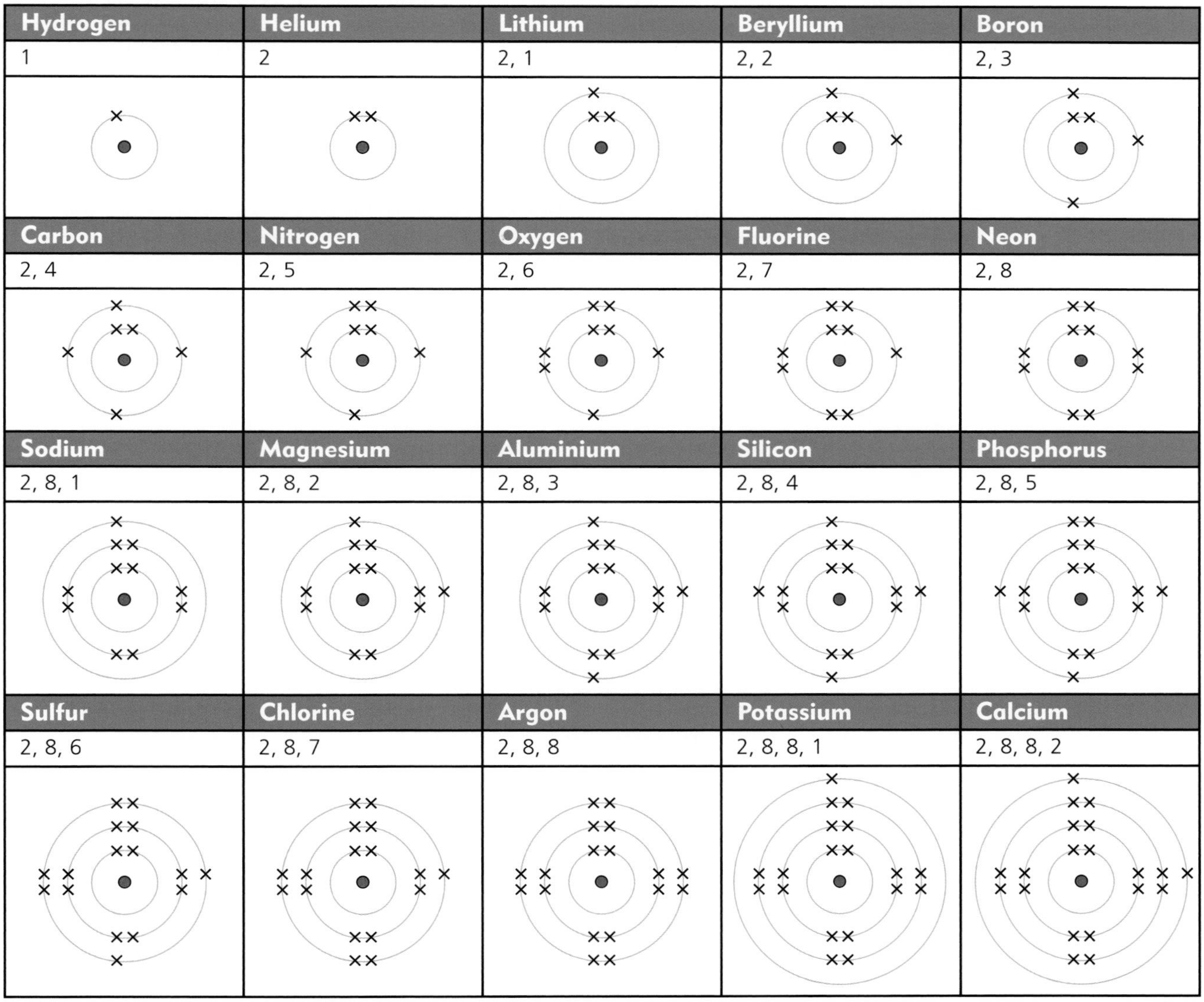

Hydrogen	Helium	Lithium	Beryllium	Boron
1	2	2, 1	2, 2	2, 3
Carbon	Nitrogen	Oxygen	Fluorine	Neon
2, 4	2, 5	2, 6	2, 7	2, 8
Sodium	Magnesium	Aluminium	Silicon	Phosphorus
2, 8, 1	2, 8, 2	2, 8, 3	2, 8, 4	2, 8, 5
Sulfur	Chlorine	Argon	Potassium	Calcium
2, 8, 6	2, 8, 7	2, 8, 8	2, 8, 8, 1	2, 8, 8, 2

Figure 9.4 The arrangement of electrons in atoms of elements 1–20

Test yourself 2

State the electronic configuration of an atom of phosphorus (atomic number 15).

▶ The Periodic Table

The **Periodic Table** lists all known elements. An element cannot be broken down into anything simpler by chemical reactions.

The modern Periodic Table is arranged in order of atomic number.

The periods are the horizontal rows of the Periodic Table.

The groups are the vertical columns of the Periodic Table.

The first period only contains two elements – hydrogen and helium.

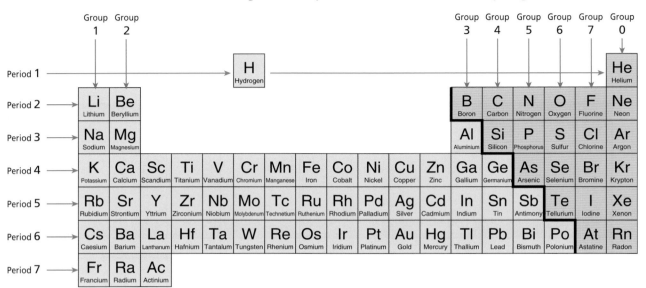

Figure 9.5 The Periodic Table

Figure 9.5 shows the symbols used as short-hand to stand for the elements and their common names.

The thick black line shown on the Periodic Table divides metals, which are listed on the left of the line, from **non-metals**, on the right. (It is shown on the Periodic Table in the Data Leaflet provided in the examination.) The metallic character of the elements decreases as you move from left to right across the Periodic Table. Silicon and germanium are called **semi-metals** as they show properties of both metals and non-metals.

In the Periodic Table, elements that have similar properties are grouped together. This means elements that react in a similar way and are similar physically are in the same vertical column or group. Each of these groups of elements has a number, like those shown above, but some of the groups also have names.

- **Group 1** is also called the **alkali metals**.
- **Group 2** is also called the **alkaline earth metals**.
- **Group 7** is also called the **halogens**.
- **Group 0** (also called **Group 8**) is called the **noble gases**, which are helium, neon, argon, krypton, xenon and radon.
- The block of elements between Group 2 and Group 3 is called the **transition metals**.

Of all the known elements, eleven are gases, two are liquids and the rest are solids.

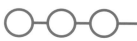

- The eleven gases are hydrogen, nitrogen, oxygen, fluorine, chlorine and the six noble gases.
- The two liquids are bromine (a non-metal), and mercury (a metal).

Some non-metallic elements exist as **diatomic molecules**. This means that two identical atoms are joined together. When you write the **formulae** for these elements, they should be written with a little $_2$ after the symbol, for example, H_2, O_2.

There are **seven** diatomic elements to remember:

Hydrogen, H_2	Nitrogen, N_2	Oxygen, O_2	Fluorine, F_2
Chlorine, Cl_2	Bromine, Br_2	Iodine, I_2	

The formula for sodium is Na but the formula for hydrogen is H_2.

The formula for magnesium is Mg but for the formula for fluorine is F_2.

▶ Compounds

A **compound** is a chemical in which two or more elements are chemically joined together. Compounds are formed when electrons move from one atom to another or when two atoms share electrons between them. It is the electrons in the outer shell that move or are shared.

Many compounds have already been named in this book. Chemists do not write the name of a compound when they can use a chemical short-hand. The symbols of the elements can be used to write **chemical formulae**. Simple compounds are formed from two elements. They can be formed from a metal and a non-metal or from two non-metals.

Simple compounds containing a metal and a non-metal:

- Sodium chloride is a simple compound of sodium and chlorine.
- Magnesium oxide is a simple compound of magnesium and oxygen.
- Copper(II) sulfide is a simple compound of copper and sulfur.

Sodium chloride

The compound sodium chloride has one sodium atom (Na) and one chlorine atom (Cl). Chemists write these together as NaCl. Compounds of Group 1 elements combined with Group 7 elements always have formulae like this, where there is one atom of each element. For example, potassium bromide is KBr.

Potassium oxide

The compound potassium oxide has two potassium atoms (K) and one oxygen atom (O). Chemists write these together as K_2O. Compounds of Group 1 elements combined with Group 6 elements always have formulae like this, where two atoms of the Group 1 element combine with one atom of the Group 6 element. For example, sodium sulfide is Na_2S.

Magnesium chloride

The compound magnesium chloride has one magnesium atom (Mg) and two chlorine atoms (Cl). Chemists write these together as $MgCl_2$. The little $_2$ after the chlorine means there are two of them. Compounds of Group 2 elements combined with Group 7 elements always have formulae like this, where one atom of the Group 2 element is combined with two atoms of the Group 7 element. For example, calcium fluoride is CaF_2.

Magnesium oxide

The compound magnesium oxide has one magnesium atom (Mg) and one oxygen atom (O). Chemists write magnesium oxide as MgO. Compounds of Group 2 elements combined with Group 6 elements always have formulae like this, where one atom of the Group 2 element is combined with one atom of the Group 6 element. For example, calcium oxide is CaO.

Aluminium chloride

The compound aluminium chloride has one aluminium atom (Al) and three chlorine atoms (Cl). Chemists write aluminium chloride as $AlCl_3$. Compounds of Group 3 elements combined with Group 7 elements always have formulae like this, where one atom of the Group 3 element is combined with three atoms of the Group 7 element. For example, aluminium fluoride is AlF_3.

Aluminium oxide

The compound aluminium oxide has two aluminium atoms (Al) and three oxygen atoms (O). Chemists write aluminium oxide as Al_2O_3. Compounds of Group 3 elements combined with Group 6 elements always have formulae like this, where two atoms of the Group 3 element are combined with three atoms of the Group 6 element. For example, aluminium sulfide is Al_2S_3.

Simple transition metal compounds

Most transition metal elements form compounds with similar chemical formulae to the Group 2 elements. (Exceptions are silver, which forms compounds like the Group 1 elements, and iron(III), which forms compounds like Group 3 elements.) The (II) in copper(II) sulfide tells you that copper is acting like a Group 2 element when it is forming compounds. Copper(II) sulfide is CuS (like magnesium oxide). Iron(III) oxide is similar to aluminium oxide so its formula is Fe_2O_3. If there is no roman numeral in brackets after the name of the transition metal element, assume it is II (except silver, which is I). For example, zinc oxide is ZnO (like MgO), copper chloride is $CuCl_2$ (like $MgCl_2$) and silver chloride is AgCl (like NaCl).

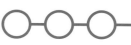
Simple compounds containing two non-metals

In a simple compound that contains two non-metals, the element that is further right in the Periodic Table (ignoring Group 0) and/or higher up changes its name to end in −IDE.

Note

If a compound's name contains 'di', this is a clue as to how many atoms of a particular element are present. 'Di' before an element's name means that there are two atoms of that element. For example, carbon dioxide contains two oxygen atoms and its formula is CO_2.

For example:

- Carbon dioxide is a simple compound formed from carbon and oxygen.
- Hydrogen chloride is a simple compound formed from hydrogen and chlorine.

Formulae of more complex compounds

The back of the Data Leaflet shows some molecular ions that may be used to write formulae. The most commonly used ones are: carbonate, hydrogencarbonate, hydroxide, nitrate and sulfate. Carbonates and sulfates form compounds with similar numbers of atoms in the formulae. Hydrogencarbonates, hydroxides and nitrates again form compounds with similar numbers of atoms in the formulae.

Carbonates and sulfates

- Group 1 elements form carbonates that have formulae like Na_2CO_3 (sodium carbonate) and K_2CO_3 (potassium carbonate). The formulae of Group 1 sulfates are similar to this. Sodium sulfate is Na_2SO_4 and potassium sulfate is K_2SO_4.
- Group 2 elements form carbonates that have formulae like $MgCO_3$ (magnesium carbonate) and $CaCO_3$ (calcium carbonate). Again, the formulae of Group 2 sulfates are similar to this. Magnesium sulfate is $MgSO_4$ and calcium sulfate is $CaSO_4$.
- Aluminium sulfate is $Al_2(SO_4)_3$ and iron(III) sulfate is $Fe_2(SO_4)_3$.

Hydrogencarbonates, hydroxides and nitrates

- Group 1 elements form hydrogencarbonates that have formulae like $NaHCO_3$ (sodium hydrogencarbonate) and $KHCO_3$ (potassium hydrogencarbonate).
- Group 1 elements form hydroxides that have formulae like $NaOH$ (sodium hydroxide) and KOH (potassium hydroxide).
- Group 1 elements form nitrates that have formulae like $NaNO_3$ (sodium nitrate) and KNO_3 (potassium nitrate).
- Group 2 elements form hydrogencarbonates that have formulae like $Mg(HCO_3)_2$ (magnesium hydrogencarbonate) and $Ca(HCO_3)_2$ (calcium hydrogencarbonate). These compounds do not exist as solids but do cause temporary hardness when dissolved in water (see Chapter 11).
- Group 2 elements form hydroxides that have formulae like $Mg(OH)_2$ (magnesium hydroxide) and $Ca(OH)_2$ (calcium hydroxide).
- Group 2 elements form nitrates that have formulae like $Mg(NO_3)_2$ (magnesium nitrate) and $Ca(NO_3)_2$ (calcium nitrate).
- Aluminium hydroxide is $Al(OH)_3$ and aluminium nitrate is $Al(NO_3)_3$.

More complex compounds of transition metals

Again, the (II) in copper(II) sulfate tells you that copper is acting like a Group 2 element when it is forming compounds. Copper(II) sulfate is $CuSO_4$ (like magnesium sulfate). Iron(III) nitrate is similar to aluminium nitrate so its formula is $Fe(NO_3)_3$. If there is no roman numeral in brackets after the name of the transition metal element, assume it is II (except silver, which is I). For example, zinc hydroxide is $Zn(OH)_2$ (like $Mg(OH)_2$), copper carbonate is $CuCO_3$ (like $CaCO_3$), and silver nitrate is $AgNO_3$ (like $NaNO_3$).

Naming compounds

Compounds can be named from their formulae. Compounds usually have two parts to their name.

- **Al_2O_3** contains 2 Al (aluminium) and 3 O (oxygen). Oxygen is further up the Periodic Table and further to the right than aluminium. Therefore its name changes from oxygen to oxide and is the second part of the name. The name of this compound is **aluminium oxide**.
- **CaF_2** contains 1 Ca (calcium) and 2 F (fluorine). Fluorine is further up the Periodic Table and further to the right than calcium. Therefore its name changes from fluorine to fluoride and is the second part of the name. The name of this compound is **calcium fluoride**.
- **K_2SO_4** contains 2 K (potassium) and 1 SO₄ (sulfate – from the back of the Data Leaflet). The name of this compound is **potassium sulfate**.

Some compounds, such as water (H_2O) and methane (CH_4), have only one name. It is important to learn the formulae of these compounds. Other compounds with special names are hydrochloric acid (HCl) and sulfuric acid (H_2SO_4).

▶ Atoms in formulae

Questions can be asked about the total number of atoms in a given formula or the total number of a specific atom.

▶ EXAMPLE 2

How many atoms are present in one molecule of sulfuric acid, H_2SO_4?
There are 2 H atoms, 1 S atom and 4 O atoms, so there are a total of 7 atoms present in one sulfuric acid molecule.

▶ EXAMPLE 3

How many oxygen atoms are present in one molecule of aluminium sulfate, $Al_2(SO_4)_3$?
The answer is the total of all the oxygen atoms in one molecule. Therefore the answer is 12, as there are three SO₄ in one $Al_2(SO_4)_3$.

Test yourself 3

Name the compound with the formula $Mg(OH)_2$.

Note

When writing formulae, make sure the correct capital and lower case letters are used. Copper sulfate is $CuSO_4$. $CUSO_4$ and $CuSo_4$ are NOT correct. Magnesium chloride is $MgCl_2$. $MgCL_2$ and $MGCl_2$ are NOT correct. The correct symbols for elements must be used. The Data Leaflet contains a Periodic Table with all the correct symbols for elements.

Test yourself 4

How many hydrogen atoms are there in one calcium hydrogencarbonate molecule, $Ca(HCO_3)_2$?

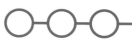

Figure 9.6 Sodium in a jar

Figure 9.7 Sodium reacting with water

Figure 9.8 Potassium reacting with water

► Group 1 (the alkali metals)

All the alkali metals are soft, grey solids. They are all very reactive metals and are stored in oil to stop them reacting with the air. They can be cut easily with a knife or a scalpel. When they are cut they show a shiny surface that starts to go dull as the metal reacts with the air. They must not be allowed to touch human skin.

All the alkali metals react with water. If a piece of lithium is added to water if floats on the surface, moves around, hisses, heat is released and a colourless solution remains. Figures 9.7 and 9.8 show sodium and potassium reacting with water.

If a small piece of sodium is added to water, it floats on the water and moves about on the surface. There is hissing as a gas is produced. It sometimes burns with a yellow flame and will eventually disappear. The reaction is very vigorous.

If a small piece of potassium is added to water, it floats on the water and moves about on the surface. There is hissing as a gas is produced. It burns with a lilac flame and will eventually disappear, with a crack. The reaction is even more vigorous than the reaction of sodium with water. Potassium is more reactive than sodium.

As you move down Group 1, the elements become more reactive. Rubidium and caesium react violently with water. The lower down the Periodic Table a Group 1 element is, the more reactive it is and so the faster and more vigorously it will react with water.

When Group 1 elements react with water, they form a solution and release a gas, which is hydrogen. The word equations for the reactions are:

lithium + water → lithium hydroxide + hydrogen

sodium + water → sodium hydroxide + hydrogen

potassium + water → potassium hydroxide + hydrogen

All Group 1 metals react with water to make a metal hydroxide (e.g. NaOH) and release hydrogen gas (H_2). The solution is the metal hydroxide and the fizzing is caused by the hydrogen gas.

The balanced symbol equations for these reactions are:

$$2Li + 2H_2O \rightarrow 2LiOH + H_2$$

$$2Na + 2H_2O \rightarrow 2NaOH + H_2$$

$$2K + 2H_2O \rightarrow 2KOH + H_2$$

All Group 1 metals react with water in a similar way. The balanced symbol equations for the reactions are always balanced using 2 before the metal, 2 before the water and 2 before the metal hydroxide.

► Other metals

All the other metals in the Periodic Table are less reactive than the Group 1 elements.

Test yourself 5

How is sodium stored safely in the lab?

93

Magnesium, zinc, iron and copper are all metals. They do not react with water but most react with dilute acids such as hydrochloric acid. When metals react with acids, hydrogen gas is produced so there are bubbles in the acid.

Figure 9.9 shows three of the elements with hydrochloric acid.

Figure 9.9 Metals with hydrochloric acid: (a) copper, (b) magnesium, (c) zinc

- Copper does not react with hydrochloric acid, so it is the least reactive of the three.
- Magnesium produces the most bubbles, so it is the most reactive.
- Zinc is more reactive than copper but less reactive than magnesium.
- If iron were included, it would be less reactive than zinc and more reactive than copper. You would see a few bubbles in the test tube.

When a metal reacts with an acid, a salt and hydrogen are produced:

zinc + hydrochloric acid → zinc chloride + hydrogen

magnesium + sulfuric acid → magnesium sulfate + hydrogen

See Chapter 7 to revise the names of salts.

The balanced symbol equations for these reactions are:

$$Zn + 2HCl \rightarrow ZnCl_2 + H_2$$

$$Mg + H_2SO_4 \rightarrow MgSO_4 + H_2$$

When a compound containing a metal is dissolved in water and another metal is added to it, a **displacement reaction** can occur. This only happens if the metal being added is more reactive than the one in the solution.

In Figure 9.10, the iron nail is placed in the solution of copper sulfate. Iron is more reactive than copper so a reaction happens. Iron, which is the more reactive metal, displaces copper, the less reactive metal. The copper coats the iron nail in the test tube.

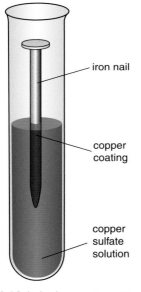

iron nail

copper coating

copper sulfate solution

Figure 9.10 A displacement reaction with iron and copper

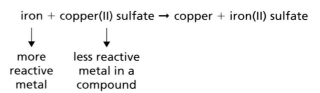

iron + copper(II) sulfate → copper + iron(II) sulfate

more reactive metal

less reactive metal in a compound

The balanced symbol equation for the above reaction is:

$$Fe + CuSO_4 \rightarrow Cu + FeSO_4$$

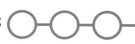

Figure 9.11 A displacement reaction with copper and silver

When a piece of copper wire is placed in a solution of silver nitrate, the copper wire becomes coated with a grey solid (Figure 9.11).

The grey solid is silver.

Copper is more reactive than silver.

copper + silver nitrate → copper (II) nitrate + silver

The balanced symbol equation for this reaction is:

$$Cu + 2AgNO_3 \rightarrow Cu(NO_3)_2 + 2Ag$$

Displacement reactions can be used to determine a **reactivity series**:

- A set of reactions between metals and their metal salt solutions is carried out.
- The metals are simply placed in a solution of the metal salt (usually the sulfate). The results are often recorded in a table like Table 9.4.

Table 9.4 Determining a reactivity series

Metal	magnesium sulfate	copper(II) sulfate	iron(II) sulfate	zinc sulfate
magnesium		✔	✔	✔
copper	✕		✕	✕
iron	✕	✔		✕
zinc	✕	✔	✔	

- A tick (✔) is used to indicate a reaction occurring. A cross (✕) indicates no reaction.
- The parts of the table that are shaded show that the metal should not be placed in a solution of its own salt. For example, magnesium is not placed in magnesium sulfate solution.
- From the table you can see that magnesium displaces the other three metals from their solutions. This shows that magnesium is the most reactive.
- Zinc displaces copper and iron from their solutions but it does not displace magnesium. This shows that zinc is the next most reactive after magnesium.
- Iron displaces only copper from its solution so iron is the third most reactive.
- Copper(II) sulfate solution is blue. When magnesium, zinc or iron react with copper(II) sulfate solution, the blue colour fades as the copper is removed. Specks of solid copper appear in the solution. All these displacement reactions release heat.
- Copper does not displace any of the other metals from their solutions. This shows that it is the least reactive in this investigation.
- The reactivity in order from most reactive to least reactive is:

magnesium   zinc   iron   copper

A typical word equation for one of these displacement reactions is:

magnesium + copper(II) sulfate → magnesium sulfate + copper

The balanced symbol equation for this reaction is:

$$Mg + CuSO_4 \rightarrow MgSO_4 + Cu$$

There will be two elements (Mg and Cu) in the balanced symbol equation and two compounds ($CuSO_4$ and $MgSO_4$), as the more reactive element displaces the less reactive one.

▶ Group 0 (the noble gases)

Group 0 (or 8) of the Periodic Table contains only gases. These are the noble gases. They are all colourless and they are called noble as they do not react very well with any other elements. Because they are so unreactive, the noble gases were discovered much later than many other elements. Although they are found in air, separating them from the air was very difficult. All of the noble gases except helium were discovered in the late nineteenth century by Lord Rayleigh. Helium, neon and argon do not form any compounds. They are **chemically inert**.

▶ History of the Periodic Table

The ancient Greeks believed that everything was made up of four different elements: Earth, Air, Fire and Water. When substances burned they released the 'Fire' element and often turned into ash or 'Earth'. Some substances released a gas on heating, which was supposed to be 'Air'. Others released 'Water' or reacted with 'Water'. As time progressed, more techniques were developed for examining elements and their compounds and more elements were discovered. For example, the discovery of electricity at the beginning of the nineteenth century allowed the extraction of more reactive elements from their compounds.

In 1864, the English chemist John Newlands arranged all the known elements in order of atomic mass. He found the first element was similar to the eighth and the second to the ninth. He called this pattern the **law of octaves**. There were no known noble gases at this stage.

Newlands' law of octaves was limited in that the noble gases had not yet been discovered. Some elements did not fit easily into the scheme (for example, oxygen, sulfur and iron were all in the same group) and Newlands did not have a block of transition metals.

In 1869, the Russian chemist Dmitri Mendeleev also arranged the elements in order of atomic mass (or atomic weight). However, he left gaps for undiscovered elements and switched the mass order to fit the patterns in the table. (The noble gases had still not been discovered.)

Newlands and Mendeleev both used observations of the physical and chemical properties of the elements, such as colour, reactivity and atomic weight, to determine their position in the Periodic Table. Mendeleev used his Periodic Table to predict the properties of elements that had not yet been discovered. These elements had almost exactly these properties when they were discovered.

Test yourself 6

Name the four elements of the ancient Greeks.

► Arrangement of electrons from the Periodic Table

You can use the Periodic Table to work out the arrangement of the electrons in an atom.

The group number gives the number of electrons in the outer shell.

The period number gives the number of shells, so the outer shell number will be the period number.

► EXAMPLE 4

From the Periodic Table on page 88, magnesium (Mg) is in Group 2 and is in period 3.

Period 3 → three shells being used

Group 2 → two electrons in outer (third) shell

The first and second shells must be full, with two and then eight electrons.

The arrangement of electrons for magnesium is 2, 8, 2.

Oxygen (O) is in Group 6 and is in period 2.

Period 2 → two shells being used

Group 6 → six electrons in the outer (second) shell

The first shell must be full, with two electrons.

The arrangement of electrons for oxygen is 2, 6.

Potassium (K) is in Group 1 and period 4.

Period 4 → four shells being used

Group 1 → one electron in the outer (fourth) shell

The first three shells must be full, with two then eight and then eight electrons.

The arrangement of electrons for potassium is 2, 8, 8, 1.

► Formation of compounds

Compounds formed from a metal and a non-metal are called **ionic** compounds. In ionic compounds, electrons are given away by one atom and these electrons are taken by another atom. Compounds that only contain non-metals are called **covalent** compounds. The atoms in covalent compounds share electrons.

Ionic compounds

Ionic compounds are compounds that contain a metal. Examples are sodium chloride (NaCl) and magnesium oxide (MgO).

Ionic compounds are made up of ions, which are charged particles. An ionic compound contains a positive ion and a negative ion.

Simple ions are those that are formed when an atom of an element gains or loses electrons, for example Na^+, O^{2-}, Mg^{2+} and Cl^-.

Formation of ions from atoms

When an ionic compound forms from the atoms of its elements, a transfer of electrons occurs. Metal atoms lose electrons and give them to non-metal atoms, which gain electrons. Each will lose or gain enough

Note

electrons to give it a full outer shell and make it more stable. When a metal atom loses electrons, it becomes a positively charged ion. When a non-metal atom gains electrons, it becomes a negatively charged ion.

There are two main combinations used:

1 Group 1 metal with Group 7 non-metal, e.g. NaCl
2 Group 2 metal with Group 6 non-metal, e.g. MgO.

Example 1: Sodium chloride

A sodium atom has an electronic configuration of 2, 8, 1.

When it reacts with a chlorine atom (electronic configuration 2, 8, 7), the single outer electron of the sodium atom is given to the outer shell of the chlorine atom.

Sodium now has only 10 electrons (2, 8) but it still has 11 protons in its nucleus so it has a charge of '+'.

The sodium atom is written 'Na'. The sodium ion is written 'Na$^+$'.

Simple positive ions have the same name as the atom, so it is called a sodium ion.

Chlorine now has 18 electrons (2, 8, 8) but it still has 17 protons in its nucleus so it has a charge of '−'.

The chlorine atom is written 'Cl'. The chloride ion is written 'Cl$^-$'.

Simple negative ions change the end of their name to −IDE, so it is called a chloride ion.

The sodium and chloride ions are attracted to each other and form the ionic compound.

An ionic bond is the attraction between oppositely charged ions in an ionic compound.

Figure 9.12 summarises the process of ion formation in sodium chloride.

The compound formed is called sodium chloride (as it contains sodium ions and chloride ions).

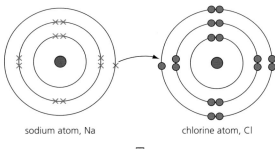

sodium atom, Na   chlorine atom, Cl

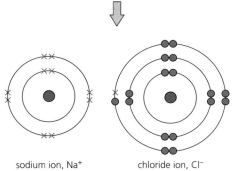

sodium ion, Na$^+$ chloride ion, Cl$^-$

Figure 9.12 Ion formation in sodium chloride

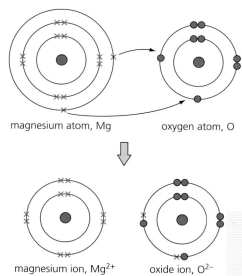

Figure 9.13 Ion formation in magnesium oxide

Example 2: Magnesium oxide

Only one magnesium atom is required for each oxygen atom when magnesium oxide forms, as each magnesium atom loses two electrons and each oxygen atom gains two electrons.

A magnesium ion is Mg^{2+} as it has 10 electrons (2, 8) but 12 protons (atomic number = 12).

An oxide ion is O^{2-} as it has 10 electrons (2, 8) but 8 protons (atomic number = 8).

The formula of magnesium oxide is MgO.

Covalent compounds

When non-metal atoms bond to form compounds they share electrons. Non-metal atoms share electrons to get a full outer shell. The shared electrons count towards the outer shell electrons for both atoms. The shared electrons make a **covalent bond** between the atoms, which holds them together.

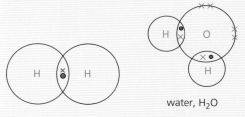

Figure 9.14 Hydrogen, H_2 **Figure 9.15** Water, H_2O

▶ Oxidation and reduction

> **Oxidation** is the gain or addition of oxygen and **reduction** is the loss or removal of oxygen.
>
> *Definition*

Oxidation is when an element gains oxygen. Reduction is when an element loses oxygen.

When magnesium burns in air it gains oxygen and forms magnesium oxide. The word equation for the reaction is:

magnesium + oxygen → magnesium oxide

The balanced symbol equation is:

$$2Mg + O_2 \rightarrow 2MgO$$

In this reaction magnesium gains oxygen. The gain of oxygen is oxidation, so magnesium is oxidised.

Copper(II) oxide reacts with hydrogen to form copper and water. The word equation for the reaction is:

copper(II) oxide + hydrogen → copper + water

The balanced symbol equation is:

$$CuO + H_2 \rightarrow Cu + H_2O$$

In this reaction the copper loses oxygen. Loss of oxygen is reduction. The hydrogen gains oxygen. Gain of oxygen is oxidation. Copper is reduced and hydrogen is oxidised.

This can be applied to any reaction where the amount of oxygen changes. A loss of oxygen is reduction and a gain of oxygen is oxidation.

▶ Exam questions

1 Some students compared the reactivity of four metals (cobalt, iron, copper and magnesium) by adding a small amount of each to sulfate solutions of the other metals. If there was a reaction they used a tick (✓); for no reaction they used a cross (✗). The results are shown below.

Solution / Metal	Cobalt sulfate	Iron sulfate	Copper sulfate	Magnesium sulfate
cobalt		✗	✓	✗
iron	✓		✓	✗
copper	✗	✗		✗
magnesium	✓	✓	✓	

a Use the information in the table and your knowledge to answer the following questions.
  i Which metal is the most reactive? *(1 mark)*
  ii Which metal is the least reactive? *(1 mark)*
  iii Give **two** observations you would make when magnesium is added to copper sulfate solution. *(2 marks)*
b Copy and complete the word equation for the reaction of magnesium with iron sulfate.
  magnesium + iron sulfate → _____ + _____ *(2 marks)*
c Elements and compounds can be represented by chemical symbols, but they must be written correctly. Give the correct formula for the compounds copper sulfate and magnesium chloride.
  (You may find your Data Leaflet helpful.)
  i copper sulfate *(1 mark)*
    Choose from: $CuSO_4$; CoSu ; $CuSO_2$; $CUSO_4$
  ii magnesium chloride *(1 mark)*
    Choose from: MGCl ; Mgcl$_2$; MC ; $MgCl_2$
  CCEA Science: Single Award, Unit 2, Foundation Tier, November 2012, Q7

2 The table shows some information about the elements that are found in Period 3 of the Periodic Table.
  Use this information and your knowledge to answer the following questions.
  a Name the **metal** which has the highest melting point. *(1 mark)*
  b Describe the trend in the metallic character across Period 3. *(1 mark)*

Name of element	Symbol	Atomic number	Melting point/°C	Boiling point/°C	Metallic character
sodium	Na	11	98	883	metal
magnesium	Mg	12	639	1090	metal
aluminium	Al	13	660	2467	metal
silicon	Si	14	1410	2680	semi-metal
phosphorus	P	15	44	280	non-metal
sulfur	S	16	113	445	non-metal
chlorine	Cl	17	−101	−35	non-metal
argon	Ar	18	−189	−186	non-metal

c Name an element from the table that is a **gas** at room temperature (25 °C). *(1 mark)*
d Name the element which is an **alkali metal**. *(1 mark)*
e What is the electronic configuration of the **semi-metal**? *(1 mark)*
  Choose from: 2, 8, 4 ; 2, 4, 8 ; 2, 8, 6
f Sodium reacts with chlorine to form the compound sodium chloride. What is the formula for **sodium chloride**? *(1 mark)*
CCEA Science: Single Award, Unit 2, Foundation Tier, November 2012, Q8

3 The diagram shows an atom of boron.

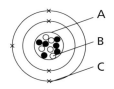

a Name the parts labelled **A**, **B** and **C** on the diagram above. *(3 marks)*
b A fluorine atom has nine electrons. Draw a diagram to show how all the electrons are arranged in an atom of fluorine. *(2 marks)*
c What is meant by the term **atomic number**? *(1 mark)*
d The table below contains information about the structure of four elements, **W**, **X**, **Y** and **Z**. (You may find your Data Leaflet helpful.)

Element	Number of protons	Number of neutrons	Number of electrons
W	2	2	2
X	11	12	11
Y	20	20	20
Z	8	8	8

i Calculate the mass number of element **Y**.
(1 mark)

ii Name the element **X**. *(1 mark)*

iii Which element (**W**, **X**, **Y**, **Z**) has six electrons in its outer shell? *(1 mark)*

iv Which element (**W**, **X**, **Y**, **Z**) is a noble gas? *(1 mark)*

CCEA Science: Single Award, Unit 2, Foundation Tier, November 2012, Q9

4 Copy and complete the diagrams below to show the arrangement of **all** of the electrons in a sodium atom and a chlorine atom.

a Sodium atom **b** Chlorine atom
(1 mark) *(1 mark)*

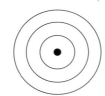 

CCEA Science: Single Award, Unit 2, Higher Tier, March 2012, Q5a

5 The Periodic Table has been developed over a period of time. Dmitri Mendeleev (see photo) was one of the chemists who helped to do this.

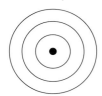

The Greeks were the first to attempt to classify the elements. They had just four elements.

John Newlands noticed a repeating pattern and he tried to put the chemical elements into a table.

Mendeleev developed the idea of a table further and left some gaps in between the elements.

Use the information given and your knowledge to answer the following questions.

You may find your Data Leaflet helpful.

a Name the four elements known to the Greeks. *(1 mark)*

b What was the repeating pattern noticed by John Newlands? *(1 mark)*

c i In what order did Mendeleev arrange the elements? *(1 mark)*

ii Why did he leave gaps between some of the elements? *(1 mark)*

d The modern Periodic Table is still very like the one produced by Mendeleev. However, much more is now known about the structure of atoms. How does the modern Periodic Table take account of what is now known about the structure of the atom?
(2 marks)

CCEA Science: Single Award, Unit 2, Higher Tier, March 2012, Q7

6 A student did an experiment to investigate which metals are the most reactive. He set up the apparatus as shown in the diagram below.

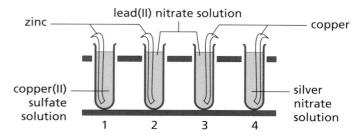

He recorded his results in a table as follows:

Test tube	Appearance of solution at start	Appearance of metal at start	Appearance of solution after 2 hours	Appearance of metal after 2 hours
1	blue	silvery colour	colourless	reddish brown deposit
2	colourless	silvery colour	colourless	greyish white deposit
3	colourless	reddish brown colour	colourless	reddish brown colour, no deposit
4	colourless	reddish brown colour	blue	greyish deposit

Use this information to answer the following questions.

a What name is given to a reaction in which one metal takes the place of another metal?
(1 mark)

b In which test tube, 1, 2, 3 or 4, was there no chemical reaction? *(1 mark)*

c Name the reddish-brown deposit on the zinc metal in test tube 1. *(1 mark)*

d The solution in test tube 1 lost its blue colour. Explain how this happened. *(1 mark)*

e Which of the metals involved is the most reactive? *(1 mark)*
Choose from: copper; silver; zinc; lead

f Explain fully what has happened in test tube 4.
(2 marks)

CCEA Science: Single Award, Higher Tier Module 3, March 2012, Q2

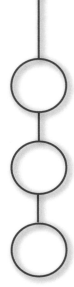

10 Oil, polymers and materials

LEARNING OBJECTIVES

By the end of this chapter you should know and understand:

- **the uses of crude oil and describe its separation into simple mixtures**
- **that fuels burn, producing oxides and releasing heat**
- **the first four alkanes and equations for their combustion**
- **how polymers are made from monomers and equations for their formation**
- **the properties and uses of materials including polymers**
- **what nanoscience is and some of its uses**
- **composite materials and their uses**
- **electrolysis including details of the extraction of aluminium from its ore.**

▶ Coal

Coal is a fossil fuel. It is formed from plants that died and were buried in swamps millions of years ago. Heat and pressure changed the plants into coal. Coal is mainly composed of the element carbon.

When a fuel burns it reacts with the oxygen in the air, producing oxides and releasing heat. The burning of any fuel is called **combustion**.

When coal is burned the main product is carbon dioxide. The equation for the burning of coal is:

carbon + oxygen → carbon dioxide

The balanced symbol equation for this reaction is:

$$C + O_2 \rightarrow CO_2$$

Carbon burns with a sooty orange flame.

In the UK in 2010, 28% of electricity was generated from burning coal.

▶ Crude oil

Many of the materials we use today come from crude oil.

Crude oil is a dark brown, thick, smelly liquid. It is another fossil fuel, formed from dead plants and animals that died millions of years ago

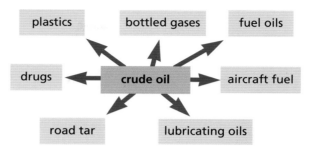

and were buried in sediment. Heat and pressure changed them into crude oil. The diagram below shows uses of crude oil.

Hydrocarbons

A **hydrocarbon** is a chemical that contains only the elements carbon and hydrogen. Crude oil is a mixture of liquid hydrocarbons, with other gases and solid hydrocarbons dissolved in it.

The following list names some hydrocarbons that are found in crude oil, with their formulae:

Methane is CH_4	Ethane is C_2H_6	Propane is C_3H_8	Butane is C_4H_{10}
Octane is C_8H_{18}	Decane is $C_{10}H_{22}$	Heptacosane is $C_{27}H_{56}$	

The only two elements in all of these hydrocarbons are carbon (C) and hydrogen (H). Methane, ethane, propane and butane are gases dissolved in crude oil. Octane and decane are liquids and are part of the liquid mixture. Heptacosane is a solid and is dissolved in the crude oil.

Table 10.1 gives the names, chemical formulae and structural formulae of methane, ethane, propane and butane, which are the first four members of the **alkanes**. The alkanes are a family of organic compounds.

Test yourself 1

What two elements are present in a hydrocarbon?

Table 10.1 The first four alkanes

Name	Molecular formula	Structural formula	State at room temperature and pressure
methane	CH_4	H │ H—C—H │ H	gas
ethane	C_2H_6	H H │ │ H—C—C—H │ │ H H	gas
propane	C_3H_8	H H H │ │ │ H—C—C—C—H │ │ │ H H H	gas
butane	C_4H_{10}	H H H H │ │ │ │ H—C—C—C—C—H │ │ │ │ H H H H	gas

Natural gas is mainly made up of the hydrocarbon methane. It is used to heat homes and for cooking. Natural gas also contains a few other hydrocarbons in small amounts.

All hydrocarbons can be burned. When hydrocarbon fuels burn, the hydrogen reacts with oxygen to form water, and the carbon reacts with oxygen to form carbon dioxide.

> hydrocarbon + oxygen → carbon dioxide + water

When methane burns, the word equation for the reaction is:

> methane + oxygen → carbon dioxide + water

All other hydrocarbons burn in the same way, making carbon dioxide and water. The process of burning hydrocarbons releases energy as heat.

Bottled gas (Figure 10.1) is mainly butane, which is a hydrocarbon. When butane burns it forms carbon dioxide and water, releasing heat:

> butane + oxygen → carbon dioxide + water

Figure 10.1 Bottled butane gas

Writing balanced symbol equations for combustion reactions

To balance a complete combustion equation:

1 Write the chemical formula of the hydrocarbon on the left and put '$+ O_2$' after it. Then put an arrow (→).

2 Write '$CO_2 + H_2O$' on the right of the arrow.

3 The number of carbon atoms in the hydrocarbon is the same as the balancing number in front of the CO_2.

4 The number of hydrogen atoms in the hydrocarbon is divided by 2 to get the balancing number in front of the H_2O.

5 Count the total number of oxygen atoms in CO_2 and H_2O (remember that CO_2 has two oxygen atoms per CO_2). Divide this total by 2 to get the balancing number in front of O_2.

6 If the balancing number in front of O_2 has a half, for example '2½', multiply all the balancing numbers by 2 to get whole numbers.

▶ EXAMPLE 1

Write a balanced symbol equation for the combustion of methane, CH_4.

STEP 1 $CH_4 + O_2 →$

STEP 2 $CH_4 + O_2 → CO_2 + H_2O$

STEP 3 There is one C atom in CH_4. This means 1 is the balancing number in front of CO_2. No number is needed as CO_2 in an equation means $1CO_2$.

$CH_4 + O_2 → CO_2 + H_2O$

STEP 4 There are 4 H atoms in CH_4. Divide this by 2 and a '2' is the balancing number in front of H_2O.

$$CH_4 + O_2 \rightarrow CO_2 + 2H_2O$$

STEP 5 There are 2 O atoms in CO_2 and 1 in each of the $2H_2O$ so there are 4 O atoms in total on the right-hand side of the arrow. Dividing this by 2 gives a '2' to go in front of the O_2 on the left-hand side.

$$CH_4 + 2O_2 \rightarrow CO_2 + 2H_2O$$

▶ EXAMPLE 2

Complete the balanced symbol equation for the complete combustion of butane.

$$C_4H_{10} + O_2 \rightarrow$$

It is common for step 1 to be given in the question and for you to complete and balance the combustion equation.

STEP 2 $C_4H_{10} + O_2 \rightarrow CO_2 + H_2O$

STEP 3 There are 4 C atoms in C_4H_{10} so 4 is the balancing number in front of CO_2.

$$C_4H_{10} + O_2 \rightarrow 4CO_2 + H_2O$$

STEP 4 There are 10 H atoms in C_4H_{10}. Divide this by 2 and a '5' is the balancing number in front of H_2O.

$$C_4H_{10} + O_2 \rightarrow 4CO_2 + 5H_2O$$

STEP 5 There are 8 O atoms in $4CO_2$ and 1 in each of the $5H_2O$ so there are 13 O atoms in total on the right-hand side of the arrow. Dividing this by 2 gives '6½' to go in front of the O_2 on the left-hand side.

$$C_4H_{10} + 6½O_2 \rightarrow 4CO_2 + 5H_2O$$

STEP 6 The above equation is perfectly correct but normally whole number balancing numbers are used. Therefore the balancing numbers are all multiplied by 2 (remember that C_4H_{10} means $1C_4H_{10}$ so it becomes $2C_4H_{10}$ when multiplied by 2).

$$2C_4H_{10} + 13O_2 \rightarrow 8CO_2 + 10H_2O$$

Separating crude oil

Crude oil is a **mixture**. It can be separated into its different constituents by **fractional distillation** (Figure 10.2).

The crude oil is heated until it becomes a gas. It is then fed into a steel tower. The tower is hotter at the bottom and cooler at the top. As the mixture of gases moves up the tower, some of them condense, changing from a gas to a liquid. These liquids form at different levels and can be collected separately.

The mixture of solids dissolved in crude oil is called **tar** or **bitumen**. It comes out of the bottom of the fractional distillation tower. The

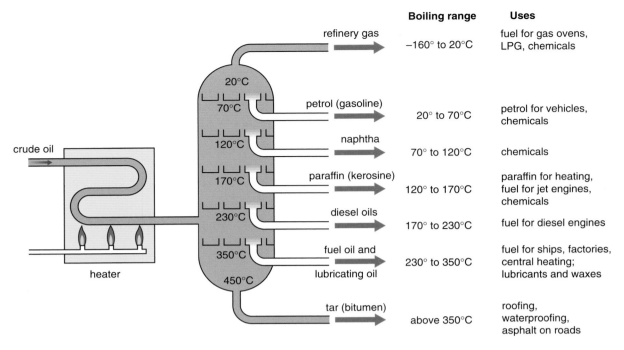

Figure 10.2 The products obtained by fractional distillation of crude oil and their major uses

mixture of gases dissolved in crude oil is referred to as **refinery gases**. They do not condense. The refinery gases come out of the top of the tower, still as gases.

The simpler mixtures of hydrocarbons produced in this way are called **fractions**. The refinery gases make up a fraction, and bitumen is also a fraction. Some of the other fractions are shown in Figure 10.2.

All of the fractions from crude oil contain hydrocarbons and they are all fossil fuels. However, some would not be very good fuels. For example, bitumen will only burn at a very high temperature.

Finding and using crude oil

Crude oil is a **finite resource**. This means that there are not limitless supplies of it – it will eventually run out. Crude oil cannot quickly be replaced because it takes millions of years to form.

It is not easy to measure the amount of crude oil left in the world. It has to be estimated. The four main factors that affect this sort of estimate are shown in the diagram and discussed below.

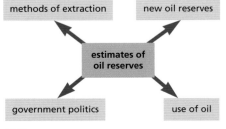

- Improved methods of extraction would allow for more oil to be taken from a reserve than was previously possible.
- New oil reserves are being discovered as methods of detecting them are getting better.
- Our use of crude oil is changing. We would use less oil if we increased the amount of plastic recycling, or if we cut down on the amount of petrol and diesel that we use.

Test yourself 2

What process is used to separate crude oil into simpler mixtures?

- Government projections on the use of crude oil may not be accurate, as they may change the numbers for political reasons:
  - If a government wants to seem more environmentally friendly it can make the figures for use of crude oil and projections for future use appear lower.
  - If the government's opponents want to make the government seem less environmentally friendly they can make the figures for use of crude oil and projections for future use appear higher.

▶ Polymers

A **polymer** is a chain of small molecules that have been bonded together (Figure 10.3). The small molecules are called **monomers**.

The monomer units in the polymer are held together by bonds. The formation of these bonds to form the polymer is called **polymerisation**. Plastics are polymers and have many uses in modern society. The monomers used to make some plastics come from crude oil.

Some common polymers and their monomer units are shown in Table 10.2.

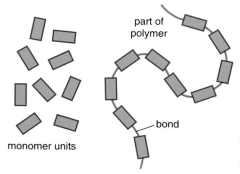

Figure 10.3 Monomers and polymers

part of polymer

bond

monomer units

> **Definition**
>
> A **polymer** is a long-chain molecule formed by joining together many small molecules called monomers.

Table 10.2 Common polymers and their monomer units

Polymer	Monomer	Uses
polythene	ethene	plastic bottles, plastic bags
polypropene	propene	shampoo bottles, plastic chairs
PVC (poly vinyl chloride)	vinyl chloride	window and door frames, clothing

> **Test yourself 3**
>
> Name the polymer formed from ethene.

The balanced symbol equations for the formation of the polymers polythene (from ethene), polypropene (from propene) and PVC (from vinyl chloride) are as shown below.

Polythene
Uses: plastic bags and bottles

$$n \quad \begin{array}{c} H \\ | \\ C \\ | \\ H \end{array} = \begin{array}{c} H \\ | \\ C \\ | \\ H \end{array} \longrightarrow \left[\begin{array}{cc} H & H \\ | & | \\ -C-C- \\ | & | \\ H & H \end{array} \right]_n$$

ethene
monomer

polythene
polymer

Polypropene
Uses: ropes, shampoo bottles, plastic crates

$$n \quad \begin{array}{c} H \\ | \\ C \\ | \\ H \end{array} = \begin{array}{c} CH_3 \\ | \\ C \\ | \\ H \end{array} \longrightarrow \left[\begin{array}{cc} H & CH_3 \\ | & | \\ -C-C- \\ | & | \\ H & H \end{array} \right]_n$$

propene
monomer

polypropene
polymer

Poly vinyl chloride (PVC)

Uses: door and window frames, clothing

$$n \quad \underset{\underset{H}{|}}{\overset{\overset{H}{|}}{C}} = \underset{\underset{H}{|}}{\overset{\overset{Cl}{|}}{C}} \longrightarrow \left[\underset{\underset{H}{|}}{\overset{\overset{H}{|}}{C}} - \underset{\underset{H}{|}}{\overset{\overset{Cl}{|}}{C}} \right]_n$$

vinyl chloride
monomer

poly vinyl chloride (PVC)
polymer

Types of plastic

There are two main types of plastic.

Thermoplastic plastics (thermoplastics)

Most modern plastics are **thermoplastics** (Figure 10.4a). Polythene, polypropene and PVC are all thermoplastics. Thermoplastics can be heated and moulded over and over again.

Thermosetting plastics (thermosets)

Many older plastics are **thermosetting** plastics (Figure 10.4b). Bakelite, melamine and epoxy are all thermosets. Thermosets set when they are heated and cannot be remoulded.

Recycling plastics

If objects made from thermoplastic plastics and thermosetting plastics are collected together, it is difficult to recycle them as they first have to be separated.

Figure 10.4 a) Thermoplastic bottles; b) Thermosetting plastic (a Bakelite telephone)

▶ Materials

The **raw materials** that are used to make everything come from five different sources:

- the Earth, for example, iron, limestone, granite, aluminium
- the sea, for example, salt, bromine
- the air, for example, oxygen, argon, helium
- crude oil, for example, plastics, drugs
- living things (plants and animals), for example, wool, cotton, wood, silk.

The raw materials may need to be processed before they are useful. Sometimes this involves some sort of chemical process.

Materials that do not need to be processed by chemical methods are called **natural** materials.

- Natural materials include wood, wool, salt, cotton, limestone and granite.

If a chemical reaction is needed to make the useful material, it is called a **synthetic** material. Synthetic materials are also called man-made materials.

- Synthetic materials include iron, aluminium, bromine and plastics.

The main types of materials we use are shown in Table 10.3.

Test yourself 4

Where do we get the raw materials to make plastics from?

Test yourself 5

Is polythene a natural or synthetic material?

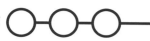

Table 10.3 Main types of materials and their uses

Type	metals	glass	ceramics	fibres	thermoplastic plastics	thermosetting plastics
Examples	iron, aluminium, copper, gold, silver	soda glass, Pyrex (heat-resistant glass)	china, bricks, pottery	nylon, cotton, silk	polythene, polypropene, PVC	bakelite, melamine
Uses	electrical wiring, saucepans, building, horse shoes, jewellery	windscreens, vases, chemical bottles	plates, cups, house bricks	clothing, curtains	plastic bags, plastic bottles, window frames	plastic cups, table tops, old light switches
Properties	good conductors of electricity, good conductors of heat, strong, hard, malleable (can be hammered into shape), ductile (can be drawn out into wires), high melting point, lustrous (shiny), some are reactive	brittle, transparent, hard, can be shaped on heating, does not conduct electricity, unreactive	brittle, hard, high melting point, unreactive, do not conduct electricity	flexible, low density, can be woven, do not conduct electricity	flexible, can be moulded on heating, do not conduct electricity, low density	strong, hard, cannot be remoulded on heating, low density, do not conduct electricity

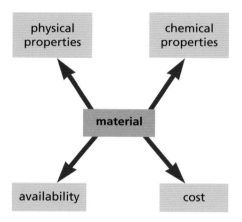

Properties related to use

The use of a material is dictated by its properties:

- A windscreen made out of aluminium would be useless.
- Electrical wires made out of nylon would not work.

The material must have the right properties for the job it is doing.

The diagram shows the factors that are used to decide on the right material for a job.

Physical properties include density, strength, hardness, flexibility, appearance and ability to conduct electricity.

Chemical properties are how the material reacts, especially with water and air, and perhaps items of food if the material is to be used in a kitchen.

Availability is a measure of how easy it would be to get the material – is it available in this country and is there enough of it?

Cost is very important because some materials are very expensive and some are much cheaper.

Decline of traditional materials

Traditional materials such as linen are not used as much nowadays because cheaper materials with better properties are now available. Linen had been used to make tablecloths, napkins and more formal clothing such as men's shirts and women's petticoats.

The decline of the linen industry in Northern Ireland began in the early 1900s, when newer materials became available and also when people started to dress less formally. Paper napkins and handkerchiefs replaced linen ones.

> **Test yourself 6**
>
> State one use of PVC.

Cotton, nylon and blends of other materials have replaced linen materials. These newer materials are easier to process, making them cheaper, and they crease less easily and are easier to iron.

Choosing a material

Scientists can examine the properties of materials. They can then make a decision about which material is best for a particular job.

Figure 10.5 is a graph comparing the stiffness of a material with its density. Materials such as metals and ceramics are stiff and heavy. Rubbers are of medium density but are very flexible.

Suppose a materials scientist is designing a set of five-a-side goal posts. The posts need to have a low density and be stiff enough to stay in shape. Wood could be a possibility but metals have higher stiffness, so a low-density metal is chosen. The metal of choice has to have high stiffness and as low a density as possible, so that it can be moved easily. From the metals in the area on the graph, the scientist chose aluminium as it is a low-density metal with good stiffness.

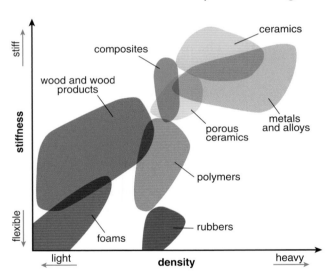

Figure 10.5 The stiffness of a material compared to its density

Composite materials

A **composite material** is one that combines the properties of more than one material to produce a more useful material for a particular purpose. Examples of common composite materials are given in Table 10.4.

> **Definition**
>
> A **composite material** is one that combines the properties of more than one material to provide a more useful material for a particular purpose.

Table 10.4 Composite materials and examples of their uses

Composite material	Made from	Examples of uses
glass fibre (glass-reinforced plastic)	fibres of glass and plastic fibres	loft insulation, boats and car bodies
reinforced concrete	steel rods inside concrete beams	construction
reinforced glass	glass with steel wires	security glass
bone	calcium phosphate and protein	skeleton

A composite material combines the best properties of each material. Glass fibre has the low density of plastic and the extra strength that the glass fibres give it, without the brittle nature of glass. Reinforced concrete has steel rods under tension inside the concrete, which gives the concrete much higher strength than normal concrete. Reinforced glass combines the transparency of glass with the strength of steel. Bone combines the strength of calcium phosphate with the flexibility of protein.

▶ Nanotechnology

Something that is described as **nano** is very small. A measure of one millionth of a millimetre is called a nanometre. The ruler in Figure 10.6 shows a millimetre (1 mm) and a centimetre (1 cm). Something the size of a nanometre cannot be seen by the naked eye. The sizes of atoms are measured in nanometres.

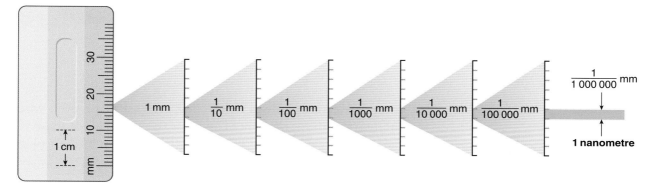

Figure 10.6 A million nanometres make up one millimetre

Nanotechnology involves the design of **nanomaterials** that are very small, often only a few nanometres across. Nanomaterials are more sensitive to light, heat, electrical conductivity and magnetism. These very small particles have a large surface area, which gives them different properties compared to traditional materials.

The latest sun-protection creams use nanotechnology. Older sun-protection creams used zinc oxide and left a white residue (Figure 10.7). Newer creams, using **nanoparticles** of zinc oxide, rub on as a clear film.

Nanoparticles of silver nitrate are used in wound dressings in hospitals. Silver nanoparticles kill bacteria and prevent wounds from becoming infected, which helps healing.

Silver nanoparticles are also used in sterilising sprays in the beauty industry and in medicine to sterilise equipment.

Figure 10.7 Conventional zinc oxide sun-protection cream

Definition
A **smart material** is one that changes its properties with changes in light or heat.

▶ Smart materials

A **smart material** is a material that changes how it behaves (its properties) as a result of a change in one of the following:

- heat
- light exposure.

Thermochromic paints and dyes change colour when heated. They are used in mood rings and in t–shirts that change colour when your body heats them up.

Photochromic paints and dyes change colour when exposed to light. They are used in glasses that darken in colour when it is sunny (Figure 10.8).

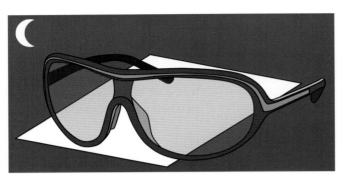

Figure 10.8 Photochromic dyes can be used in sunglasses

Shape-memory alloys retain their original shape, even when you try to bend them out of shape. The most common use of these is in the frames of glasses that can be bent and will return to their original shape.

▶ Electrolysis

Two graphite rods, placed in a liquid and connected externally to a power supply such as a battery or a power pack, can be used to test whether the liquid conducts electricity. If the liquid conducts electricity and is decomposed by it, then **electrolysis** is taking place.

The **electrolyte** is the liquid or solution that conducts electricity and is decomposed by it. The graphite rods used are called **electrodes**. Graphite is used because it conducts electricity and is unreactive.

The negative electrode is called the **cathode**. The positive electrode is called the **anode**.

How electrolysis works

- All electrolytes conduct electricity as they have free ions that can move and carry charge.
- When these positive and negative ions are free to move, the positive ions (called **cations**) move to the negative electrode (called the **cathode**). The negative ions (called **anions**) move to the positive electrode (called the **anode**).

> **Definition**
>
> **Electrolysis** is the decomposition of a liquid electrolyte using a direct current of electricity.

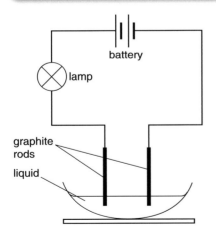

Figure 10.9 The apparatus used to test whether a liquid conducts electricity

Test yourself 7

Explain how electrolysis happens in a molten ionic compound.

Extraction of aluminium from its ore

- Aluminium metal is extracted from its ore using electrolysis. The ore is called bauxite.
- Bauxite is purified to form aluminium oxide (called alumina). The alumina is dissolved in molten cryolite to reduce its melting point and increase the conductivity.
- The crust of aluminium oxide keeps heat in. The operating temperature is 900 °C. The cathode and anode are made of carbon.
- The reaction at the cathode is: $Al^{3+} + 3e^- \rightarrow Al$.
- The carbon anode has to be replaced periodically as it wears away because of its reaction with oxygen. The equation for this reaction is: $C + O_2 \rightarrow CO_2$.
- The extraction of aluminium is expensive because the cost of electricity is high and a high temperature is needed to keep the aluminium oxide molten. The use of cryolite increases the conductivity and reduces the operating temperature, saving money. The aluminium oxide crust keeps some of the heat in, again saving money.
- The expense of recycling aluminium is only a fraction of the cost of producing new aluminium from bauxite. This is why it is important to recycle materials such as aluminium. It saves resources, saves energy, prevents waste going to landfill and costs less.

Figure 10.10 shows the apparatus used to extract aluminium from its ore.

Test yourself 8

Write an ionic equation for the reaction that occurs at the cathode during the extraction of aluminium from its ore.

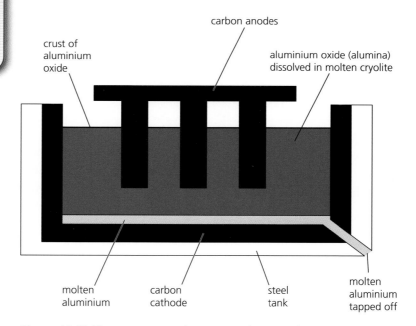

Figure 10.10 The apparatus used to extract aluminium from its ore

► Exam questions

1 a Below are four common materials.
nylon; silk; cotton; polythene
Place each material in the correct column of a copy of the table below. *(2 marks)*

Natural	Synthetic

b Most modern watering cans are made from plastic rather than metal.
Give **one** reason why plastic is a better material for making watering cans.
(1 mark)

CCEA Science: Single Award, Unit 2, Foundation Tier, November 2012, Q1

2 In an investigation the same amount of each of five hydrocarbon fuels was burnt. The amount of energy released was measured and recorded below.

Fuel	Number of carbon atoms	Energy released/kJ
methane	1	900
ethane	2	1500
propane	3	2200
butane	4	2900
pentane	5	3500

a Plot and draw a line graph for these results on a copy of the grid below.
The first point is plotted for you. *(3 marks)*

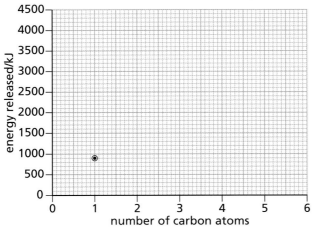

b i State **one** thing that was done in this investigation to make it a fair test. *(1 mark)*
ii Describe the trend shown in these results by copying and completing the following sentence.
As the number of carbon atoms in the fuel increases _____. *(1 mark)*
iii Use the information given to suggest how much energy (in kJ) would be released if hexane, C_6H_{14}, was burnt. *(1 mark)*

CCEA Science: Single Award, Unit 2, Foundation Tier, November 2012, Q4

3 a Aluminium sulfate has the chemical formula $Al_2(SO_4)_3$.
i How many different elements are present in this formula? *(1 mark)*
ii How many oxygen atoms are there in this formula? *(1 mark)*
iii What is the total number of atoms in this formula? *(1 mark)*

Aluminium metal is produced by passing electricity through a cell containing molten aluminium oxide.

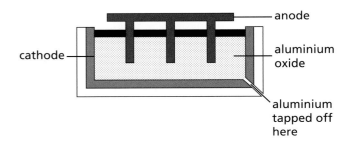

b Describe how the aluminium is extracted from the aluminium oxide by copying and completing the following sentences.
In this extraction process the cathode is _____ charged and is made of _____.
The aluminium ions travel to the _____ where they are discharged and form _____ metal. Oxide ions travel to the _____ where they form _____ gas.
(6 marks)

CCEA Science: Single Award, Unit 2, Higher Tier, March 2012, Q3

4 The properties of four metals are shown in the table below.

Metal	Density/ g/cm³	Relative strength	Melting point/ °C	Relative electrical con- ductivity	Cost per tonne/ £
iron	7.9	1.0	1535	1.0	130
aluminium	2.7	0.3	660	3.7	950
copper	8.9	0.6	1083	5.8	3100
silver	10.5	0.4	962	6.1	250 000

a Use the information in the table to answer the following questions.

i Explain fully why the properties of aluminium make it more suitable than copper for use in overhead electrical cables in the National Grid. *(3 marks)*

ii Explain why iron is used to make bridges. *(2 marks)*

b The table below gives some information about materials A, B, C and D. These could be metals, metal compounds or non-metals.

Metal compounds can only conduct electricity in the liquid state.

Material	Electrical conductivity in solid state	Electrical conductivity in liquid state	Melting point/°C
A	poor	poor	3550
B	good	good	327
C	poor	good	808
D	good	good	1540

Use this information to answer the following questions.

i Which material (A, B, C or D) is a metal with a low melting point? *(1 mark)*

ii Which material (A, B, C or D) is a metal compound? *(1 mark)*

iii Which material (A, B, C or D) is a non-metal? *(1 mark)*

c Silver is used in sterilising sprays and wound dressings.

The silver has to be specially prepared to give it new properties for these specialised uses. Fully describe the silver particles that are used in sterilising sprays. *(2 marks)*

d Some newly developed materials are described as smart materials.

Explain fully what is meant by the term 'smart material'. *(2 marks)*

CCEA Science: Single Award, Unit 2, Higher Tier, March 2012, Q4

5 The following chemical compounds are important hydrocarbons.

methane : ethane : propane : ethene : butane

a i Which one of these compounds is **not** an alkane? *(1 mark)*

ii Propane has the molecular formula C_3H_8. Draw the **structural** formula of propane. *(1 mark)*

iii Give the molecular formula for:
1 butane
2 ethene *(2 marks)*

b Vinyl chloride can be polymerised to form the well known polymer PVC.

Copy and complete the equation for the formation of PVC. *(3 marks)*

CCEA Science: Single Award, Unit 2, Higher Tier, March 2012, Q8

6 Crude oil is made up of many hydrocarbons and these can be separated using fractional distillation.

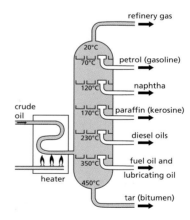

a i Describe how fractional distillation separates the fractions in crude oil. *(3 marks)*

ii Give **one** use of the paraffin fraction. *(1 mark)*

b Ethene is an important hydrocarbon which is used to make polythene.

Describe what happens to ethene molecules when they are polymerised to form polythene. *(2 marks)*

CCEA Science: Single Award, Module 4, Foundation Tier, March 2011, Q6a and b

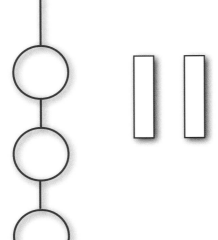

11 Hard water, recycling and exploitation of Earth's resources

▶ Water – soft or hard?

- **Soft water** forms a lather easily with soap.
- **Hard water** will not readily form a lather with soap. Hard water forms a scum with soap.

Activity 1

Testing a sample of water to see if it is hard or soft

1 Place 10 cm³ of water in a test tube.
2 Add 10 drops of soap solution.
3 Put a stopper in the test tube and shake it vigorously for 1 minute.
4 If the water forms lots of bubbles of lather, the water is soft. If the water does not form a good lather, the water is hard.

When comparing the hardness of different samples of water it is important that the experiment is a fair test. This means that only one thing is changed (the type of water) and all other factors such as the volume of water, number of drops of soap solution and time for which it is shaken are kept the same.

The two main types of hardness in water are:

- **temporary** hardness
- **permanent** hardness.

Removal of hardness from water is called **softening**. Temporary hardness can be removed by **boiling**. Permanent hardness cannot be removed by boiling.

Causes of hardness in water

Hardness in water is caused by **dissolved** compounds. Table 11.1 shows various compounds and indicates which are soluble or insoluble in water and which cause hardness in water.

Table 11.1 Compounds, their solubility in water and whether they cause hardness in water

Compound	Soluble in water	Causes hardness in water	Type of hardness
calcium chloride	yes	yes	permanent
sodium chloride	yes	no	–
calcium hydrogencarbonate	yes	yes	temporary
magnesium oxide	no	no	–
magnesium sulfate	yes	yes	permanent
magnesium hydrogencarbonate	yes	yes	temporary
magnesium chloride	yes	yes	permanent

Hardness in water is caused by dissolved calcium and magnesium compounds.

- Only some compounds of calcium and magnesium are soluble.
- Permanent hardness is caused by magnesium or calcium chloride, or magnesium or calcium sulfate, dissolved in water.
- Temporary hardness is caused by magnesium or calcium hydrogencarbonate dissolved in water.
- An ion is a charged particle. A calcium ion is Ca^{2+} and a magnesium ion is Mg^{2+}.
- Calcium compounds contain calcium ions and magnesium compounds contain magnesium ions.

Test yourself 1

Name the two types of hardness found in water.

▶ Softening hard water

Temporary hardness can be removed by boiling the water. Boiling causes the calcium hydrogencarbonate or magnesium hydrogencarbonate dissolved in the hard water to break down. Breaking down a compound by heating it is called **thermal decomposition**.

$$\text{magnesium hydrogencarbonate} \rightarrow \text{magnesium carbonate} + \text{carbon dioxide} + \text{water}$$

$$\text{calcium hydrogencarbonate} \rightarrow \text{calcium carbonate} + \text{carbon dioxide} + \text{water}$$

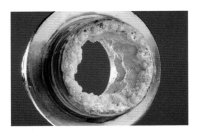

Figure 11.1 Fur inside a hot water pipe

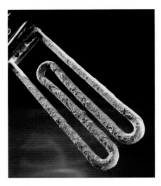

Figure 11.2 Limescale on the heating element of a washing machine

> **Test yourself 2**
>
> State two advantages of hardness in water.

The balanced symbol equations for these reactions are given below:

$$Mg(HCO_3)_2 \rightarrow MgCO_3 + CO_2 + H_2O$$

$$Ca(HCO_3)_2 \rightarrow CaCO_3 + CO_2 + H_2O$$

The problem with boiling to remove temporary hardness in water is that it will produce calcium carbonate and magnesium carbonate, which are insoluble solids. These solids cause **limescale deposits** inside kettles, water pipes and hot water tanks. This may be referred to as **furring up**.

Limescale can stop a kettle working properly. Furring inside pipes cuts down the flow of water. Pipes that become **furred**, as shown in Figure 11.1, may have to be replaced. A heating element like the one in Figure 11.2 will waste energy. Hard water can also leave white marks on clothes that have been washed. These marks are deposits of calcium and magnesium carbonate.

If you live in a hard–water region you have to accept these problems, but there are benefits as well. Hard water tastes better and is useful for making beer. It is good for keeping your bones and teeth strong, as it contains a source of calcium, and it can help prevent heart disease.

Carbonates and hydrogencarbonates

Many metals form compounds called **carbonates** and a few metals form compounds called **hydrogencarbonates**.

Calcium carbonate ($CaCO_3$) and magnesium carbonate ($MgCO_3$) are common compounds found in rocks such as limestone and marble. Magnesium carbonate and calcium carbonate react with acids such as hydrochloric acid:

$$\text{metal carbonate} + \text{acid} \rightarrow \text{salt} + \text{carbon dioxide} + \text{water}$$

When hydrochloric acid is used, the salt formed is a metal **chloride**.

When metal carbonates react with hydrochloric acid, bubbles of carbon dioxide can be seen in the solution.

$$\text{calcium carbonate} + \text{hydrochloric acid} \rightarrow \text{calcium chloride} + \text{carbon dioxide} + \text{water}$$

$$\text{magnesium carbonate} + \text{hydrochloric acid} \rightarrow \text{magnesium chloride} + \text{carbon dioxide} + \text{water}$$

All other carbonates react in the same way with hydrochloric acid.

The balanced symbol equations for the reactions above are:

$$CaCO_3 + 2HCl \rightarrow CaCl_2 + CO_2 + H_2O$$

$$MgCO_3 + 2HCl \rightarrow MgCl_2 + CO_2 + H_2O$$

These equations are identical except for the metal in the carbonate and in the salt. They balance in exactly the same way so only one equation needs to be learned.

Metal hydrogencarbonates are less common. Only sodium hydrogencarbonate and potassium hydrogencarbonate are common. Calcium and magnesium hydrogencarbonates only exist in solution. Calcium hydrogencarbonate solution or magnesium hydrogencarbonate solution is temporary hard water.

Other methods of softening hard water

Boiling will soften temporary hard water but it has no effect on permanent hard water. The other methods of water softening, which work on both temporary and permanent hard water, are:

- adding washing soda (causing a precipitation reaction)
- ion exchange
- distillation.

Washing soda

Washing soda (Figure 11.3) is hydrated sodium carbonate. *Hydrated* means that it contains water of crystallisation, which is water that is bonded into the crystals when they form.

Figure 11.3 Washing soda

Adding washing soda to hard water removes the calcium or magnesium ions of the compounds dissolved in the water. The carbonate ion of the washing soda joins up with the calcium or magnesium ions of the compound in the hard water to form solid calcium carbonate or magnesium carbonate. This means that the calcium and magnesium compounds are not dissolved in the water any more and the water has become soft.

A solid that appears on mixing two solutions is called a precipitate. In this reaction calcium carbonate is the precipitate and the reaction is described as a precipitation reaction.

| **calcium chloride** (calcium compound – causes the hardness in the water) | + | **sodium carbonate** (washing soda – dissolves in the water) | → | **calcium carbonate** (calcium ion of the compound causing the hardness – removed as a solid) | + | **sodium chloride** (left in the water after the reaction) |

The balanced symbol equation for the above reaction is:

$$CaCl_2 + Na_2CO_3 \rightarrow CaCO_3 + 2NaCl$$

Ion exchange

The calcium (Ca^{2+}) and magnesium (Mg^{2+}) ions that cause the hardness in water can also be removed by **ion exchange**.

Hard water is poured into the top of the ion-exchange column. The column has lots of sodium (Na^+) ions attached to the little beads inside it.

As the water passes through, the calcium and magnesium ions are removed and replaced or **exchanged** with the sodium ions. The water

---

Test yourself 3

Name all the products when magnesium carbonate reacts with hydrochloric acid.

Test yourself 4

What is the common name for hydrated sodium carbonate used to soften hard water?

coming through is soft as it does not contain calcium ions or magnesium ions. The sodium ions in the water do not cause hardness.

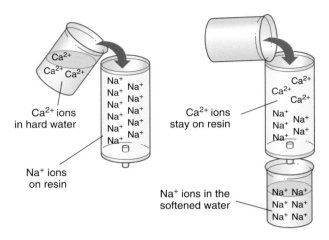

Figure 11.4 Using an ion-exchange column

Ion-exchange columns are used in dishwashers to make the water soft. Dishwashers need to have salt added to them. This salt contains sodium ions that attach to the ion-exchange column and replace the sodium ions that have been used to soften the water. Adding salt to the ion-exchange column ensures that it can be used again.

Distillation

Distillation is the process of heating and condensing a solution such as hard water.

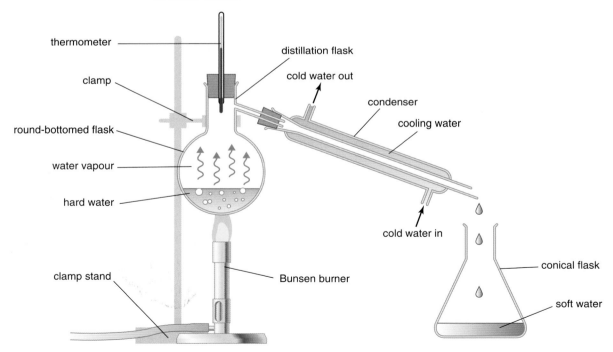

Figure 11.5 Distilling hard water to produce soft water

The hard water is heated, using either a Bunsen burner or an electric heating mantle.

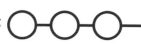

The water boils and water vapour moves up and into the condenser. The cool sides of the condenser make the water vapour change to liquid water.

The liquid water runs down into the conical flask. The calcium and magnesium compounds do not boil, so they are left behind in the round-bottomed flask.

▶ Hard water regions

Hard water occurs in regions where there is a lot of chalk or limestone. Rainwater has carbon dioxide dissolved in it, so it is acidic. The acidic rainwater reacts with limestone and chalk, and the calcium and magnesium ions in these rocks are dissolved into the water. This makes the water hard. Because the rainwater reacts with the limestone, it causes several geological features that are common in hard water regions. These include **caves**, **stalagmites** and **stalactites**, as shown in Figure 11.6.

Caves form because the rainwater makes its way down through limestone and chalk rocks and reacts with these rocks underground. The rainwater eventually eats away an underground cave.

Northern Ireland has the Marble Arch Caves in County Fermanagh. The region has very hard water, caused by the rainwater reacting with the limestone rocks in the area. The caves were sculpted from the limestone by rainwater. They are very important as a tourist attraction in Fermanagh, bringing money into the area.

In some caves, water drips from the roof of the cave and lands on the floor. As the water drips from the roof, it leaves behind some calcium or magnesium carbonate. This builds up as a growth from the roof of the cave. This is called a stalactite. Stalactites hang down from the roof of the cave.

As the water hits the floor of the cave, calcium and magnesium carbonate get deposited on the floor. This eventually builds up as a growth on the floor. This is called a stalagmite.

Figure 11.6 Geological features: a cave with stalagmites and stalactites

Test yourself 5

Name three geological features of a hard water region.

▶ Recycling and exploitation of Earth's resources

The Earth only contains a certain amount of natural resources or materials. Some of these materials, such as crude oil, are non-renewable. This means they cannot be made again in a short period of time. Other renewable materials, such as wood, can be produced again in a reasonably short time.

Some materials can be recycled so that they can be used again and again. This means that we do not waste the Earth's resources. Items that can be recycled for the materials they contain are:

* paper
* aluminium

- glass
- iron/steel
- plastic
- tin cans
- batteries.

Many local councils are promoting the 3R approach to recycling. This is a scheme to reduce the amount of rubbish that goes into landfill sites. The three Rs stand for **reduce**, **reuse**, **recycle**, as explained in Figure 11.7, with some examples of what we can do.

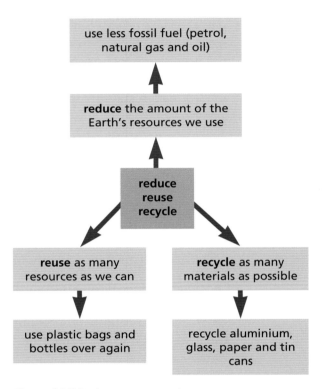

Figure 11.7 Reduce, reuse, recycle

Biodegradable and non-biodegradable materials

Plastics are made from crude oil and are **non-biodegradable**. This means that microbes cannot break them down in the earth.

Non-biodegradable materials will not break down if they are buried in the ground. This means that it is better not to put this type of material into landfill. Plastics can be **incinerated** (burned) but this releases gases into the air. These gases are polluting and some can increase the greenhouse effect.

Neither dumping in landfills nor incineration is a good way of getting rid of plastics. It is better to recycle them. Chemists have also developed **biodegradable** plastics that can be disposed of in landfill sites and can be decomposed by microbes.

Table 11.2 shows some materials that are biodegradable and some that are non-biodegradable.

Definition

A **biodegradable** material is one that can be broken down by microbes in the environment.

Test yourself 6

What do the three Rs stand for?

Table 11.2 Biodegradable and non-biodegradable materials

Biodegradable materials	Non-biodegradable materials
wood	plastics
paper	glass
garden waste	metals

All the materials in Table 11.2 can be recycled in one way or another. Recycling prevents waste of the Earth's resources and limits how much goes into landfill sites. Recycling also saves energy as it takes more energy to make a material from scratch than to recycle it.

- Garden waste can be made into garden mulch or compost.
- Wood and paper can be recycled to make new paper.
- Plastics are sorted into different types and the thermoplastics are melted down and remoulded.
- Glass is sorted into different colours, melted and remoulded.
- Metals are sorted into different types, melted and remoulded.

Environmental advantages of recycling

Recycling reduces the use of the Earth's resources, which in turn reduces energy use. Most energy is produced from fuels that burn to produce carbon dioxide. Carbon dioxide is a greenhouse gas. When resources are put into landfill sites, they begin to break down and produce methane gas, which is also a greenhouse gas. Foul-smelling water from landfill sites can leach into rivers and lakes. Landfill sites are also unsightly. Therefore it is better to recycle materials, reduce the amount of materials used and reuse materials such as plastics if they cannot be recycled.

Promoting recycling

The government has set local councils **targets** for recycling and landfill. The aim is to limit the amount of recyclable waste that ends up in landfill. Local councils will be fined heavily if the targets are not met.

Local councils provide special bins for recyclable waste such as plastics, paper, aluminium, iron/steel and food cans. Separating these types of waste from normal waste stops them being put into landfill.

They also provide brown bins for collecting garden waste such as grass cuttings, which are used to make mulch. People are also encouraged to produce their own mulch from garden waste.

Businesses are charged by the local council for disposing of their waste that goes to landfill, which encourages recycling. Councils and government are advertising about recycling in newspapers, magazines and on television. They are trying to educate people and encourage them to recycle. People may be fined for not recycling and/or rewarded for carrying out correct recycling.

Test yourself 7

State one advantage of recycling materials.

Glass recycling

Glass makes up 7% of household waste. This is a large percentage, so it makes sense to recycle glass to save resources and limit the amount of non-biodegradable material that goes into landfill sites.

Glass recycling is described in Figure 11.8. The glass is collected from door-steps in some areas of Northern Ireland. Most regions have bottle banks operated by the local council. These bottle banks are often found in car parks. The glass is separated depending on its colour. The glass is broken up into smaller pieces called cullet, which is used to form new glass.

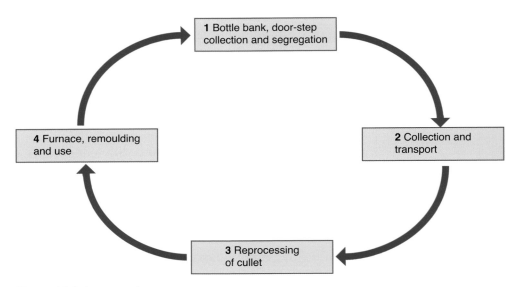

Figure 11.8 Glass recycling

Plastics recycling

The methods used to recycle plastics depend on the type of plastic. Thermoplastics are separated from thermosetting plastics and recycled.

Thermoplastics (Figure 11.9) can be melted and **remoulded**. The lids and sprays will be removed as they may be made of a different plastic.

Figure 11.9 Plastic bottles

The different bottles can be melted together and dyes can be added to colour the plastic a solid colour such as black or green. The dyed plastics are remoulded into objects such as bin bags, plastic pipes and carrier bags (Figure 11.10).

The new objects all have to be dyed a completely new colour because the dyes that made the old objects their original colours cannot be removed.

Making plastics from potatoes

Potatoes contain starch, which is a natural polymer. It is made up of lots of glucose monomers bonded together. If the G stands for glucose, the starch molecule looks like Figure 11.11.

Figure 11.10 A shopping bag made from recycled plastic

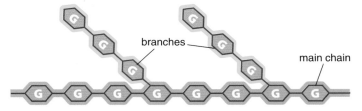

Figure 11.11 Starch is a natural polymer that contains branches

Starch has branches along its chains. These branches stop the main chains getting close enough together to form a solid polymer. Treating the starch with hydrochloric acid cuts off the branches. The main chains can then pack closely together and this makes a good polymer (Figure 11.12).

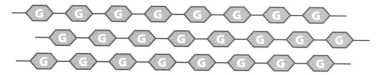

Figure 11.12 Starch forms a brittle polymer when its branches are removed

When the chains line up this well, the plastic is brittle and not flexible. A small molecule such as glycerol is added to the plastic before it forms. Glycerol is a **plasticiser**. This means it stops the chains from getting too close together and this makes a better, more flexible plastic (Figure 11.13).

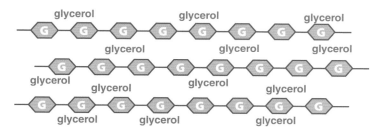

Figure 11.13 Glycerol acts as a plasticiser and makes starch a flexible polymer

Plasticisers are sometimes used in poly vinyl chloride (PVC) to make it less rigid. The PVC that is used to make window frames does not contain any plasticisers. It is often called **unplasticised PVC** or **uPVC**.

Activity 2

Making a starch polymer

1 Clean a couple of small potatoes.
2 Grate them into a mortar and add about $100\,cm^3$ of deionised water.
3 Use a pestle to grind them.
4 Pour off the liquid carefully into a beaker, making sure no potato pieces get into the beaker. Use a sieve to stop the potato getting into the beaker.
5 Add another $100\,cm^3$ of deionised water to the potato pieces and grind again. Pour off the liquid into the beaker again.
6 Repeat this with another $100\,cm^3$ of deionised water.
7 Leave the water in the beaker for about 10 minutes. The insoluble starch will settle to the bottom.

8 Carefully pour off the water and keep the white solid in the bottom of the beaker.
9 Add 100 cm³ of deionised water to this solid and stir again.
10 Let the white solid settle to the bottom of the beaker again and pour off the water. This solid is insoluble starch.
11 Using a measuring cylinder, measure out 25 cm³ of deionised water.
12 Weigh 2.5 g of the insoluble starch and add it to the water.
13 Add 3 cm³ of hydrochloric acid.
14 Add 2 cm³ of glycerol (plasticiser).
15 Put a watch glass over the beaker and heat the beaker for 15 minutes but do not let it boil dry.
16 Check the pH of the solution by dipping a glass rod into it and putting a drop onto universal indicator paper.
17 Add (0.1 M) sodium hydroxide solution, drop by drop, and keep checking the pH in the same way until the pH is 7 (universal indicator is green).
18 Pour the final mixture into a Petri dish and make sure that it forms a thin layer.
19 Leave it until the mixture dries.

You will have a biodegradable plastic made from starch.

Activity 3

Using a measuring cylinder

When you put water in a measuring cylinder, the water forms a **meniscus**. The level of the water should always be read at the bottom of the meniscus. The measuring cylinder should be at eye level.
The measuring cylinder shown in Figure 11.14 contains a volume of 76 cm³.

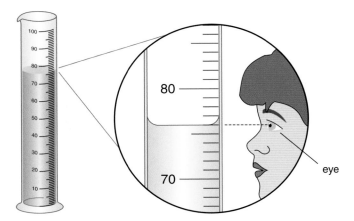

Figure 11.14 Reading the meniscus at eye-level

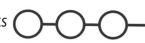

▶ Exam questions

1 The Marble Arch Caves are found in Fermanagh, which is a hard water area.

   a Give an **economic** benefit that the caves bring to the Fermanagh area. *(1 mark)*

   b Other than taste, give an **advantage** of drinking hard water. *(1 mark)*

   c Hard water forms undesirable deposits of calcium carbonate in kettles and hot water pipes. Copy and complete the **balanced symbol equation** for this reaction. *(3 marks)*

   $Ca(HCO_3)_2 \rightarrow$ _____ + _____ + _____

   d The deposits of calcium carbonate inside a kettle are often described as 'fur'. Kettle 'fur' can be removed by reacting it with an acid. Copy and complete the word equation below for this reaction. *(2 marks)*

   Calcium carbonate + hydrochloric acid → _____ + water + _____

   e A student conducted the following investigation into the hardness of different samples of water. She put 25 cm³ of four different samples, **P**, **Q**, **R** and **S**, into separate flasks. She added soap solution to each flask and shook until a lather was formed. She repeated the experiment with boiled samples. The results are shown below.

Sample	Height of lather before boiling/mm	Height of lather after boiling/mm
P	5	5
Q	20	19
R	28	28
S	4	20

   i The student concluded that samples **Q** and **R** were soft water.
   Using the information in the table explain why she is correct. *(2 marks)*

   ii What can be concluded about the type of water in sample **S**?
   Explain your answer. *(2 marks)*

   CCEA Science: Single Award, Unit 2, Higher Tier, November 2012, Q6

2 Mineral water contains many different ions which give it a characteristic taste. The table below gives the information shown on the label of a popular brand of mineral water.

Ions present	Concentration/arbitrary units
magnesium	18
potassium	3
calcium	113
sodium	17
chloride	32
hydrogencarbonate	430
nitrate	11
phosphate	1
sulfate	2

   a i Using the information in the table, calculate the total concentration of the ions causing this mineral water to be hard. (Show your working out.) *(2 marks)*

   ii Name the ion in the table which would be thermally decomposed if the water was boiled. *(1 mark)*

   b Hard water can cause undesirable deposits of calcium carbonate, called 'fur', in kettles.
   Copy and complete the word equation to show how the 'fur' forms in kettles. *(3 marks)*

   _____ → calcium carbonate + _____ + _____

   c Explain what is meant by the term **hard water**. *(2 marks)*

   d Describe an experiment you could carry out in the laboratory to compare the hardness of bottled water to the hardness of the tap water in your school.
   In this question you will be assessed on your written communication skills including the use of specialist terms. *(6 marks)*

   e Give **one** advantage of drinking hard water. *(1 mark)*

   CCEA Science: Single Award, Unit 2, Higher Tier, March 2012, Q2

3 The photograph below shows the Marble Arch Caves in County Fermanagh. The water in this area is described as being hard.

a What is meant by the term **hard water**?

(2 marks)

The table below gives the results of an experiment to test the hardness of different water samples.

Water sample	Volume of soap solution needed to form a lather before boiling/cm³	Volume of soap solution needed to form a lather after boiling/cm³
A	20	15
B	4	3
C	14	2
D	24	11

b Use this information to answer the following questions.

i Which sample, **A**, **B**, **C** or **D**, of water is the least hard? *(1 mark)*

ii Which sample, **A**, **B**, **C** or **D**, contains only temporary hardness? *(1 mark)*

iii Which **two** samples, **A**, **B**, **C** or **D**, contain both temporary and permanent hardness? *(1 mark)*

c Hard water can be softened by using an ion exchange column.

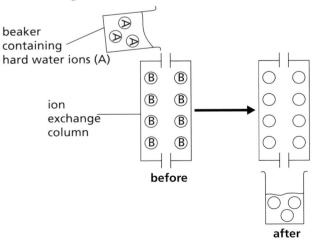

Copy and complete the diagram to show the position of the ions after the water has passed through the column. *(2 marks)*

d Hard water can cause unwanted deposits in hot water pipes.

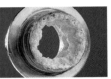

Copy and complete the word equation for the reaction that forms the unwanted deposits.

calcium hydrogencarbonate → _____

+_____ + _____ *(3 marks)*

CCEA Chemistry: Unit 2, Higher Tier, February 2013, Q2

4 Copy and complete the following diagram showing the steps in recycling glass. *(3 marks)*

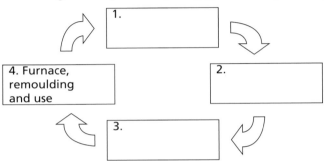

CCEA Science: Single Award, Unit 2, Foundation Tier, November 2012, Q5b

5 The graph below shows the percentage of household waste in Northern Ireland that has been recycled over seven years.

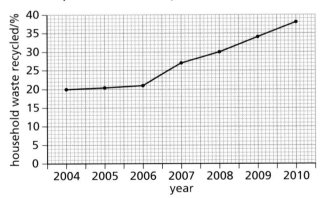

Use the graph and your knowledge about recycling to answer the following questions.

a Calculate the increase in the percentage of waste recycled between 2004 and 2010. (Show your working out.) *(2 marks)*

b Suggest the year that local councils first provided recycling bins to households. Explain your answer. *(2 marks)*

CCEA Science: Single Award, Unit 2, Foundation Tier, November 2012, Q6

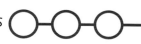

6 Given below is some information on the disposal of waste in Northern Ireland.

Wheelie bins contain many different kinds of waste including food waste, paper, glass, metal, textiles and household dust.

In Northern Ireland 85% of waste goes into landfill sites where it is buried and covered with clay. The rest is recycled.

Some of the waste decomposes giving off the polluting gas methane, and also produces foul-smelling liquids that are unpleasant and can leak into water supplies.

The table below shows the time it takes for some waste items to break down.

Waste item	Time taken
aluminium can	80–100 years
apple core	8 weeks
glass bottle	500 years
newspaper	6 weeks
plastic bag	10–20 years
plastic bottle	greater than 500 years

Use the information provided and your own knowledge to answer the following questions.

a Name the item which will lie in the landfill site for the longest period of time. *(1 mark)*

b Apart from newspapers list all the other materials in the table which should be recycled. Explain fully why you have chosen these materials. *(3 marks)*

c i Apple cores are described as biodegradable. Explain fully what is meant by the term biodegradable. *(2 marks)*

ii Suggest another material from the table which could also be biodegradable. *(1 mark)*

d Apart from the time taken to decompose, use the information to give **two** other **disadvantages** of burying waste in landfill sites. *(2 marks)*

e i Calculate the percentage of waste in Northern Ireland that is recycled. (Show your working out.) *(2 marks)*

ii Give **two** ways local authorities can encourage people to recycle more waste.

(2 marks)

CCEA Science: Single Award, Unit 2, Foundation Tier, March 2012, Q4

12 Using materials to fight crime

▶ Forensic science

Forensic science is used to help fight crime. There are lots of ways in which science can help solve crimes. More and more of the evidence that is used in court to identify a criminal is scientific.

Using fingerprints

Everyone has different patterns of lines in the skin on their fingers. These patterns leave a mark on any surface they touch. There are four main types of fingerprint ridge pattern (Figure 12.1). They are **arch**, **loop**, **whorl** and **composite**.

arch   loop   whorl   composite

Figure 12.1 The four fingerprint pattern types

Criminals can be identified by matching their fingerprint patterns with fingerprints taken at the crime scene. This system was adopted by Scotland Yard in 1901. Fingerprints are almost invisible and forensic scientists have to dust powder over them to make them visible. The powder they use depends on the surface the fingerprint is on (Table 12.1). Powders are used as the solid particles are very small and can stick to the pattern, displaying it clearly.

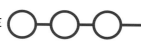

Table 12.1 Revealing fingerprints

Surface	Powder	Example of print	
white	carbon black powder	whorl ridge pattern taken from a white door, using carbon black powder	
black or mirrored	aluminium powder	loop ridge pattern taken from a mirror, using aluminium powder	

Test yourself 1

What type of powder would be used to show a fingerprint on a piece of white paper?

Chemical methods of revealing fingerprints

Fluorescent dyes that glow under ultraviolet light can also be used to show up a fingerprint more clearly. If fingerprints are on a surface where they cannot be shown clearly by dusting, forensic scientists have to treat them with substances such as iodine fumes or superglue vapour to make them clearer. Iodine fumes are used to show up fingerprints on paper, clothing and even on skin. They stain the print brown. Figure 12.2 shows an iodine vapour fingerprint on a scrap of paper.

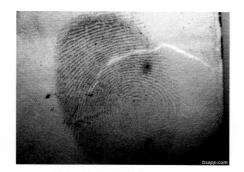

Figure 12.2 Iodine fumes stain a fingerprint brown

Collecting fingerprints for analysis

Once a fingerprint is dusted on a surface, it has to be transferred. The excess dust is brushed off and sticky tape is pressed over the print. The print will transfer to the tape and the tape can then be put on a piece of card. White card is used for carbon black prints and black card for aluminium prints. Some prints are photographed digitally at the scene of the crime. Others, such as those on paper or clothing, can be taken away to a laboratory.

The fingerprints are scanned into a computer that will compare them with a fingerprint database of known criminals and also with any suspects. A 16-point system is used to compare the lines and patterns on fingerprints, to make sure the match is right. If the match is not exact, experts will examine the fingerprints by eye to try to verify the match.

Fingerprints are unique to each individual person and good fingerprint evidence means that the person was at the scene of the crime. It does not mean that they actually committed the crime, so fingerprint evidence is used with other evidence to obtain a conviction. A national fingerprint database would hold everyone's fingerprint data. It would mean that more crimes would be solved. They would also be solved more quickly, so making better use of police time.

Test yourself 2

Name the four different types of fingerprints.

▶ Crime prevention

There are many ways to protect your valuables in the home:

- Do not leave doors or windows unlocked.
- Mark electrical equipment with a security pen.
- Fit alarm systems that are linked to a security centre or the police.
- Neighbourhood watch schemes can help prevent crime.
- When on holiday, inform the police and cancel deliveries to your home. Get a friend to check the house and remove any post.
- Use lights, set up to come on randomly and controlled by timers, to give the impression that someone is at home.

Shops can help prevent crime by:

- using ultraviolet light to check for forged bank notes (Figure 12.3)
- training staff to look for forged bank notes, checking:
  - the metal strip
  - the hologram
  - the quality of the paper
  - watermarks
  - bar codes
- using online bank training
- using security tags for products
- having security guards on the doors.

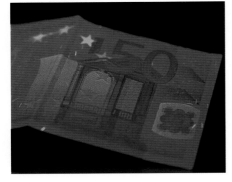

Figure 12.3 A €50 note under UV light

▶ Clothing fibres

There are many different types of fibres used in clothing nowadays. Someone who commits a crime will leave some clothing fibres at the scene of the crime. These can be collected and examined using a powerful microscope called a **scanning electron microscope** (Figure 12.4). They can be compared with fibres from the clothing of the suspects.

Forensic scientists will look at:

- the mixture of fibres, for example, nylon mixed with cotton
- the colours of the fibres, for example, red fibres mixed with white
- the twist pattern of the fibres, for example, how tightly the fibres are twisted
- the weave pattern of the fibres, for example, how the material is woven together
- stains within the fibres, for example, blood, saliva, sweat.

A light microscope on high magnification can see some of these features of fibres. Hair is also a natural fibre that can give a lot of information about the criminal. Hair found at the scene can be compared with hair from a suspect in a similar way to the way fibres are compared.

Figure 12.4 Clothing fibres viewed by means of a scanning electron microscope

► Genetic fingerprinting (DNA profiling)

DNA is the genetic material found in cells in the body. It can be extracted from hair, blood or semen found at a crime scene, and compared to a suspect's DNA profile. The DNA is compared using a technique called **DNA fingerprinting**. If the genetic fingerprint matches, then the DNA is from the suspect.

The DNA samples are cut into small fragments. The fragments are then placed in a gel and separated using an electric current. Different DNA samples give their own unique patterns. A typical genetic fingerprint will appear as a series of bands. All the bands should match if the DNA is from the same person. Many different types of DNA fingerprinting are carried out to ensure that the match is correct.

An example of a genetic fingerprint from DNA found at a crime scene is shown in Figure 12.5. Also shown are the genetic fingerprints of four different suspects. Each column contains bands that show the genetic fingerprints. It is clear that the DNA of suspect 3 matches the DNA found at the crime scene. Again, as with fingerprint evidence, this means that the suspect was there but more investigative work would be carried out to prove whether he or she committed the crime.

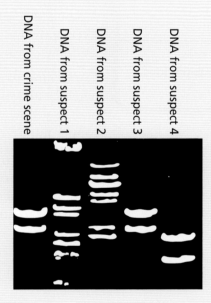

Figure 12.5 Genetic fingerprints from DNA at a crime scene and from four suspects

The DNA profile of any person who provides DNA evidence, even if it is just to eliminate them from an investigation or because they were at a crime scene, is stored in a database. Many people are worried about the genetic profiles of innocent people being kept in a database.

Figure 12.6 A flame test

Test yourself 3

State the flame test colour observed when potassium ions are present.

▶ Flame tests

Some metal ions will produce a coloured flame when they are heated in a blue Bunsen flame (Figure 12.6). A flame-test rod is dipped in deionised water or hydrochloric acid and placed in the sample which is then heated in a blue Bunsen flame to clean it. It can then be put into the sample and heated in the flame. Some ions will give a very characteristic coloured flame (Table 12.2). The flame-test rod should be cleaned between each sample. Safety glasses should be worn and care taken when using a Bunsen burner.

Table 12.2 Metal ions and the colours of flames

Ion	Flame colour
lithium (Li^+)	red
sodium (Na^+)	orange-yellow
potassium (K^+)	lilac
calcium (Ca^{2+})	brick-red
lead (Pb^{2+})	blue-white
copper (Cu^{2+})	blue-green

As an alternative to a flame-test rod, nichrome wire may be used, in which case it is dipped into concentrated hydrochloric acid.

A flame test can be used to identify metal ions found at the scene of a crime. They can then be compared to those found on a suspect's clothing.

Compounds containing these ions also give these characteristic colours when heated in a flame. For example, sodium chloride will give an orange-yellow colour when heated in a roaring Bunsen flame, while copper nitrate will give a blue-green flame test colour.

As the colour of the flame test depends on the observer, often **emission spectroscopy** is used to positively identify the presence of these ions at a crime scene. Their emission spectroscopy spectra are compared to known spectra from a database.

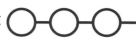

▶ Exam questions

1 Flame tests can be used to identify the metal in a compound.

Explain how you would carry out a flame test experiment on solutions of potassium chloride and sodium chloride.

Your answer should include:
- any safety precautions
- the results you would expect to see.

In this question you will be assessed on your written communication skills including the use of specialist scientific terms. *(6 marks)*

CCEA Science: Single Award, Unit 2, Foundation Tier, November 2012, Q10

2 The fingerprint shown below was found on a stolen black TV set.

There are four types of fingerprints.

a Name the type of fingerprint shown above.
(1 mark)

Choose from: arch; whorl; loop; composite

b What type of powder would be used to show the fingerprint on the TV set? *(1 mark)*

c Explain fully how a fingerprint could be obtained from the TV set for evidence use.

(3 marks)

CCEA Science: Single Award, Unit 2, Foundation Tier, March 2012, Q6

3 Forensic scientists can help to solve crime by taking and analysing fingerprints found at the scene.

Explain fully why fingerprints are so important. Your answer should include:
- the different types of fingerprints
- how to obtain a fingerprint from different surfaces
- how they are used in the court system.

In this question you will be assessed on your written communication skills including the use of specialist scientific terms. *(6 marks)*

CCEA Chemistry: Unit 2, Higher Tier, February 2013, Q3

4 a The following two fingerprints were found on the window of a stolen car.

A **B**

i Name the two types of fingerprint patterns found on the stolen car. *(2 marks)*

ii Name a suitable powder for obtaining fingerprints on the window of the car.

(1 mark)

iii How can forensic scientists use the fingerprints found at the scene of the crime to convict the person who has committed the crime? *(2 marks)*

b The government has discussed the possibility of having a national database of fingerprints.

i Suggest what the national database would contain. *(1 mark)*

ii Suggest one advantage of a national database. *(1 mark)*

CCEA Science: Single Award, Module 4, Higher Tier, March 2011, Q3

13 Electrical circuits

LEARNING OBJECTIVES

By the end of this chapter you should know and understand:

- the directions of electron motion and conventional current flow
- how to interpret simple series and parallel electrical circuits
- the effect of switches
- the use of ammeters and voltmeters in circuits
- how to use Ohm's law
- what is meant by electrical resistance
- what a variable resistor is and how it works
- the effect of material and length on the resistance of a wire
- the effect of cross-sectional area on the resistance of a wire.

▶ Electrical circuits

An electrical **circuit** is a path along which electricity can flow. It may consist of **batteries**, **wires**, **bulbs** and **switches**.

Circuit diagrams, using symbols for the components, are often used to represent electrical circuits. Figure 13.1 shows some commonly used symbols.

Component	Symbol	Function
battery		to supply electricity
bulb		to convert current to light
switch		to control the flow of current
fuse		to stop too much current flowing
voltmeter	V	to measure voltage
ammeter	A	to measure current
resistor		to cut down the amount of current flowing

Figure 13.1 Circuit symbols

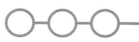

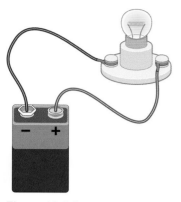

Figure 13.2 A picture of a circuit

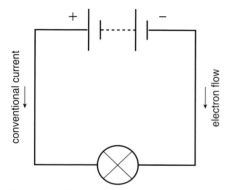

Figure 13.3 A circuit diagram of a complete circuit; current will flow

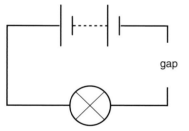

Figure 13.5 An incomplete circuit; current will not flow

Circuit diagrams

Circuit diagrams are used because they are easier to understand than pictures and are universally understood. Figures 13.2 and 13.3 show the difference between pictures and circuit diagrams.

Conventional current and electron flow

Chemical reactions inside the battery push electrons from the negative terminal round to the positive terminal. Figure 13.4 shows how electrons flow in a wire connected across a battery. Electrons are repelled from the negative terminal of the battery and are attracted to the positive terminal. Electrons therefore flow through a circuit from the negative terminal to the positive terminal.

Scientists in the nineteenth century thought that an electrical current consisted of a flow of positive charge from the positive terminal of the cell to the negative terminal. Although this idea is now known to be wrong, it is useful to think of conventional current flowing through the circuit from the positive terminal of the battery to the negative terminal.

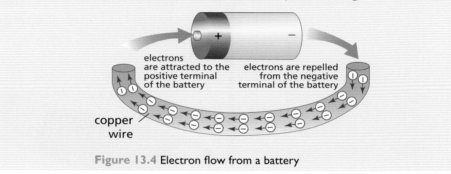

electrons are attracted to the positive terminal of the battery

electrons are repelled from the negative terminal of the battery

copper wire

Figure 13.4 Electron flow from a battery

Electricity can only flow around a complete circuit, which is one with no gaps.

Electricity will flow around the circuit in Figure 13.3 because it is a complete circuit. Electricity will not flow around the circuit in Figure 13.5 because there is a gap in it.

▶ Simple circuits

There are two types of simple circuit: **series** and **parallel**.

Figure 13.6 shows two bulbs connected in series, side by side.

Figure 13.7 shows two bulbs connected in parallel, one under the other.

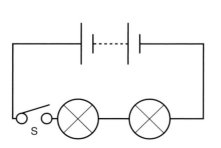

Figure 13.6 Two bulbs connected in series

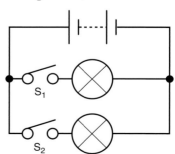

Figure 13.7 Two bulbs connected in parallel

Table 13.1 summarises the features of series and parallel circuits.

In Figure 13.6 both bulbs will light when switch S is closed. Both bulbs will go out when switch S is open.

In Figure 13.7 the upper bulb will light only when switch S_1 is closed. The lower bulb will light only when switch S_2 is closed. This means that each bulb is controlled by its own switch. Opening or closing S_1 has no effect on the lower bulb. Opening or closing S_2 has no effect on the upper bulb.

Table 13.1 Comparing series and parallel circuits

	Series	Parallel
bulbs are connected	side by side	one under the other
adding more bulbs	bulbs get dimmer	brightness stays the same
unscrewing one bulb	all bulbs go out	other bulbs remain lit

▶ Batteries and voltage

Batteries supply **electrical energy** to a circuit. They must always be connected side by side and nose to tail (positive to negative), as shown in Figure 13.8.

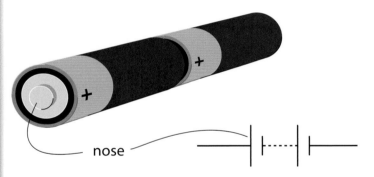

Figure 13.8 Batteries connected side by side and nose to tail

Voltage

Batteries supply **voltage** to a circuit. The more batteries there are, the more volts and so the brighter the bulbs appear. Voltage is the amount of **electrical energy** supplied to a circuit or component. It is measured with a **voltmeter**. The unit of voltage is the **volt** (**V**).

Figure 13.9 shows digital and analogue voltmeters and the voltmeter symbol.

In a series circuit, as in Figure 13.10, the total voltage from the batteries is shared among the bulbs. If there are two bulbs, they will each receive half the battery voltage.

If there are more than two bulbs, as in Figure 13.11, the voltage is shared equally:

$$V_b = V_1 + V_2 + V_3$$

Test yourself 1

In a hairdryer, a fan and a heater are wired in parallel across a battery. There are two switches. When the fan alone is on, the hairdryer blows cold air. When both the fan and the heater are on, the hairdryer blows warm air. This arrangement of the switches protects the hairdryer from overheating.

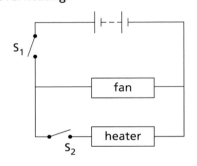

(a) Copy and complete the table below to show how the hairdryer works for different switch settings.
(b) How does the arrangement of the switches protect the hairdryer from overheating?
(c) Mark with an arrow on a copy of the diagram the direction in which electrons flow through the fan.

Switch S_1	Switch S_2	Fan (off/ on)	Heater (off/ on)	Hairdryer (off/blows cold air/ blows warm air)
open	open			
open	closed			
closed	open			
closed	closed			

In a parallel circuit, as in Figure 13.12, each bulb receives the total voltage from the batteries.

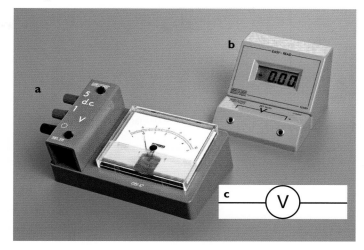

Figure 13.9 (a) An analogue voltmeter (b) A digital voltmeter (c) The symbol for a voltmeter

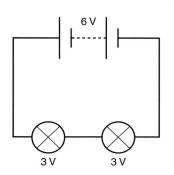

Figure 13.10 The total voltage from the batteries is shared among the bulbs

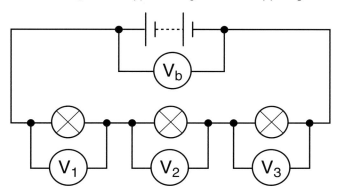

Figure 13.11 A circuit with three bulbs in series

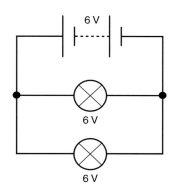

Figure 13.12 A circuit with two bulbs in parallel

Current

The **current** is a measure of the amount of electricity flowing around a circuit or through a component. The unit of current is the **amp** (**A**).

Current is measured with an **ammeter**. Figure 13.13 shows digital and analogue ammeters with the ammeter symbol.

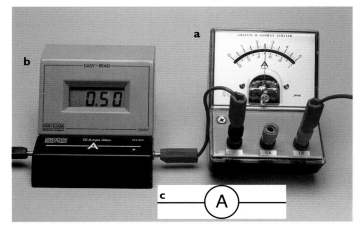

Figure 13.13 (a) An analogue ammeter (b) A digital ammeter (c) The symbol for an ammeter

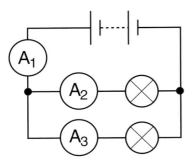

Figure 13.14 Measuring current in a parallel circuit

The current flowing in a series circuit is the same all the way round.

In a parallel circuit, as in Figure 13.14, the current is shared among the branches:

$$A_1 = A_2 + A_3$$

Table 13.2 summarises the features of voltage and current.

Table 13.2 Comparing voltage and current

	Voltage	Current
What is it?	the 'force' that pushes the electrons through a circuit or component	the amount of electricity flowing through a circuit or component
Measured using	voltmeter (connected in parallel)	ammeter (connected in series)
Units	volts (V)	amps (A)
In series circuits	shared among the bulbs	same all around the circuit
In parallel circuits	total voltage supplied to each branch	shared among the branches

Both Foundation and Higher level students have to plan and carry out investigations on how current and voltage vary in simple series and parallel circuits. You also have to be able to draw diagrams of these types of circuits using the correct circuit symbols. When preparing for the exam, be sure you are able to describe in detail exactly what you did in your investigation.

Resistance

Resistance is the amount of opposition a component or circuit gives to the flow of electrical current through it. The units of resistance are **ohms** (Ω).

higher resistance → less current flowing → dimmer bulbs

lower resistance → more current flowing → brighter bulbs

In a series circuit, the bulbs become dimmer each time another one is added. This is because each time you add a bulb you add more resistance.

Insulators have very high resistances – so high that electricity cannot flow through them. Conductors have low resistances.

You can test materials to find out if they are conductors or insulators using the circuit shown in Figure 13.15.

If the bulb lights up, the material is a conductor as it allows electricity to flow through it. All metals are conductors and copper is the most commonly used conductor.

If the bulb does not light up, the material is an insulator. Nearly all non-metals are insulators and plastic is the most commonly used insulator.

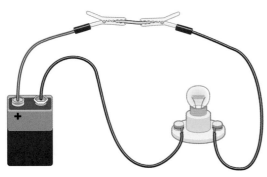

Figure 13.15 A continuity tester circuit

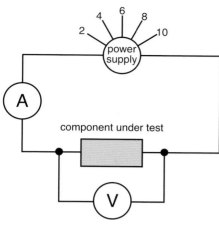

Figure 13.16 Measuring resistance: ammeter–voltmeter method

Note

Remember that if you are a Higher Tier student you must be able to rearrange the equation you are given. If you are a Foundation student you will never have to rearrange the equation you are given.

Resistance is the opposition to the flow of electrical current. It can be found by dividing voltage by current.

Definition

Test yourself 2

Two wires are made of the same material.
Wire A has a resistance of 4 Ω.
Wire B is twice as long as Wire A and has double the cross-sectional area.
What is the resistance of Wire B in ohms?

► Ohm's law

The three properties of electricity, voltage (V), current (I) and resistance (R), are linked by **Ohm's law**, which states that:

$$V = I \times R$$

You can use the circuit shown in Figure 13.16 to investigate how voltage and current are related. As you increase the voltage output of the power supply, the current flowing around the circuit will also increase.

► *EXAMPLE*

Use the equation $V = I \times R$ to calculate the resistance of the filament (fine wire) in an electric light bulb if it takes a current of 0.25A when connected to a 220V supply.

Solution

From Ohm's law, $V = I \times R$
Rearranging gives $R = V/I = 220/0.25 = 880\,\Omega$

Factors affecting a wire's resistance

There are three factors that can affect the resistance of a wire.

Length

The longer a wire is, the greater its resistance will be. In fact, the resistance of a wire is **directly proportional** to its length. This means that if the length of a wire is doubled, its resistance will double too. If the length is trebled, its resistance will treble, and so on.

Cross-sectional area

The thicker a wire is, the smaller its resistance will be. In fact, the resistance of a wire is **inversely proportional** to its cross-sectional area. This means that if the cross-sectional area is doubled, the resistance will halve. If the cross-sectional area is trebled, its resistance will only be a third of its previous value, and so on.

Material

Some conductors have greater resistance than others. Think about a copper wire and an iron wire of the same length and the same cross-sectional area. The iron wire will have a greater resistance than the copper wire. This simply means that copper wires are better conductors than iron wires because they have a smaller resistance.

The wires commonly used in experiments on resistance are **constantan** and **nichrome**. Constantan is a mixture of nickel and copper, while nichrome is a mixture of nickel and chromium. However, a metre of constantan wire has only about half the resistance of a metre of nichrome wire of the same thickness.

Fixed and variable resistors

Table 13.3 shows the symbols of fixed and variable resistors and what they are used for.

Table 13.3 Fixed and variable resistors

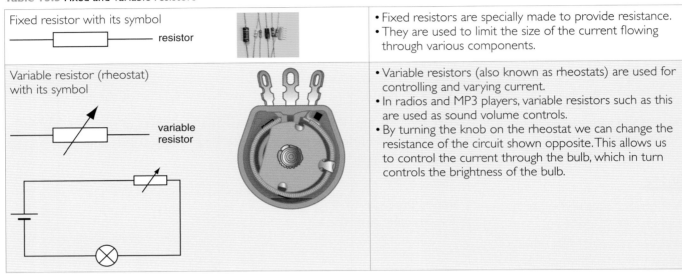

Fixed resistor with its symbol ——[ ]—— resistor		• Fixed resistors are specially made to provide resistance. • They are used to limit the size of the current flowing through various components.
Variable resistor (rheostat) with its symbol variable resistor		• Variable resistors (also known as rheostats) are used for controlling and varying current. • In radios and MP3 players, variable resistors such as this are used as sound volume controls. • By turning the knob on the rheostat we can change the resistance of the circuit shown opposite. This allows us to control the current through the bulb, which in turn controls the brightness of the bulb.

Figure 13.17 Appliances that use electrical resistance: (a) a kettle (b) a heater (c) a toaster

Resistance can be useful

Whenever electricity flows through any component or circuit, resistance tries to stop it. You might think that this is not useful. However, as resistance tries to stop the current flow, heat is produced. This heating effect of resistance is very useful. We use the heating effect of resistance in kettles, electrical fires, toasters, ovens and hairdryers (Figure 13.17).

bigger resistance → more heat

Elements in fires, kettles and toasters have high resistances.

Insulators have such a high resistance that electricity cannot flow through them. If we did not know about resistance, we would not know about insulators and therefore we would not be able to protect ourselves from electricity.

Table 13.4 Resistance – a summary

What is it?	the amount of opposition given to the flow of electricity through a circuit or component
Units	ohms (Ω)
Calculated using	Ohm's law: $V = I \times R$; or rearranged: $R = V/I$
Used for	heating effect in kettles, toasters, fires; insulators such as the plastic coating on wires

▶ Exam questions

1 Given below are some electrical properties and their units. Copy the lists and match each property to its correct unit.
The first one is done for you. *(2 marks)*

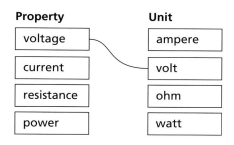

CCEA Science: Single Award, Module 5, Foundation Tier, November 2007, Q1c

2 Below is shown a simple circuit which includes a variable resistor.

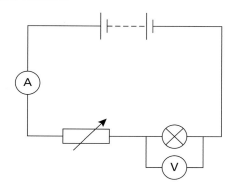

a What name is given to the apparatus:
  i in series with the battery, the variable resistor and the bulb? *(1 mark)*
  ii in parallel with the bulb? *(1 mark)*
b Draw an arrow on a copy of the diagram to show the direction of conventional current flow. *(1 mark)*
c What is the purpose of the variable resistor? *(1 mark)*

The table shows the results obtained from the circuit when the variable resistor is adjusted.

Voltage/V	Current/A
2	0.10
3	0.15
5	0.25
7	0.30

d State the trend shown by these results. *(1 mark)*
e Use the appropriate numbers in the table and the equation

$$\text{voltage} = \text{current} \times \text{resistance}$$

to calculate the resistance of the bulb's filament when the current flowing through it is 0.25A. *(2 marks)*

CCEA Science: Single Award, Revised Unit 3, Higher Tier, March 2012, Q5 (modified)

3 The diagram shows four identical bulbs connected in series across a battery.

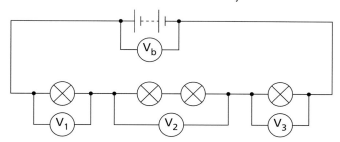

Voltmeter V_1 gives a reading of 1.5V.
a What readings would be observed on voltmeters:
  i V_2 *(1 mark)*
  ii V_3 *(1 mark)*
  iii V_b? *(1 mark)*
b The filament of the bulb in parallel with V_1 breaks and the bulb goes out.
  i What effect, if any, would this have on the brightness of the other bulbs? *(1 mark)*
  ii What reading would now be observed on voltmeter V_1? *(1 mark)*

4 Pupils set up the circuit below to investigate the effect of adding extra batteries.

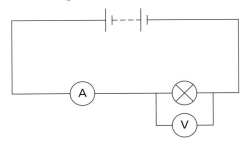

The pupils' results are shown in the table.

Number of batteries	Voltage/V	Current/A
1	1.5	0.10
2	3.0	0.19
3	4.5	0.30
4	6.0	0.41
5	7.5	0.50

a State two trends shown by these results.

(2 marks)

b The pupils then used a light meter to measure how the brightness of a bulb was affected by the number of batteries. The results are shown below.

Number of batteries	Bulb brightness/lux
1	14
2	22
3	35
4	35
5	35

i Explain the advantage of using only three batteries with this bulb. *(2 marks)*

ii Use the table in **a** and the equation:

Power = voltage × current

to calculate the power used when three batteries are connected to this bulb.

(2 marks)

CCEA Science: Single Award, Unit 3, Higher Tier, February 2013, Q1

14 Household electricity

▶ What makes electricity the most useful form of energy?

Electricity is the energy form most easily transferred into heat, kinetic (movement) energy, sound and light. Table 14.1 lists some of the many electrical devices in our homes and shows the energy transfer each is designed to bring about.

Table 14.1 Uses of electricity in the home

Devices found in the home	Converts electrical energy mainly to ...
electric kettle, toaster, iron, heater, oven	heat
fan, CD/DVD motor, washing machine motor, pump in fridge	kinetic (movement)
loudspeaker in radio/TV, doorbell, earpiece	sound
energy efficient bulb, LED, TV screen	light

In devices that are designed to produce movement, sound or light, some of the electrical energy will also be wasted as useless heat.

The wiring inside a three-pin plug

The three-pin plug, shown in Figures 14.1 and 14.2, is the easiest and safest way to connect any electrical appliance to the electricity supply. In this section we investigate its safety features.

Each wire is also coated with plastic insulation for protection.

Figure 14.1 A three-pin plug

Colour	Name	Connection
blue	neutral	left
brown	live	right
green and yellow	earth	top

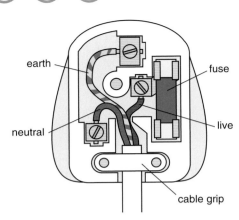

Figure 14.2 The wiring inside a three-pin plug

Test yourself 1

(a) Which wire *normally* has no current flowing through it?
(b) Which wires *normally* have the same current flowing through them?

Figure 14.3 Fuses

If a fault develops in an appliance that has any metal parts, the metal could become live, which means electricity could flow through it. Then anyone who touched the metal parts would get an electric shock. The earth wire stops this from happening as it offers an escape route, to earth, for the current. This is instead of the current going through a person to earth.

Fuses

Fuses, as shown in Figure 14.3, are safety devices. They are short lengths of resistance wire, which stop too much current flowing in a circuit.

- The more current that flows, the hotter the fuse wire becomes.
- When the current is bigger than the fuse size, the fuse wire melts and breaks.
- This creates a gap in the circuit.
- This stops the flow of current and so protects both the appliance and the user.

Extra design features of the three-pin plug

The cable grip inside the plug prevents the cable from being pulled out. It also helps to prevent the wires being pulled out of their connections inside the plug.

The outside of the plug is made of plastic, an insulator.

Finding the right fuse

To find the right fuse for any appliance, follow these steps:

1 Find the power (P) of the appliance.
   This can usually be found on a label on the back of the appliance.
   The units of power are **watts (W)** or **kilowatts (kW)**.
   1000 watts = 1 kilowatt
2 Find the voltage (V) of the supply, usually 220 V in the UK.
3 Start with the formula:
   power (P) = voltage (V) × current (I)
   $P = V \times I$
   Rearrange this to get:
   $$I = \frac{P}{V}$$
   to calculate the current needed by the appliance.
4 Use the fuse that takes a current just higher than the value you have found.

   The most common fuse sizes are 1 A, 2 A, 3 A, 5 A and 13 A.

▶ EXAMPLE 1

Find the fuse required for a 500 W television.
Power = 500 W and voltage = 220 V.

$$P = V \times I$$

$$I = \frac{P}{V} = \frac{500}{220} = 2.273 \text{ A}$$

Choose the 3 A fuse.

Fitting the wrong fuse

If the fuse fitted is too big, in the event of a fault developing, it will allow too much current through to the appliance. This will cause damage to the appliance or the user.

If the fuse fitted is too small the appliance will not work properly as the fuse cannot carry enough current. The fuse will blow immediately.

Residual current circuit-breakers

In a house, the main fuses are near the electricity meter. They protect the house wiring from overheating if too much electricity flows or if there is a fault. A house usually has separate fuses for sockets, lights, cooker, shower and heating. Modern houses have **circuit-breakers** instead of fuses. They are easy to check and reset. Modern homes also have **residual current circuit-breakers** (RCCB) that can detect fault conditions in a circuit and switch off the current very quickly (Figure 14.4).

Figure 14.4 A circuit-breaker

> **Definition**
>
> A **watt** is a unit of power and represents 1 joule per second.
> A **kilowatt** (kW) is 1000 watts or 1000 joules per second.

> **Definition**
>
> A **kWh** is the energy used in 1 hour by a device using 1000 joules per second.

▶ Paying for electricity

Electricity companies bill customers for the electrical energy they use in units known as **kilowatt-hours** (**kWh**). These are sometimes called 'units' of electricity.

One kilowatt-hour is the amount of energy transferred when 1000W is delivered for 1 hour. The joule is much too small a unit for this purpose. You should prove for yourself that 1 kWh = 3 600 000 joules, using the equation:

$$\text{energy (in J)} = \text{power (in W)} \times \text{time (in seconds)}.$$

Look at the electricity bill in Figure 14.5.

Northern Electricity Board				Customer account no: 3427 364
Present meter reading	Previous meter reading	Units used	Cost per unit (incl. VAT)	£
57139	55652	1487	11.0p	163.57

Figure 14.5 Electricity bill

The difference between the present reading and the previous reading is the number of units used.

In this particular example: 57 139 − 55 652 = 1487 units (kWh)

So, 1487 units have been used.

Since each unit costs 11.0p, the total cost is 1487 × 11.0p = 16 357p = £163.57.

The kilowatt-hour (kWh)

We can work out the energy used by an appliance in kilowatt-hours by using the equation:

$$\text{energy in kWh} = \text{power in kW} \times \text{time in hours}$$

▶ EXAMPLE 2

Calculate the cost of using a 2500 W immersion heater for 30 minutes if electricity costs 12 pence per kWh.
First note that 2500 watts = 2.5 kW and 30 minutes = 0.5 hours.
Now apply the energy equation above.

Energy used in kWh = 2.5 kW × 0.5 hours = 1.25 kWh

Cost = 1.25 kWh at 12 pence per kWh = 1.25 × 12 = 15 pence

Reducing energy bills

The only way to reduce energy bills is to use less energy. This can be done by:

- draught-proofing windows and doors
- fitting cavity-wall and loft insulation to stop heat loss
- blocking up unused chimneys
- turning off electrical equipment – do not leave on 'stand by'
- using low-energy light bulbs
- fitting double-glazed windows
- turning lights off when no-one is in the room
- using energy-efficient appliances.

▶ Making electricity

As shown in Figure 14.6, electricity can be made very easily, using:

- a coil of wire
- a magnet
- movement between the coil and the magnet.

When the magnet moves in and out of the coil, a current is made to flow. This process is called **electromagnetic induction**. It is the basic principle behind the generation of electricity in dynamos (Figure 14.7) and power-station generators.

Using a stronger magnet, a coil with more turns or moving the magnet faster will make more electricity.

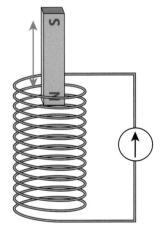

Figure 14.6 Making electricity with a magnet and a coil of wire

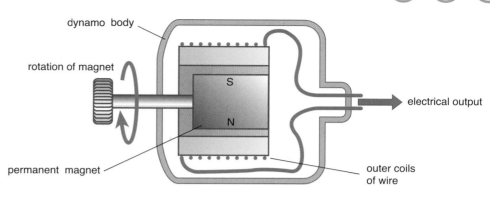

Figure 14.7 A dynamo uses a magnet and a coil to produce electricity

Power stations

Most power stations use the principle of electromagnetic induction (moving a magnetic field relative to a coil of wire) to make electricity. Figure 14.8 shows what happens inside a typical fossil fuel (coal, oil or gas) power station.

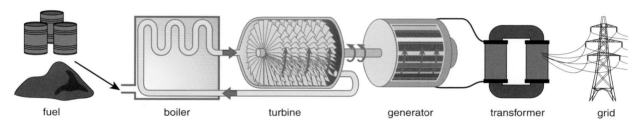

Figure 14.8 What happens inside a fossil-fuel power station

Figure 14.9 The National Grid for the UK

Inside the power station, the process has several stages:

* The fuel is burned, releasing heat.
* The heat is used to turn water into steam.
* The steam is used to drive a turbine, which is connected to a generator.
* The generator makes electricity when it is moved.

► Electricity transmission

Electrical power from power stations is distributed around the country through a grid of high-voltage power lines. The electricity in overhead power lines is transmitted to our homes and industry at 275 kV or 400 kV. The grid ensures that when a local power station is switched off for maintenance, electricity can still reach all the consumers in the area.

Why use high voltages?

The high voltages used to transmit electrical power around a country are extremely dangerous. That is why the cables that carry the power are supported on tall pylons high above people, traffic and buildings.

Sometimes the cables are buried underground, but this is much more expensive, and the cables must be safely insulated.

High voltages are used because it means that the current flowing in the cables is relatively low. When a current flows in a wire or cable, some of the energy it is carrying is lost because of the cable's resistance – the cable gets hot. A small current produces less heat and therefore wastes less energy than a large current.

Transformers

Power stations typically generate electricity at about 30 kV. This is then converted to the grid voltage, usually 275 kV or 400 kV, using a **step-up transformer**. Near the electricity user, such as a factory or a home, the voltage is then stepped down in stages using a number of **step-down transformers**. Heavy industry often takes its electricity at 415V, while equipment in a person's home usually requires the voltage to be reduced to 220V.

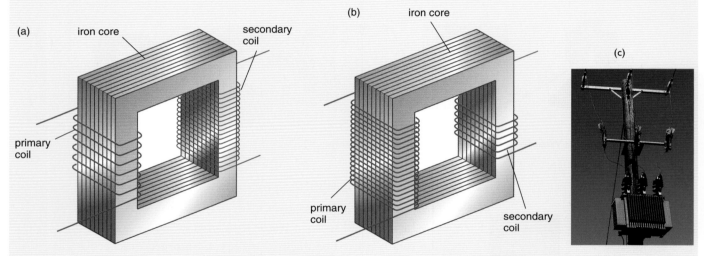

Figure 14.10 Transformers: (a) Step-up transformer (b) Step-down transformer (c) This transformer delivers power to users from the grid

All transformers have three parts:

1 Primary coil – the input voltage is connected across this coil.
2 Secondary coil – the output voltage is across the secondary coil.
3 An iron core – this links the coils magnetically. No current flows in the iron core.

Summary

A step-up transformer:

- increases the voltage
- decreases the current (to reduce heat losses in the grid)
- has more turns on the secondary coil than on the primary
- can always be found between the power station and the grid.

Electricity from the grid is passed first through a step-up transformer and then later through a step-down transformer before it reaches the consumer.

(a) What change, if any, does the step-up transformer make to:
   i   the current
   ii the voltage?

(b) Why is it necessary to pass the electricity through the step-down transformer?

Figure 14.11 A wind turbine

Figure 14.12 A light powered by a solar cell

Note

Solar heating panels made in Bangor in Northern Ireland are exported all over the world.

A step-down transformer:

* decreases the voltage for safety reasons
* has fewer turns on the secondary coil than on the primary
* can always be found between the grid and the electricity users.

▶ Renewable energy

Fossil fuel and nuclear energy are described as **non-renewable** as they will run out. There is a limited supply of each in the Earth's crust.

Renewable energy sources will not run out. The main sources are wind, waves, tides, solar and hydroelectric.

The blades of the windmill (Figure 14.11) act as the turbine. This turns the generator when the wind blows, producing electricity. Wind energy is free, non-polluting and renewable. The disadvantages of using windmills are that they can be ugly and noisy and they only produce electricity when there is a strong enough wind.

Solar cells (Figure 14.12) directly convert light energy into electricity. Solar energy is free, non-polluting and renewable. The major disadvantage of solar cells is that they only produce electricity when they receive sunlight.

Solar panels can be placed on the roof of a building to provide hot water. Solar panels trap the heat energy from the Sun, as shown in Figure 14.13.

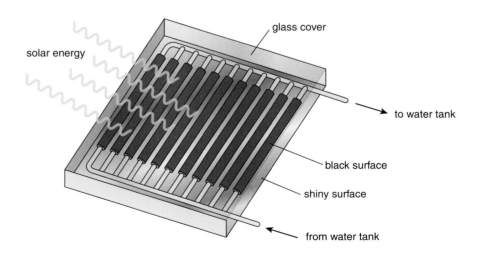

Figure 14.13 The solar panel traps solar energy and can heat the water in the house

Hydroelectric power involves building a dam to trap water, as shown in Figure 14.14. Water is allowed to flow through tunnels in the dam. This turns turbines and thus drives generators. Once

Note

Northern Ireland has an experimental tidal energy generator at the mouth of Strangford Lough. Tidal energy is reliable and the generator is mostly submerged so it is not visually polluting.

the dam is built, the energy is virtually free. No waste or pollution is produced. The major disadvantage is that the area behind the dam is flooded and this may formerly have provided habitats for endangered plants or animals.

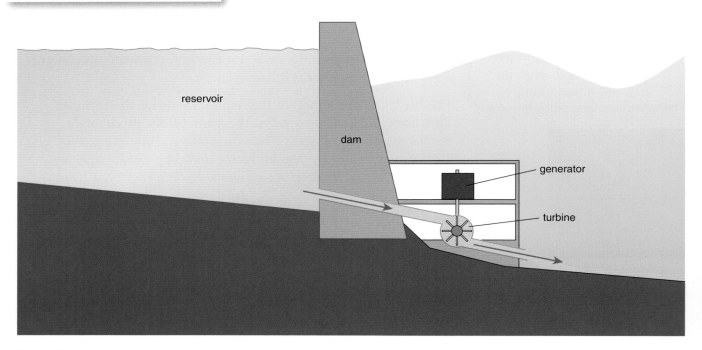

Figure 14.14 Hydroelectric power from a reservoir

► Exam questions

1 The picture below shows a three-pin plug.

X

a Trace or copy the diagram and draw a line from X to the earth pin. *(1 mark)*

b i What structure, inside the plug, connects the live wire to the live pin? *(1 mark)* Choose from:

neutral wire	fuse	earth wire

ii State **two** other safety features of the plug. *(2 marks)*

c Using any appliance for less time will reduce household electricity bills. Suggest two other ways of reducing household electricity bills. *(2 marks)*

CCEA Science: Single Award, Module 5, Foundation Tier, February 2008, Q2

2 a An investigation was carried out, using a bicycle dynamo, to find how the amount of current produced depends on the speed of rotation. The experiment results are given in the table below.

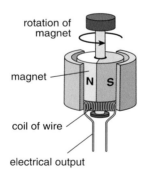

rotation of magnet

magnet

N S

coil of wire

electrical output

Magnet speed (revolutions per minute)	Number of coils	Current produced (mA)
20	30	2
30	30	3
40	30	4

i State the conclusion that can be drawn from these results. *(1 mark)*

ii Suggest the effect on the current produced if:

1 A stronger magnet is used. *(1 mark)*

2 Fewer coils of wire are used. *(1 mark)*

b Thirty years ago most bicycles would have been fitted with dynamo-powered lights. These were soon replaced with battery-powered lights, which were safer.

Suggest a reason why battery-powered lights were safer. *(1 mark)*

c Below is a diagram of a power station.

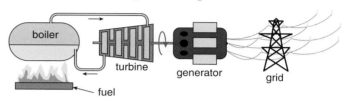

boiler

turbine generator grid

fuel

Name the part of the power station that does the same job as the dynamo. *(1 mark)*

d Fossil fuels and nuclear power are classed as non-renewable energy sources.

i Explain the term **non-renewable**. *(1 mark)*

ii Even though renewable energy sources are better for the environment, there can also be disadvantages to using them. State **two** disadvantages of using wind power. *(2 marks)*

CCEA Science: Single Award, Module 5, Foundation Tier, November 2007, Q6

3 a Describe fully two energy changes that occur in a fossil fuel power station during the production of electricity. Your answer must specify where these changes take place. *(2 marks)*

Before being distributed along the grid, the electricity leaving the power station must pass through a transformer.

b Name the type of transformer the electricity must past through and explain why it is used. *(3 marks)*

CCEA Science: Single Award, Revised Unit 3, Specimen Paper, Higher Tier, 2011, Q6 (modified)

4 Dara needs to replace the fuse in the plug connected to her television.

Below is a copy of the label stuck to the back of the television.

Voltage: 240V	Power: 600W	Supply: 50Hz

Warning: This appliance is double insulated. Unqualified personnel must not attempt to repair this appliance.

a Use the equation below to calculate the current flowing to the television. *(2 marks)*

power = voltage × current

b The most common fuse sizes sold are 1A, 2A, 3A, 5A and 13A.

Which fuse size is correct for this television? *(1 mark)*

c Explain how the television is protected by fitting the correct fuse. *(2 marks)*

d The television is on for 6 hours each day and each unit of electricity costs 12p.

Use the equation below to calculate the weekly cost of using this television. *(3 marks)*

weekly cost = power × time × cost per unit

CCEA Science: Single Award, Revised Unit 3, Specimen Paper, Higher Tier, 2011, Q4 (modified)

15 Waves and communication

▶ Waves

A **wave** is a series of disturbances or **vibrations** that carry energy from one place to another. Waves can travel through solids, liquids, gases and empty spaces or **vacuums**.

There are two types of wave: longitudinal waves and transverse waves.

- In **longitudinal waves** the particles vibrate in the same direction as the wave is travelling, as shown in Figure 15.1. Sound travels as longitudinal waves.

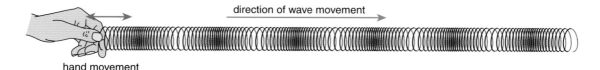

direction of wave movement

hand movement

Figure 15.1 A longitudinal wave

- In **transverse waves** the particles vibrate at right angles to the direction of travel, as shown in Figure 15.2. Light, water ripples and electromagnetic waves travel as transverse waves.

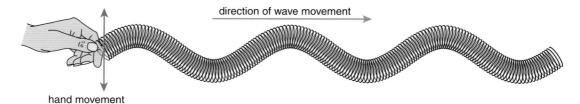

direction of wave movement

hand movement

Figure 15.2 A transverse wave

Wave features

- **Wavelength (λ)** is the distance between two successive crests or troughs, as shown in Figure 15.3.
- Wavelength is the length of one complete vibration.
- Wavelength is measured in millimetres (mm), centimetres (cm) or metres (m).

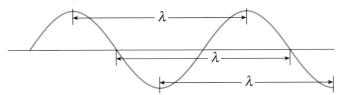

Figure 15.3 Wavelength, measured between two successive crests or troughs

- **Amplitude (A)** is the maximum height of the wave, as shown in Figure 15.4.
- Amplitude is measured from the mid-line, in millimetres (mm), centimetres (cm) or metres (m).

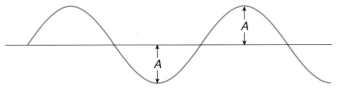

Figure 15.4 Amplitude, the maximum height of the wave

- **Frequency (f)** is the number of vibrations that pass a particular point in one second.
- Frequency is measured in **hertz (Hz)**. 1 vibration per second = 1 Hz.

▶ The wave equation

Imagine a wave with wavelength λ (metres) and a frequency f (hertz). Then the speed of the wave, v, is given by

speed = frequency × wavelength

or $v = f\lambda$

Note that the units used in this equation must be consistent as shown in Table 15.1.

Table 15.1 Units in the wave equation

Frequency	Wavelength	Speed
Always in hertz	cm	cm/s
	m	m/s
	km	km/s

▶ *Example 1*

What is the speed of a wave of frequency 4 Hz and wavelength 3 cm?
Solution
$v = f\lambda = 4 \times 3 = 12$ cm/s

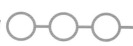

> ### ► *Example 2*
> Find the frequency of radio waves of wavelength 1500 m if their speed is 300 000 km/s.
> **Solution**
> First note that $v = 30000$ km/s $= 300\,000\,000$ m/s
> Then make the substitutions:
> $v = f\lambda$ so $300\,000\,000 = f \times 1500$
> Rearranging gives
> $$f = \frac{300\,000\,000}{1500} = 200\,000 \text{ Hz} = 200 \text{ kHz}$$

► Sound

* Sounds are produced by vibrating objects.
* Sound is a longitudinal wave.
* Sound can travel through solids, liquids and gases but it cannot travel through a vacuum (empty space).
* Sound travels most quickly through solids and most slowly through gases.
* Sound travels at 330 metres per second through air.
* Bigger vibrations make louder sounds. This can be seen on a graph as a bigger amplitude (Figure 15.5).

Slower vibrations produce sounds of lower frequency or pitch. The lower the frequency, the longer the wavelength (Figure 15.6).

Hearing

* The frequency range of human hearing is from 20 Hz to 20 kHz.
* This is called the **audible hearing range**.
* As we get older our upper limit decreases. Older people can find it difficult to hear sounds above 14 000 Hz (14 kHz).

The factors that affect a person's hearing include:

* birth defects
* damage to the eardrum
* prolonged exposure to a noisy environment
* age.

Earplugs and protectors are required in noisy environments and on building sites to prevent hearing damage.

Echoes

Like all waves, sound can be reflected off a surface. A reflected sound is called an **echo**. The best reflectors of sound are hard surfaces. This is why the bathroom and kitchen are usually the 'loudest' rooms in your home. Soft surfaces are good absorbers of sound.

Echoes can be both very useful and a real nuisance. They are a nuisance in concert halls and theatres, where the music reaches the

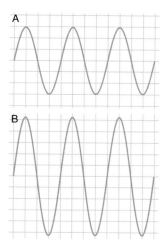

Figure 15.5 Wave A is quieter than wave B as its amplitude is smaller

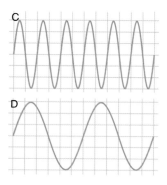

Figure 15.6 Wave D has a longer wavelength than wave C

audience not only from the stage but also as echoes created by the walls, floor and ceiling. This causes reverberation and can reduce quality. The problem is overcome in auditoria by using soft, sound-absorbing materials in the walls and ceilings.

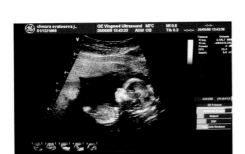

Figure 15.7 Ultrasound used to scan a foetus in the womb

Ultrasound

- Sounds with a frequency higher than 20 000 Hz (20 kHz) are known as **ultrasound**.
- The human ear cannot hear these sounds.

Uses of ultrasound

Ultrasound is used extensively in medicine because it is much safer than X-rays.

It is used in medicine:

- for scanning the developing foetus in the womb (Figure 15.7)
- for early diagnosis (e.g. to detect the presence of gall stones in the gall bladder)
- to check for internal bleeding in an organ
- to scan veins and arteries for clots
- to remove plaque from teeth in dentistry
- to see in real time the working of the heart (e.g. the opening and closing of cardiac valves).

Ultrasound is used extensively in industry to:

- clean delicate articles of jewellery, watches and lenses
- create the controllable heat needed to weld plastics
- detect micro-cracks in railway lines
- find distances (e.g. the depth of the ocean or the distance from one end of a room to the other)
- find fish and submarines.

Using ultrasound and echoes

Bats use echoes and ultrasound to navigate and to find the flying insects that they eat. Dolphins also use ultrasound to find their prey.

▶ EXAMPLE 3

A pulse of ultrasound takes 4 seconds to travel from a dolphin to its prey and back again. The speed of sound in sea water is 1500 m/s.
Use the equation to calculate how far away the dolphin is from its prey.

$$\text{distance} = \text{speed} \times \text{time} = 1500 \times 4 = 6000 \, \text{m}$$

But this is the distance from the dolphin to its prey and back again.
Divide 6000 by 2.
The answer is therefore 3000 m.

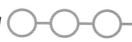

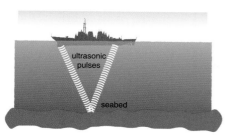

Figure 15.8 A ship using ultrasound to chart the seabed

Ships use echoes and ultrasound to chart the seabed (Figure 15.8).

▶ *EXAMPLE 4*

A ship sends out a pulse of ultrasound that takes 0.6 seconds to return. How deep is the seabed beneath the surface?

distance = speed × time = 1500 × 0.6 = 900 m

Remember to divide the answer by 2.
The seabed is 450 m beneath the surface.

Measuring the speed of sound

The echo method can be carried out as an experiment (Figure 15.9).

▶ *EXAMPLE 5*

Two pupils have been asked to go outside to estimate the speed of sound. One hits two wooden blocks together. The other measures the time between the bang and hearing the echo. The wall is 300 m away and the average time found was 2 seconds.

Use the equation: $\text{speed} = \dfrac{\text{distance}}{\text{time}}$

to calculate the speed of sound from the pupils' results.
Time to the wall and back = 2 s so the time to the wall = 1 s.

So $\text{speed} = \dfrac{300}{1} = 300 \text{ m/s}$

Figure 15.9 Using the echo method to measure the speed of sound

Flash-bang method

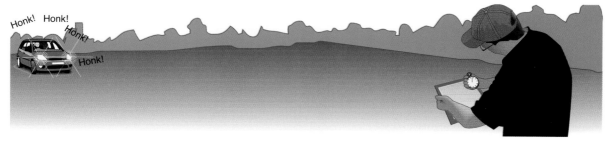

Figure 15.10 The flash–bang method of measuring the speed of sound

This involves two people being about a kilometre or so apart. Typically, one person stands with a stop watch at one end of a large field. The other person sets the distance meter to zero and drives a kilometre away. With the two people facing each other, the person with the car simultaneously flashes the car headlights and sounds the horn. Immediately the headlights are seen, the person with the stop watch starts the watch, and then stops it when the sound is heard. This is repeated several times and the average time to the sound to travel the known distance is calculated. This reduces the effect of human error. To reduce possible error due to the wind, the two people reverse positions and measure the time of travel of the sound in the opposite direction. The speed of sound is then taken as the average of the two calculated speeds. Typical results are shown in the Table below.

	Distance travelled by sound in m	Average time taken in s	Speed in m/s	Average speed in m/s
With the wind	990	2.9	341	330
Against the wind	990	3.1	319	

Note

Electromagnetic waves travel at 300 000 000 metres per second. This is so fast that they can go around the Earth seven times in just one second. In the same time, sound can only travel a mere 330 metres.

▶ The electromagnetic spectrum

The **electromagnetic spectrum** is the full spread of all known electromagnetic waves.

The part of this spectrum that can be seen is called the visible spectrum. Other parts of the electromagnetic spectrum include gamma rays, X-rays, ultraviolet light, infrared and radio waves. The full spectrum is shown below. Figure 15.11 and Table 15.2 show some uses of electromagnetic waves.

gamma rays	X-rays	ultraviolet (UV)	visible light	infrared	microwaves	radio waves

◀ Increasing frequency   Increasing wavelength ▶

All electromagnetic waves:

- carry energy
- are transverse waves
- can travel through a vacuum
- travel at the same speed in a vacuum.

Figure 15.11 Uses of electromagnetic waves

Table 15.2 Uses of electromagnetic waves

Wave	Effect on living cells	Main applications
gamma rays	can kill cells, can cause cancer	cancer treatment (radiotherapy), sterilisation of equipment
X-rays	can kill cells, can cause cancer	food preservation, cancer treatment, diagnosis of broken bones and dental problems
ultraviolet	causes a sun tan, can cause skin cancer	sun beds, detecting forged banknotes
visible light	allows us to see, helps skin cells produce vitamin D	lamps, photography, photosynthesis, used in telephone networks in optical fibres
infrared	produces a sensation of warmth, can cause burns	heaters, security detectors, remote controls, optical-fibre communications
microwaves	can cause burning under the skin	cooking food, fast satellite communications, mobile phone communications, speed cameras
radio waves	little effect on human body	long-range communication, radio and TV broadcasting

Dangers associated with electromagnetic waves

The electromagnetic waves that cause cancer are gamma rays, X-rays and ultraviolet light. These are the electromagnetic waves that have the highest frequency and carry the most energy. It is because they have so much energy that these particular waves are capable of disrupting the DNA in living cells and causing cancer.

How do microwaves heat up food?

Most foods contain some water. Microwaves have continuously changing electric and magnetic fields associated with them and can readily penetrate food. When a microwave comes across a water molecule, the electric field causes the water molecule to oscillate about 2 billion times a second. This rapid movement of the water molecule is observed as an increase in temperature. Microwaves therefore work best when heating foods that contain a lot of water. This is why they work so well when re-heating ready meals, soups and stews.

Test yourself

Explain why gamma radiation can produce cancer deep inside the body, but ultraviolet light tends to produce cancer of the skin.

► Communications

Telephone messages can be sent along copper wires or optical fibres (Figure 15.12). Signals along optical fibres are sent through the cable as pulses of either visible light or infrared.

Optical fibres are better for several reasons:

- They can carry much more information.
- The signals are more secure.
- The signals are not as prone to interference.
- The signals do not need to be boosted as often.

Figure 15.12 Communications cables consisting of optical fibres

Mobile phones

A mobile phone sends and receives messages carried by microwaves. The signal is sent from the mobile phone to the nearest mast. From there it is passed on to the next mast and so on until it reaches its destination (Figure 15.13).

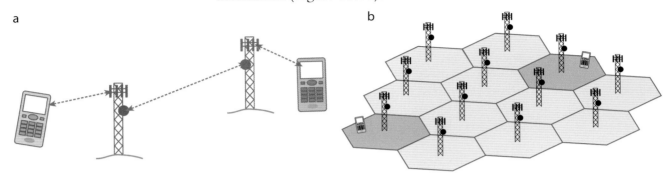

Figure 15.13 (a) How a mobile phone works (b) A cell network

The area around a mobile phone mast is called a **cell**. Each cell acts as a repeater station. Without these repeater stations the signals would have to be much stronger and this would make mobile phones much bigger.

Long-distance calls will involve satellite transceivers (Figure 15.14).

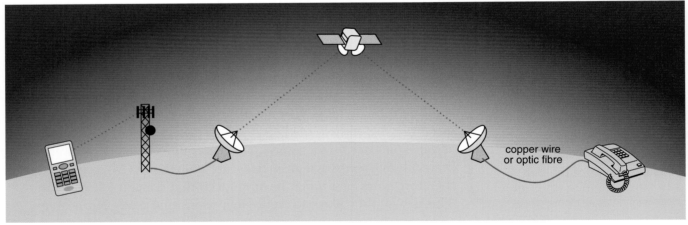

copper wire or optic fibre

Figure 15.14 Long-distance calls involving satellite transceivers

Health risks of mobile phones and communication masts

Mobile phones and mobile phone masts emit and receive microwaves and many people have suggested there may be a link between microwave radiation and cancer. There are claims that because mobile phones use microwaves, holding the phone close to your ear can cause the brain to be damaged.

Independent Expert Groups set up by Britain, the USA and the European Union have reported that there is no *proven* case of damage being done to people either by communication masts or by mobile phones. However, most expert groups have recommended the **precautionary principle** is followed. This states that even if the chances of negative health effects are low, it makes sense to avoid unnecessary risk. This means:

- young children should use mobile phones very sparingly, because their small body mass would make any possible harm to them more severe
- people should be encouraged to use mobile phones with headsets or speaker-phones whenever possible, so as to keep their heads as far as possible from the radiation-emitting handset
- mobile phone masts should not be erected close to schools or hospitals.

▶ Exam questions

1 a Copy and complete the paragraph below using the following words.

| vibrations   transverse   energy   wavelength |

A wave is a series of ___ . Waves carry ___ from one place to another. There are two types of wave, longitudinal and ___ . The three features of waves are frequency, speed and ___ .

(2 marks)

b Shown below are four waves taken over the same time.

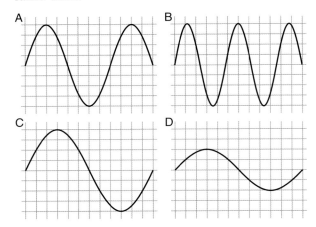

Which diagram (A, B, C or D) shows the wave with the:

i lowest amplitude *(1 mark)*
ii shortest wavelength? *(1 mark)*

c The diagram below represents a longitudinal wave.

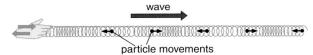

Use the diagram above to explain what a longitudinal wave is. *(1 mark)*

CCEA Science: Single Award, Module 5, Foundation Tier, November 2007, Q2

2 a The diagram below represents a sound wave.

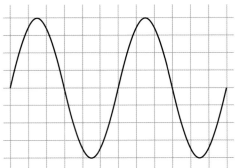

Copy or trace the diagram.
Using arrowed lines (↔), mark and label the following accurately on the diagram.

i amplitude (label A) *(1 mark)*
ii wavelength (label W) *(1 mark)*

b Choose from the following words to answer questions **i** and **ii** below.

| transverse   longitudinal   electromagnetic |

i What type of wave is sound? *(1 mark)*
ii What type of wave vibrates at right angles to the direction of travel? *(1 mark)*

c Which two types of electromagnetic radiation are commonly used inside optic fibres? *(2 marks)*
Choose from:

| microwaves   radio waves   visible light   gamma rays   infrared |

CCEA Science: Single Award, Module 5, Foundation Tier, February 2008, Q3

3 The graph shows how the frequency of electromagnetic waves changes with wavelength.

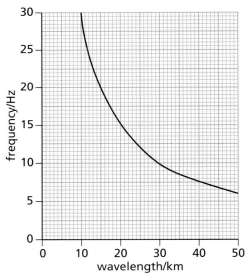

a State the conclusion that can be drawn from this graph. *(1 mark)*

b i Use the graph to find the wavelength of an electromagnetic wave with a frequency of 7.5 kHz. *(1 mark)*

ii Use your answer to part **i** and the equation:
wave speed = frequency × wavelength
to calculate the speed of this wave in metres per second (m/s). *(2 marks)*

c State two features of electromagnetic waves. *(2 marks)*

d Name two types of electromagnetic wave that can be used in mobile phone communications. *(2 marks)*

CCEA Science: Single Award, Unit 3, Higher Tier, March 2012, Q4

4 The electromagnetic spectrum is shown below.

gamma rays	X-rays	ultra-violet	visible light	infrared	micro-waves	radio waves

wavelength →

a Name the electromagnetic radiation that is most dangerous to human tissue. Explain why. *(2 marks)*

b Explain fully how microwaves can be used to cook food. *(2 marks)*

CCEA Science: Single Award, Specimen Paper, Higher Tier, 2011, Q6 (modified)

5 Two pupils were sent out to the playground to carry out an experiment to find the speed of sound. They were given a stopwatch and two wooden blocks. The children are 100 m from a wall.

a Describe a method that would allow these pupils to find the speed of sound. *(3 marks)*

b The pupils' recorded time was 0.6 seconds. Use the equation below to calculate the speed of sound from their results.

$$\text{speed} = \frac{\text{distance}}{\text{time}}$$

Answer in metres per second (m/s). *(3 marks)*

c The experiment was repeated the next day, giving different results. Suggest one reason why. *(1 mark)*

d Reflected sounds can cause problems in concert halls (auditoria). Explain fully one way to counteract this problem. *(2 marks)*

CCEA Science: Single Award, Module 5, Foundation Tier, February 2008, Q6 (modified)

6 a Given below are some sound wave frequencies.
200 Hz   20 Hz   2000 Hz   30 kHz   2 kHz

i Which frequency is the lowest humans can hear? *(1 mark)*

ii Which two frequencies are the same? *(1 mark)*

iii Which frequency is in the ultrasound range? *(1 mark)*

b The diagrams below represent sound waves taken over the same time.

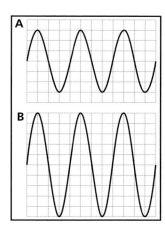
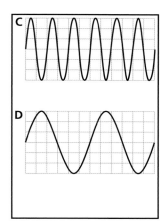

Which wave, A, B, C or D, has:

i the longest wavelength? *(1 mark)*

ii the biggest amplitude? *(1 mark)*

c i Copy and complete the following sentence. Sound is an example of a longitudinal wave whereas light is an example of a _____ wave. *(1 mark)*

ii What do waves carry from one place to another? *(1 mark)*

CCEA Science: Single Award, Unit 3, Foundation Tier, February 2013, Q2

 *Vision*

> **LEARNING OBJECTIVES**
>
> **By the end of this chapter you should know and understand:**
>
> - **the action of converging and diverging lenses**
> - **the structure of the human eye**
> - **how images are produced on the retina**
> - **short sight and long sight and how they are corrected.**

▶ Light and vision

Visible light is the only part of the electromagnetic spectrum that humans can see. The Sun, flames and burning candles are called sources of light as they emit their own light. Things that do not emit light are visible because light reflects or bounces off them.

We see things when light enters our eyes, either from a source or when it has been reflected off an object.

Light travels in straight lines, but it can change direction by being bent. This happens when light passes from one material into another. It occurs because light travels at different speeds in different materials. The bending of light is called **refraction**. Lenses refract or bend light.

Lenses are usually made of glass or plastic and their surfaces are curved. There are two types of lens:

- **Convex** or converging lenses are thicker in the middle than at the outside. Convex lenses bring rays of light closer together. The rays **converge** (Figure 16.1). Convex lenses are found in the eye and are used in cameras.
- **Concave** or diverging lenses are thinner in the middle than at the outside. Concave lenses refract or bend light outwards. They make rays of light spread out or **diverge** (Figure 16.2).

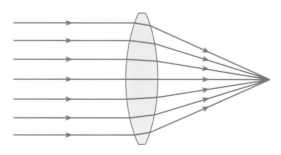

Figure 16.1 Convex lenses bring rays of light closer together

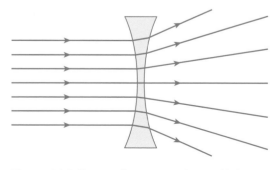

Figure 16.2 Concave lenses spread rays of light apart

The human eye

Figure 16.3 shows the main features of the eye.

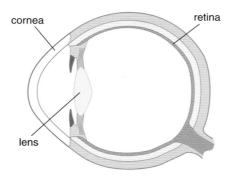

Figure 16.3 **The human eye**

Rays from an object are refracted to form an image on the **retina**. The image is upside down but the brain turns it the right way up. Most of the refraction occurs as the light passes through the cornea. Some refraction also occurs as the light passes through the lens.

To get a sharp image, the light must be focused onto the retina by the lens (Figure 16.4).

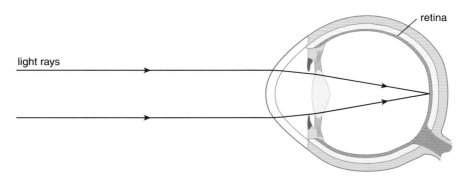

Figure 16.4 **The light is focused onto the retina by the lens**

The lenses in some people's eyes are too strong and so the light is bent too much. This causes a blurred image to be formed before the retina. This is called **short sight** (Figure 16.5) and it can be corrected by means of a concave lens (Figure 16.6). A person with short sight can see close objects clearly but distant objects appear blurry.

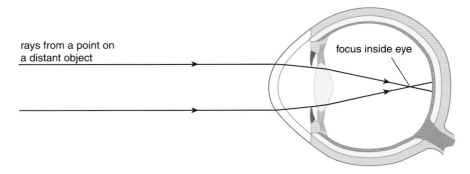

Figure 16.5 **Short sight – a blurred image may be formed before the retina**

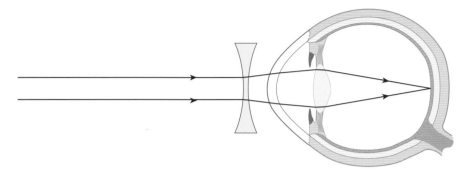

Figure 16.6 Short sight corrected by a concave lens

Long sight occurs when the eye lens is too weak to converge the light. This causes blurred vision as the rays are brought to a focus behind the retina (Figure 16.7). A convex lens can be used to correct this condition (Figure 16.8). A person with long sight can see distant objects clearly but close objects appear blurry.

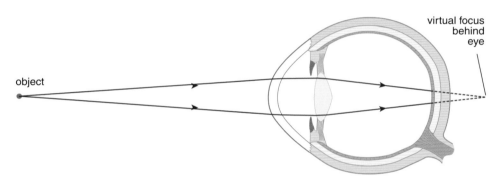

Figure 16.7 Long sight – the image is formed behind the retina

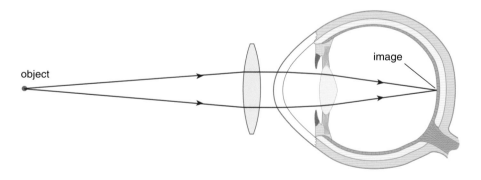

Figure 16.8 Long sight corrected by a convex lens

Exam questions

1 a The diagram below shows the structure of the human eye.

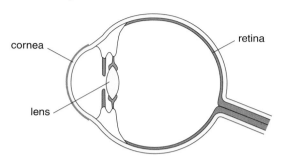

Match each part with its correct function.

(3 marks)

Part	Function
Cornea	Image is formed here
Retina	Focuses light
Lens	Controls amount of light entering the eye
	Light is bent most

b Below is a diagram showing the eye of someone who has an eye defect.

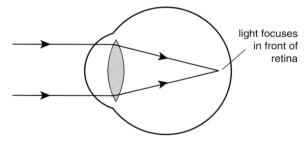

light focuses in front of retina

i Name this type of eye defect. *(1 mark)*

ii Below is a diagram of the lens needed to correct this defect.

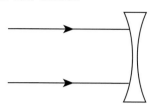

Name this type of lens. *(1 mark)*

iii Copy and complete the diagram to show the path of the rays out of the lens. (Use a ruler.) *(1 mark)*

CCEA Science: Single Award, Module 5, Foundation Tier, May 2007, Q1

2 a The diagram below shows three glass shapes.

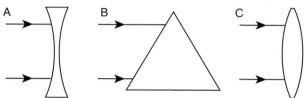

Which diagram (A, B or C) shows:

i a prism *(1 mark)*

ii a concave lens? *(1 mark)*

b State what a convex lens does to parallel rays of light. *(1 mark)*

c Describe fully what happens to light on its path through the eye. *(3 marks)*

CCEA Science: Single Award, Module 5, Foundation Tier, February 2008, Q5

3 a Describe fully the cause and effect of short sight. *(3 marks)*

b Explain how short sight is corrected. *(1 mark)*

CCEA Science: Single Award, Unit 3, Higher Tier, February 2013, Q10

17 Energy

▶ Fossil fuels

The most common fuels used in the world today are fossil fuels. Of these, the most important are **coal**, **oil** and **natural gas**. Other fossil fuels include **peat** and **lignite** but these are not used in such large quantities.

They are called fossil fuels because they were made over millions of years from the remains of plants and animals. Plant remains have produced the coal while animal remains have produced the oil and natural gas. Fossil fuels are non-renewable fuels, which means that eventually the Earth's stores of them will run out.

Fossil fuels in Ireland

Ireland has very few fossil fuel resources and continues to import increasing quantities of fuel, particularly oil and coal. In recent years we have exploited natural gas reserves discovered in the Celtic Sea.

Northern Ireland has substantial deposits of lignite around Crumlin and Ballycastle but, as yet, these deposits have not been exploited commercially. To do so would involve open-cast mining (Figure 17.1), with significant noise and dust pollution. It would also destroy areas of natural beauty. However, those in favour of commercial development of lignite say we would have:

- increased employment
- a stronger local economy
- cheaper fuels.

Figure 17.1 Open-cast mining

Increasing use of fossil fuels

All fossil fuels are non-renewable and will eventually run out, as there are only limited world reserves.

Burning any fossil fuel also produces carbon dioxide, a major contributor to increased global warming.

We are using more and more fossil fuels every day as developing countries are becoming industrialised and need fuel and electricity. There is also a worldwide increase in the number of cars and other vehicles on the roads, which increases our use of oil.

▶ What can be done?

1 Use more renewable energy sources for electricity and home heating

Possible alternative sources of renewable power (Figure 17.2) include:

- tidal
- geothermal
- wind
- solar
- hydroelectric.

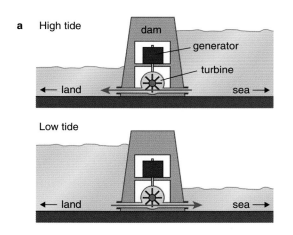
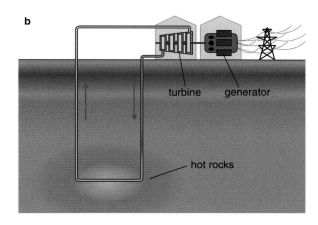

Figure 17.2 Renewable energy sources (a) tidal power (b) geothermal power

2 Develop alternative fuels for transport

Biofuel

Biofuel can be produced from vegetable oil extracted from the seeds of oilseed rape. It is almost carbon neutral, contributing less than fossil fuels do to the greenhouse effect. The plants from which biofuels are made take in as much carbon dioxide as the fuel gives out when it is burned, which is why they are largely '**carbon neutral**'.

Gasohol

In Brazil and Thailand the oil companies produce **gasohol** by adding alcohol to petrol. This extends their oil supplies. The alcohol is made from sugar beet, rice, wheat, barley, sugar cane, potatoes, corn and other biomass materials.

Other new fuels include the use of hydrogen gas and methanol (see below).

Regenerative hybrid systems

For many years London buses used regenerative braking systems. The buses had electrical generators attached to the wheels. When the bus braked, its kinetic (movement) energy was converted to electricity. This recharged the battery.

The Toyota Prius and several other cars have an ordinary petrol engine and a high-voltage rechargeable battery. As far as possible, all wasted energy is used to recharge the battery, which can be used at times to power the vehicle.

Using fuel cells

Ordinary batteries convert chemical energy into electrical energy. When the chemicals inside the battery are used up, the battery is returned for recycling. **Fuel cells** are a special type of battery in which the chemicals are supplied continuously by the user, in much the same way as petrol is supplied to keep a car engine working. A car using a fuel cell is therefore an electric car in which the user tops up the battery by adding the fuel as needed. Many car manufacturers are currently researching the use of fuel cells to power their vehicles.

Fuel cells can use many different chemicals. One type uses methanol, which is readily made from ordinary alcohol and steam. The alcohol needed to make the methanol is produced from renewable biomass. The use of renewable methanol fuel can therefore replace fossil fuels directly.

Inside the cell the methanol 'burns' to produce electricity. The waste products are carbon dioxide, water and heat. Liquid methanol fuel can be purchased from a filling station in much the same way as petrol.

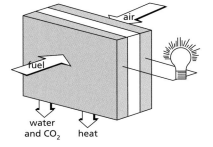

Figure 17.3 How a methanol fuel cell works

Figure 17.4 Buying methanol fuel at a filling station

Test yourself

Give one possible disadvantage of making renewable methanol from biomass.

Figure 17.5 A traditional filament light bulb

Figure 17.6 Energy-saving bulbs: (a) A low-energy compact fluorescent tube light bulb (b) A low-energy LED (light-emitting diode) bulb

3 Use fuels more efficiently

The **efficiency** of any device describes how good it is at transferring energy in the intended way.

The equation for efficiency is

$$\text{efficiency} = \frac{\text{useful energy output}}{\text{total energy input}}$$

Light bulbs are designed to convert electricity to light. Unfortunately they also produce heat. The bulb shown in Figure 17.5 is not very efficient as it produces more heat than light.

Energy-saving bulbs, like those shown in Figure 17.6, produce less heat and so they are more efficient.

▶ EXAMPLE 1

A 40 watt light bulb uses 144 000 joules of electrical energy per hour. If it produces 9600 joules of light, what is the efficiency of the light bulb?

$$\text{efficiency} = \frac{\text{useful work (energy) output}}{\text{total energy input}} = \frac{9600}{144\,000} = 0.07 = 7\%$$

▶ EXAMPLE 2

A car does 360 000 joules of useful work driving to town. The efficiency of its petrol engine is 0.26. How much chemical energy was there in the petrol used?

$$\text{efficiency} = \frac{\text{useful work (energy) output}}{\text{total energy input}}$$

Rearrange this equation

$$\text{total energy input} = \frac{\text{useful work (energy) output}}{\text{efficiency}} = \frac{360\,000}{0.26} = 1384615 \text{ joules}$$

▶ Law of Conservation of Energy

One of the fundamental laws of physics is the **Law of Conservation of Energy**. This states that:

Energy can neither be created nor destroyed, but it can change its form.

If energy cannot be destroyed, where does it go? The answer is that both the useful and wasted energy are *eventually* transferred to their surroundings as heat. This causes the environment to become warmer. In this way energy is continually becoming more and more diluted and hence less useful.

▶ EXAMPLE 3

A microwave oven converts electrical energy into useful microwave energy and other forms of energy that are wasted.

Complete the box below by adding the appropriate number.

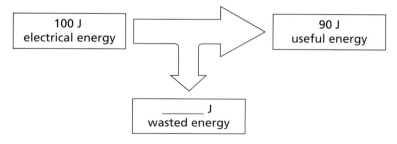

Total input electrical energy = total output energy

100 J = 90 J (useful energy) + wasted energy

wasted energy = 100 − 90 = 10 J

► Exam questions

1 The picture shows a television, an energy changing device.

a Copy and complete the following sentences. Choose from:

light   heat   chemical   sound   electrical

The energy input into the television is _____ energy.

The useful energy output from the screen is _____ energy.

Some energy is wasted in the form of _____ energy. *(3 marks)*

b The table below shows the energy input and output figures for three televisions. However, one value has been recorded incorrectly.

Television	Energy input/J	Useful energy output/J
A	480	100
B	350	500
C	600	400

Which set of figures, **A, B** or **C**, is incorrect? Explain your answer. *(2 marks)*

c An energy-efficient television saves £12 per year in running costs compared to a less efficient model. However, it costs £60 more to buy.

Calculate how many years it takes to save the extra £60. *(1 mark)*

CCEA Science: Single Award, Unit 3, Foundation Tier, February 2013, Q1

2 The table below gives information for two different types of light bulb.

	Low-energy bulb	Ordinary bulb
electrical power input	15W	60W
light power output	3W	3W
cost to buy	£3.50	£0.50
expected lifetime	8 years	1 year
annual running cost	£1.00	£4.00

a i Give two reasons for choosing a low-energy light bulb. *(2 marks)*

ii Give one reason for choosing the ordinary light bulb. *(1 mark)*

b Calculate the efficiency of the low-energy bulb using the equation below: *(2 marks)*

$$\text{efficiency} = \frac{\text{light power output}}{\text{electrical power input}}$$

CCEA Science: Single Award, Unit 3, Foundation Tier, March 2012, Q3

3 a The table below gives information about four types of electric lights.

Light	Power input/ watts	Light power output/ watts	Average lifetime/ hours	Cost to buy/£	Efficiency/ %
filament bulb	100	30	1000	0.5	
halogen lamp	40	30	10000	4	75
LED spotlight	10	7	30000	6	70
fluorescent tube	15	10	5000	5	67

i Use the equation

$$\text{efficiency} = \frac{\text{useful power output}}{\text{total power input}}$$

to calculate the efficiency of the filament bulb. *(2 marks)*

ii The total cost of lighting includes the cost to buy and the cost of electricity used. You need to provide 30000 hours of lighting for the lowest overall cost.

Explain fully why you might choose the LED spotlight rather than the halogen lamp. *(2 marks)*

b State the law of conservation of energy. *(2 marks)*

CCEA Science: Single Award, Unit 3, Higher Tier, March 2013, Q8

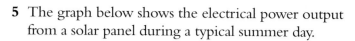

4 a The diagrams show a filament lamp, a halogen lamp and a compact fluorescent lamp (CFL).

filament lamp   halogen lamp   CFL
(wire inside)   (filled with argon)

The graph shows how the light output for each type changes with power input.

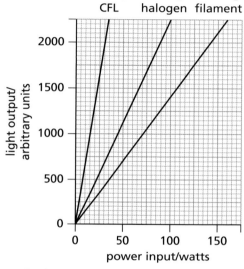

i At 25 watts calculate how much more light a halogen lamp produces compared with a filament lamp. *(1 mark)*

ii State two trends that the graph shows. *(2 marks)*

b The government is promoting the use of CFL bulbs and the production of filament bulbs is about to stop. Use the information provided to explain why this is the best course of action. *(3 marks)*

c State the law of conservation of energy. *(2 marks)*

CCEA Science: Single Award, Unit 3, Higher Tier, March 2012, Q6

5 The graph below shows the electrical power output from a solar panel during a typical summer day.

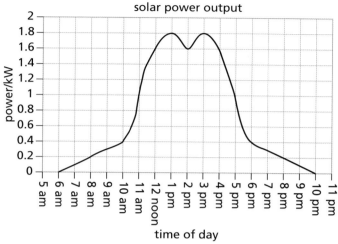

a This solar panel is to be used to supply electricity to a 1 kW water pump. How many hours each day will the pump work? *(2 marks)*

b Suggest one reason for the drop in power output during the mid–afternoon. *(1 mark)*

c Draw a line on a copy of the graph to show what the power output might be on a typical winter day. *(2 marks)*

d Solar power is described as a renewable energy source. Why are renewable energy sources better for the environment than fossil fuels? *(1 mark)*

CCEA Science: Single Award, Unit 3, Specimen Paper, Foundation Tier, 2011, Q8

6 Coal, oil, solar, nuclear and wind are examples of energy resources used in the United Kingdom to generate electricity.

a i Write down an example of a non-renewable energy resource from the list above. *(1 mark)*

ii Explain the meaning of the term non-renewable energy resource. *(1 mark)*

b i Write down an example of a renewable energy resource from the list above. *(1 mark)*

ii Explain the meaning of the term renewable energy resource. *(1 mark)*

CCEA Science: Double Award, Forces & Energy, Foundation Tier, June 2012, Q2

18 Transport and road safety

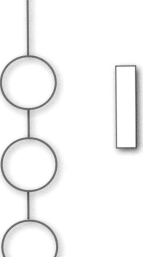

LEARNING OBJECTIVES

By the end of this chapter you should know and understand:

- about thinking distance, braking distance and stopping distance
- that friction opposes motion and the role it plays in braking
- what is meant by reaction time and how it can be measured
- the use of seatbelts, airbags and crumple zones to reduce injuries to road users
- how speed restrictions, speed bumps and traffic cameras contribute to road safety
- how to interpret straight line graphs of distance against time
- the difference between instantaneous and average speed
- what is meant by momentum and how momentum transfer causes a force
- the effect of balanced forces on an object
- that a resultant force is necessary to produce an acceleration.

▶ Road safety

One cause of road accidents is driving too close to the vehicle in front. If the leading vehicle brakes suddenly there will be a crash. According to the *Highway Code*, you should leave enough space between you and the vehicle in front so that you can pull up safely if it suddenly slows down or stops (Figure 18.1). The safe rule is never to get closer than the overall stopping distance.

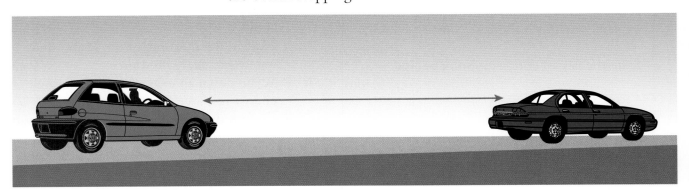

Figure 18.1 Stopping distance

Stopping distance

The **stopping distance** is how far a vehicle travels from the time the driver sees a reason to stop until the vehicle reaches a complete stop. It is made up of the **thinking distance** and the **braking distance**.

Thinking distance

The thinking distance is how far the vehicle travels while the driver is thinking about what to do. It is the distance the car travels from when the driver sees the danger until the brakes are applied.

Braking distance

The braking distance is how far the vehicle travels after the brakes are applied, until it comes to a complete stop.

Table 18.1 gives the typical thinking, braking and stopping distances at different speeds, on dry roads with good tyres and brakes.

Table 18.1 Typical thinking, braking and stopping distances

Speed/miles per hour and metres per second	Thinking distance/metres	Braking distance/ metres	Stopping distance/metres
20 mph (9 m/s)	6	6	12
40 mph (18 m/s)	12	24	36
60 mph (27 m/s)	18	55	73

What affects thinking distance?

Anything that slows the driver's brain will increase the thinking distance. It will take the driver longer to think what they should do and so the car travels further. The major factors that increase thinking distance are:

- **speed** – the higher the speed, the greater the distance the vehicle travels in a certain time
- **alcohol** – slows down the brain and impairs judgement
- **tiredness** – slows down the brain and impairs judgement
- **illegal drugs** – slow down the brain and impair judgement
- **prescribed medicines** – may slow down the brain. (If there is any danger you will be warned by the chemist's label.)

What affects braking distance?

Anything that reduces the amount of friction or grip of the brakes and between the tyres and the road will increase the braking distance. The major factors increasing braking distance are:

- **speed** – the higher the speed, the greater the distance the vehicle travels in a certain time
- **state of tyres** – bald tyres give less grip between tyres and road
- **weather** – wet or icy roads give less grip between tyres and road
- **state of the brakes** – poor brakes reduce grip between brakes and wheels
- **state of the road** – poor road surfaces reduce grip between tyres and road.

▶ Physics and car accidents

Crumple zones are areas at the front and rear of a car that are designed to absorb the huge amount of kinetic energy lost in an accident. Crumple zones collapse relatively easily and slowly. The car's

Figure 18.2 Crumple zones make forces on car passengers smaller

Figure 18.3 Drivers and passengers, by law, must wear seatbelts

Figure 18.4 Airbags are fitted in most modern cars

cabin is much stronger, so it does not crumple around the passengers. Crumple zones spread the collision over a longer time and so reduce the force on the passengers. Hopefully this reduces the chance of serious injuries.

Seat belts provide a restraining force and reduce the risk that drivers and passengers will be thrown forward and seriously injured. Drivers and passengers, by law, must wear seatbelts (Figure 18.3).

Airbags in cars give extra protection in collisions. Front airbags are fitted in the steering wheel or in the dashboard. The shock of a front-end collision sets off a controlled explosive chemical reaction inside the bag. The reaction forms a large volume of gas very quickly. The gas fills the bag, which then holds a passenger in their seat. The bags are porous and go down quickly after the accident. Many cars also have airbags fitted to the sides. These reduce the number of crush injuries that occur from the side impact of another vehicle.

Motorway crash barriers are designed to prevent vehicles from crossing from one carriageway to the other. They also prevent vehicles from impacting or entering roadside hazards. The barriers absorb some of the kinetic energy from the impact caused by the vehicle striking them. They also redirect the vehicle along the line of the barrier so that it does not turn around, turn over or re-enter the stream of traffic. Motorway designers call this Road Traffic Accident Containment.

Speed limits

The speed limit on any road depends on the type of road and type of vehicle. The speed limits for UK roads are summarised in Table 18.2.

The two main reasons for speed limits are:

- to make accidents less likely
- to reduce the risk of fatal injury if an accident occurs.

Table 18.2 Speed limits for roads in the UK

Type of vehicle	In built-up area / mph	On single carriageway / mph	On dual carriageway / mph	On motorway / mph
cars and motorcycles	30	60	70	70
cars towing trailers or caravans	30	50	60	60
buses and coaches	30	50	60	70
goods vehicles	30	50	60	70
heavy goods vehicles	30	40	50	60

Police and local councils attempt to enforce these speed restrictions, using a variety of methods.

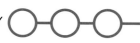

a

b

Figure 18.5 Different types of speed camera (a) a hand-held speed camera (b) an instantaneous speed camera

Figure 18.6 A speed bump used to slow vehicles down in built-up areas

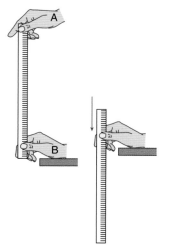

Figure 18.7 Using a metre stick to measure reaction time

Speed cameras

Speed cameras are used to photograph speeding vehicles and those jumping traffic lights. There are hand-held, instantaneous speed (Figure 18.5) and average speed varieties. **The instantaneous speed is the rate of change of distance travelled with time.** Instantaneous speed is shown on a car's speedometer. It shows the speed of the car at that moment in time.

The owner of a speeding vehicle will be identified by means of the registration number. The driver will be penalised with a fine and/or penalty points on their licence.

Speed bumps

Speed bumps, as shown in Figure 18.6, are used to slow vehicles down in built-up areas. Drivers are forced either to slow down or risk a bumpy ride with possible damage to their vehicle.

Calming measures

Speed cameras, speed bumps and road-narrowing schemes are commonly called **traffic calming measures**. The advantage of these measures is that drivers are forced to slow down and this leads to fewer and less serious accidents. The major disadvantage of such measures is that they increase the time taken to provide emergency services.

▶ Reaction time

When reading about stopping distance, you learned that it has two parts – thinking and braking distances. Thinking distance was how far the vehicle travelled while the driver was thinking what to do. It depended on the speed of the driver's brain.

Reaction time is the time that passes between an observation and the start of the body's response to that observation. Reaction times can be measured roughly using a metre stick, as shown in Figure 18.7.

The metre stick is held vertically, by person A, against person B's outstretched hand. The zero on the metre stick must be level with the tip of B's index finger. A lets go of the metre stick and B tries to catch it as soon as possible. The distance the stick falls can be used to calculate reaction time, using the following equation:

$$t^2 = \frac{d}{4.9}$$

where d = distance travelled by the metre stick and t = reaction time.

To ensure a reliable, accurate result, this experiment must be carried out several times and then an average of all the results should be taken.

▶ Friction

Braking distance is how far the vehicle travels, from when the driver applies the brakes until the vehicle comes to a complete stop. Braking distance depends on **friction**. Friction is the force that opposes motion (Figure 18.8). It is measured in **newtons (N)**.

- Friction is produced when two surfaces rub together.
- The rougher the surfaces, the more friction is produced.
- The greater the weight of an object, the more friction is produced.

friction ← → motion

Figure 18.8 Friction opposes motion

Is friction a help or a hindrance?

Friction produces grip and heat. Grip is useful as it allows us to get things moving, as well as slow them down. It also allows us to walk and to write.

Friction is a nuisance when it wears out moving parts and causes them to heat up. We have to get rid of this heat or reduce the friction.

Braking distance and friction

When the brakes of a vehicle are applied, friction is produced between the brake pads and the brake discs to slow the vehicle down. It is essential, therefore, to have good brakes.

Friction is also produced between the tyre and the road surface. The more friction there is, the faster the vehicle will stop and so the shorter the braking distance.

Good tyres and good road conditions produce more friction and so a shorter braking distance. In Figure 18.9, the summer tyres have different tread patterns from the winter tyres.

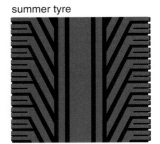

summer tyre

winter tyre

Figure 18.9 Tyres can have different treads for different conditions

▶ Speed

When an object travels, its **average speed** can be calculated from the equation:

$$\text{average speed} = \frac{\text{total distance travelled}}{\text{total time taken}}$$

When distance is measured in metres (m) and time is measured in seconds (s), the units of speed are metres per second (m/s). Other common speed units are kilometres per hour (km/h) and miles per hour (mph). Remember that average speed is not the same as instantaneous speed (page 179).

▶ *EXAMPLE 1*

A car travels 600 m in 30 s. Calculate its average speed.

$$\text{average speed} = \frac{\text{total distance travelled}}{\text{total time taken}} = \frac{600\,\text{m}}{30\,\text{s}} = 20\,\text{m/s}$$

▶ EXAMPLE 2

An athlete runs at an average speed of 6 m/s for 2 minutes. How far does she travel?

$$\text{average speed} = \frac{\text{total distance travelled}}{\text{total time taken}}$$

Rearranging gives:

$$\text{total distance travelled} = \text{average speed} \times \text{total time taken}$$
$$= 6 \times 120 = 720\,\text{m}$$

▶ Distance–time graphs

A **distance–time graph** is a graph of distance on the y-axis versus time on the x-axis. Three rules will help with the interpretation of such graphs:

- Horizontal lines mean the object is stationary (not moving, zero speed).
- Diagonal lines mean the object is moving with constant speed.
- The steeper the diagonal line, the faster the object is moving.

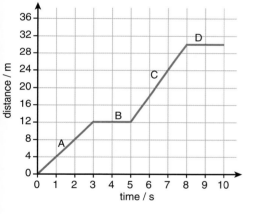

Figure 18.10 Distance–time graph

▶ EXAMPLE 3

Refer to Figure 18.10.

- In section A, the object is moving at a constant speed (diagonal line) of 4 m/s.
- In section B, the object is stationary (horizontal line).
- In section C, the object is moving at a constant speed (steeper diagonal line) of 6 m/s.
- In section D, the object is again stationary (horizontal line).

Using a data-logger to measure speed

Figure 18.11 shows how to measure the speed of a moving trolley using a data-logger and computer.

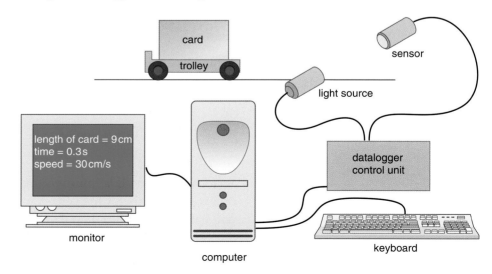

Figure 18.11 Measuring the speed of a trolley

A beam of light passes between the two sensors. The card on the trolley breaks the beam as the trolley passes through. The computer software will ask you to input the length of the card (its distance). The computer will then time how long it takes the card to pass between the sensors and calculate its speed using the equation:

$$\text{average speed} = \frac{\text{total distance travelled}}{\text{total time taken}}$$

▶ Momentum

Any moving object is said to have **momentum**. Momentum is defined as the mass of a body multiplied by its velocity:

$$\text{momentum} = \text{mass} \times \text{velocity}$$

Since mass is measured in kg and velocity is measured in m/s, momentum is measured in kg m/s.

Like force, momentum has both size and direction. Its direction is the direction of the velocity.

▶ EXAMPLE 4

Calculate the momentum of a 750 g ball travelling north at 120 cm/s. Give your answer in kg m/s.
First convert the units for mass and velocity:

$$750\,g = 0.75\,kg \text{ and } 120\,cm/s = 1.2\,m/s$$

Now make the substitutions:

$$\text{momentum} = \text{mass} \times \text{velocity} = 0.75\,kg \times 1.2\,m/s = 0.9\,kg\,m/s \text{ due north}$$

▶ EXAMPLE 5

Calculate the velocity of a 800 kg car that has a momentum of 10 400 kg m/s due west.

$$\text{momentum} = \text{mass} \times \text{velocity}$$

$$10\,400 = 800 \times v$$

$$v = \frac{10\,400}{800} = 13\,m/s \text{ due west}$$

When objects collide, momentum is generally transferred from one object to the other. One object will lose momentum and the other will gain momentum. It is this transfer of momentum that causes the objects to exert a force on each other. The longer it takes for the momentum to be transferred, the smaller the force that the objects exert on each other. We use this idea when designing cars to reduce the injuries to passengers in car accidents.

▶ Acceleration

The **acceleration** is the rate of change of the speed of an object. If an object is getting faster, it is accelerating. If an object is slowing down, it is decelerating.

▶ Balanced and unbalanced forces

If the forces on an object are equal in size but opposite in direction, then the forces are said to be **balanced**. If the forces on an object are balanced, then its velocity remains constant. This means that the object will either remain at rest or move in a straight line with a constant speed.

The **unbalanced force** on an object is known as the **resultant force** and it causes the object's speed or direction to change. The object therefore accelerates. This is illustrated in Examples 6 and 7.

▶ EXAMPLE 6

A lorry is moving at a constant speed in a straight line.

backward force   forward force

a The forward force due to the engine is 30 000 N.
  i Which one of the following statements is correct?
    ● The backward force is less than 30 000 N
    ● The backward force is equal to 30 000 N
    ● The backward force is greater than 30 000 N
  ii What is the name of the backward force acting on the lorry?
b The forward force due to the engine increases to 50 000 N. If the backward force does not change, what happens to the speed of the lorry?

Solution

a i The lorry is moving at a constant speed so the forces are balanced. This means the backward force and the forward force are equal in size. The backward force is therefore equal to 30 000 N.
  ii Friction
b The forces are now unbalanced so the lorry accelerates, getting faster and faster.

▶ *EXAMPLE 7*

A car is travelling in a straight line on a level road. The force of friction at the wheels is 2000 N. The force provided by the car's engine is 2400 N.

a Calculate the resultant (unbalanced) force, if any, on the car.
b Describe the motion of the car.

The car then passes over a stretch of rough road, so that the friction force increases from 2000 N to 2400 N. The engine force is unchanged.

c Calculate the new resultant (unbalanced) force, if any, on the car.
d Describe the motion of the car.

Solution

a Resultant (unbalanced) force = 2400 − 2000 = 400 N forwards.
b The car is accelerating since there is a forward resultant force of 400 N.
c There is now no resultant (unbalanced) force. The engine force (2400 N) and friction force (2400 N) are the same in size, but opposite in direction. They are balanced.
d The car moves at a steady speed in a straight line.

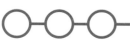

▶ Exam questions

1 a The diagram shows the total stopping
distances for cars travelling at different speeds.

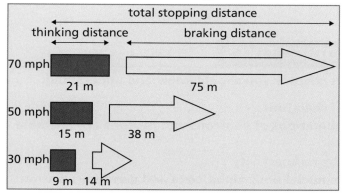

i Calculate the total stopping distance at
70 mph. *(1 mark)*

ii From the diagram state two effects of
increasing speed. *(2 marks)*

b Copy and complete the table below to show
what effect (if any) each condition may have
on thinking and braking distance.

Choose from: increased none decreased

(2 marks)

Condition	Thinking distance	Braking distance
wet road surface		
worn tyres	none	increased
driver has been drinking alcohol		

c i Name the force that opposes motion. *(1 mark)*
ii Name the unit for force. *(1 mark)*
CCEA Science: Single Award, Unit 3, Foundation Tier, February 2013, Q4

2 a The diagram below shows Julie's journey to
school.

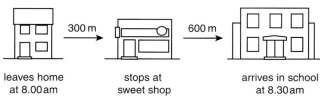

i What distance (in metres) did Julie walk to
school? *(1 mark)*

ii How long, in minutes, did it take Julie to
get to school? *(1 mark)*

iii Use the equation:

$$\text{average speed} = \frac{\text{total distance travelled}}{\text{total time taken}}$$

to calculate Julie's average speed, in m/minute.
(1 mark)

iv If Julie does not stop at the shop but walks
straight to school, what, if anything, will
happen to her average speed? Choose from:
decrease stay the same increase *(1 mark)*

b Robin is investigating friction. He uses a
newtonmeter to measure the force needed to
pull a block of wood across different surfaces.

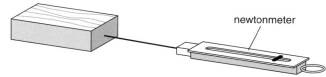

Here are his results.

Surface	Force needed/N
wooden bench	2.5
tiled floor	2
tarmac	4
carpet	3.5

i Which surface has the lowest friction?
(1 mark)

ii What could Robin do to reduce the
friction of the wooden bench? *(1 mark)*

iii Robin gives the block the same size of
push across each surface. On which surface
would the block travel the shortest distance?
Explain your answer. *(1 mark)*
CCEA Science: Single Award, Module 6, Foundation Tier, February 2008, Q4

3 a During a cycle race a cyclist of mass 60 kg
travelled at a velocity of 15 m/s on a bicycle of
mass 10 kg.

i Use the equation:

momentum = mass × velocity

to calculate the momentum at this
velocity. *(2 marks)*

ii State the units of momentum. *(1 mark)*

b Explain the terms average and instantaneous
speed. *(2 marks)*

c Explain fully, in terms of forces and their
effects, the differences between cyclists A
and B shown in the diagram. *(6 marks)*

CCEA Science: Single Award, Unit 3, Higher Tier, February 2013, Q9

19 *Radioactivity*

LEARNING OBJECTIVES

By the end of this chapter you should know and understand:

- the structure of the atom
- that some combinations of neutrons and protons are unstable and disintegrate
- what is meant by radioactivity
- that radioactive nuclei emit alpha, beta and gamma radiation
- the properties of alpha, beta and gamma radiation and how they can be stopped
- what background radioactivity is and its sources
- how to carry out simple calculations involving half-life
- the link between half-life and background activity and the time taken for a radioactive source to become safe
- ionising radiation, its uses and dangers.

▶ Structure of the atom and radioactivity

All matter is made up of tiny particles called **atoms**. Inside every atom there are three types of particle, which are **protons**, **neutrons** and **electrons** (Figure 19.1). The properties of these particles are summarised in Table 19.1.

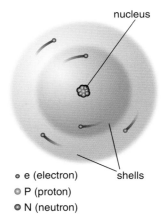

nucleus

- e (electron)
- P (proton)   shells
- N (neutron)

Figure 19.1 The structure of an atom

Table 19.1 Properties of particles

Particle	Charge	Mass	Position
proton	+1	1	nucleus
neutron	0	1	nucleus
electron	−1	1/1840	shell

Radioactive elements have atoms with large, unstable nuclei. The unstable nuclei will **disintegrate** or **decay** (split up) into smaller, more stable atoms. When this happens, the atom emits **radiation** with large unstable nuclei that contain too many protons and neutrons.

▶ Radiation

Background radiation

Radioactive material is found naturally all around us and even inside our bodies. This type of radiation is called **background radiation** with large unstable nuclei that contain too many protons and neutrons. Sources of background radiation are:

- carbon 14 – a type of carbon found inside all living organisms
- a radioactive gas called radon, emitted from granite rocks

- measurable traces of potassium contained in some foods
- waste products from nuclear power stations
- radioactive materials used in medicine in hospitals
- cosmic rays striking the Earth from space.

Types of radiation

The three types of radiation that can be emitted from radioactive nuclei are summarised in Table 19.2 and Figure 19.2.

Table 19.2 Types of radiation

Name	Description	Stopped by	Charge
alpha (α)	large, heavy, slow particles like a helium atom that has lost its two electrons	a few centimetres of air or millimetres of paper	+2
beta (β)	small, light and fast-moving electrons	a few metres of air or a few millimetres of aluminium	−1
gamma (γ)	electromagnetic radiation (invisible, fast and powerful)	a few centimetres of lead or metres of concrete	0

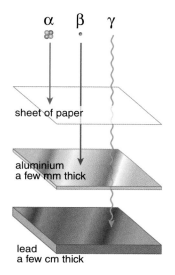

Figure 19.2 Protecting against the different types of radiation

Half-life

Radioactivity is a completely random process. We cannot say which atom in a piece of radioactive material will disintegrate next but we can count the number of disintegrations per second.

The term **half-life** is used to describe how radioactive a substance is. The half-life is the amount of time taken for half of the atoms in a piece of radioactive material to disintegrate. It is the time taken for the level of radioactivity to fall by half (Figure 19.3).

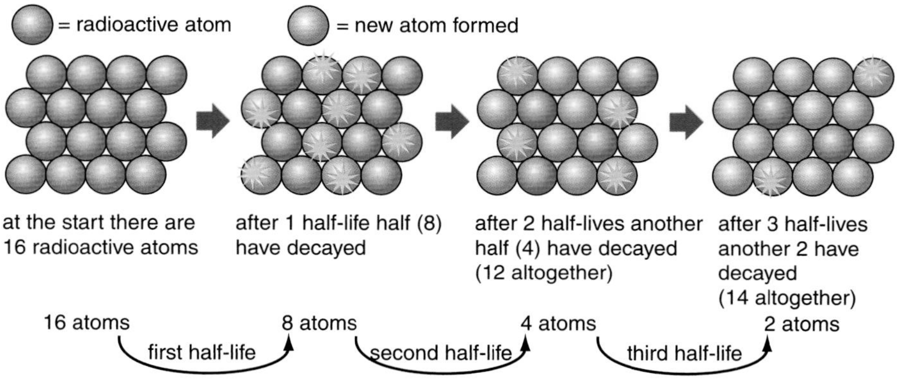

= radioactive atom   = new atom formed

at the start there are 16 radioactive atoms

after 1 half-life half (8) have decayed

after 2 half-lives another half (4) have decayed (12 altogether)

after 3 half-lives another 2 have decayed (14 altogether)

16 atoms   8 atoms   4 atoms   2 atoms
first half-life   second half-life   third half-life

Figure 19.3 Half-life

The greater the half-life of a radioactive source, the more slowly it is decaying and therefore the longer it will take to become safe. Some sources have half-lives of tens of thousands of years, so it will take a very long time indeed for these materials to become safe. But what exactly do we mean by 'become safe'?

There is no agreed answer as to what is meant by 'safe'. But, in general, a radioactive material is not considered safe if the activity around it is above background radiation. In Northern Ireland the background radiation level is about 15 disintegrations per minute.

Unit of radioactivity

The activity of a radioactive material is often measured in units called **becquerels** (Bq). One disintegration per second is 1 becquerel. So,

> ### Definition
>
> The **half-life** of a radioactive material is the time taken for its activity to fall to half of its original value. Learn this definition so that you can quote it accurately in an exam.

> ### Test yourself
>
> What fraction of a radioactive source remains undecayed after three half-lives?

if a radioactive material emits 1200 α-particles every minute, then 20 nuclei decay every second and its activity is 20 Bq.

Graphical representation

Figure 19.4 shows how the activity of a radioactive material varies with time. Notice that its activity falls from 1800 counts/minute to 900 counts/minute in 2 hours. This means its half-life is 2 hours.

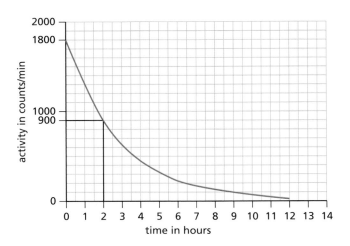

Figure 19.4 Graph of activity against time for a radioactive source

The big advantage of a graph like this is that we can use it to state the activity at any time, not just whole numbers of half-lives. For example, the activity after 3 hours (1½ half-lives) is about 640 counts/minute.

▶ EXAMPLE

Calculations of half-life

A certain radioactive material has a half-life of 5 days. When delivered to a hospital its activity is 5120 disintegrations per second. Find:

a its activity 15 days after it arrives at the hospital
b the time taken for its activity to fall to 80 disintegrations per second
c its activity 10 days before it arrived at the hospital.

Solution

Questions on half-life are best answered using a table as shown below.

a

Activity in disintegrations/second	Number of half-lives elapsed	Time in days	Comment
5120	0	0	Arrival
2560	1	5	Every half-life causes the activity to fall to half of its previous value.
1280	2	10	
640	3	15	So, the activity is 640 disintegrations per second after 15 days.

b We continue with the table to find the time taken to reach 80 disintegrations per second.

Activity in disintegrations/second	Number of half-lives elapsed	Time in days	Comment
640	3	15	Last entry in previous table.
320	4	20	Every half-life causes the activity to fall to half of its previous value.
160	5	25	
80	6	30	So, after 30 days the activity is 80 disintegrations per second.

c To find the activity 10 days before arrival, we work backwards in time.

Activity in disintegrations/second	Number of half-lives elapsed	Time in days	Comment
5120	0	0	Arrival
10240	−1	−5	The minus sign shows events before the arrival.
20480	−2	−10	So, 10 days before arrival the activity was 20480 disintegrations per second.

Dangers of radiation

When alpha (α), beta (β) and gamma (γ) radiation collide with atoms, they are most likely to hit the outer electrons, knocking them out of their orbit.

All atoms are **electrically neutral** as they have equal numbers of protons and electrons. This means that there are equal numbers of positive and negative charges. When electrons are knocked out, the atom becomes positively charged as it loses negative charge. This is illustrated in Figure 19.5.

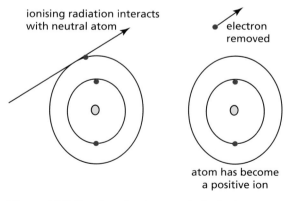

ionising radiation interacts with neutral atom

electron removed

atom has become a positive ion

Figure 19.5 Showing what is meant by ionisation

Charged atoms are called **ions** and the process of turning neutral atoms into charged ions is called **ionisation**. This is why alpha, beta and gamma radiation are also called **ionising radiation**.

When radiation ionises the molecules of living cells it causes cancers and kills healthy cells. The larger the dose of radiation, the greater the

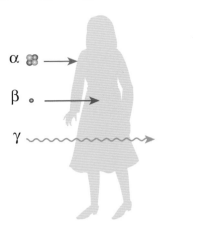

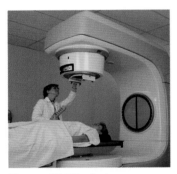

Figure 19.6 Radiation and the human body

risk. Outside the body, β and γ are more dangerous as α-radiation is blocked by the skin. Inside the body an α source causes the most damage because it is the most ionising. This is summarised in Figure 19.6.

Uses of radiation

Radiotherapy is the use of radiation to kill cancer cells, as shown in Figure 19.7. Powerful X-rays or gamma rays are targeted at the tumour, as in Figure 19.8.

The dose must be just enough to kill the cancer cells and not enough to kill the healthy cells surrounding the tumour.

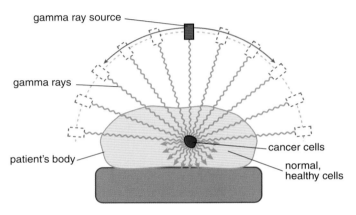

gamma ray source

gamma rays

patient's body

cancer cells

normal, healthy cells

Figure 19.8 Gamma rays can kill tumours

Figure 19.7 Radiotherapy

Gamma radiation is also used to sterilise surgical instruments. It will kill any bacteria, viruses or fungi found on them.

Gamma radiation can also be used to treat fresh food. The radiation will kill any bacteria and fungi on the food, stopping it from decaying. This means the food will stay fresher for longer, extending its shelf-life. Figure 19.9 shows strawberries that have not been treated in this way and strawberries that have been treated with gamma radiation.

Figure 19.9 Gamma rays can treat fresh food to prevent it decaying

Exam questions

1 a The graph below shows how the activity of a radioactive isotope varies with time.

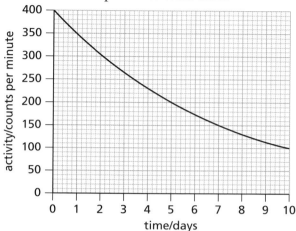

i What is the activity at 7 days? *(1 mark)*

ii Describe the trend shown by this graph. *(1 mark)*

iii Use the graph to give the half-life of this isotope. *(1 mark)*

b Explain fully why some nuclei are radioactive. *(1 mark)*

The isotope produces gamma radiation.

c Explain fully why gamma radiation can be used to treat cancer within the body. *(2 marks)*
CCEA Science: Single Award, Unit 3, Foundation Tier, February 2013, Q6

2 Radon is a naturally occurring radioactive gas. Some parts of the United Kingdom are at risk from higher levels of radon than previously thought, according to the Health Protection Agency.

a Radon gas is a source of background radiation.

i What is meant by background radiation? *(1 mark)*

ii Explain fully why someone living in an area with a high concentration of radon could be concerned about their health. *(1 mark)*

iii Why is radon considered more dangerous than solid radioactive materials like uranium? *(1 mark)*

b Gamma radiation can be used to check for leaks in water pipes.

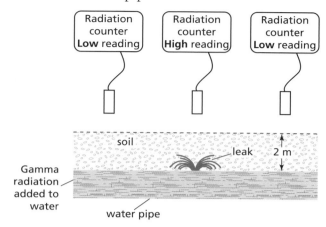

Explain fully why gamma radiation is the best source to use. *(2 marks)*
CCEA Science: Single Award, Unit 3 Physics Foundation, May 2013, Q1 (amended)

3 The diagram below shows how a radioactive source is used to monitor the thickness of an aluminium sheet during manufacture. If the thickness of the aluminium sheet changes, the force applied to the rollers will adjust to maintain the correct thickness.

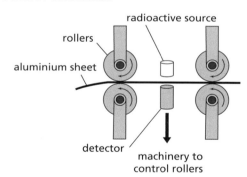

a Beta is the best type of radiation to use as a source. With reference to the penetration properties of all types (alpha, beta and gamma) explain fully why beta is the best.

In this question you will be assessed on your written communication skills including the use of specialist science terms. *(6 marks)*

b Radiation is used to kill bacteria and fungi found in fresh food to stop decay. The radiation is applied after packaging. The table below gives details of some isotopes.

Isotope	Type of radiation emitted	Half-life
radon-220	alpha	54.5 seconds
polonium-210	alpha	138 days
bismuth-83	beta	61 minutes
hydrogen-3	beta	12 years
technetium-99	gamma	6 hours
cobalt-60	gamma	5 years

Which isotope would be best for a food producer to use with a packet of fresh strawberries? Explain your answer. *(3 marks)*

CCEA Science: Single Award, Unit 3, Foundation Tier, March 2012, Q8

4 a A radioactive atom of uranium decays by emitting a beta (β) particle. From what part of the atom does the beta (β) particle come?
(1 mark)

b Alpha radiation (α), beta radiation (β) and gamma radiation (γ) are all emitted by radioactive materials.

Copy and complete the table below by writing a description of each type of radiation in the spaces that are blank. *(3 marks)*

Radiation	Description
alpha (α)	
beta (β)	
gamma (γ)	

c A radioactive source is known to emit two types of radiation. To find out which types, the apparatus shown below was set up. Three different materials were, in turn, placed between the source and the detector. The results are shown in the table.

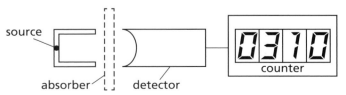

	Number of counts per minute
no material present	600
thin sheet of paper	310
aluminium 1 cm thick	308
lead 1 cm thick	145

Which radiations did the source emit? Explain your answer fully. *(6 marks)*

d The results of the experiment in part **c** have been adjusted to allow for the background radiation. State the meaning of the term background radiation. *(1 mark)*

CCEA Science: Double Award, Unit 3, Specimen Assessment materials, Foundation Tier, 2011, Q3 (part)

5 Radioactive substances emit up to three types of radiations, alpha, beta and gamma. These radiations can travel different distances in air. A source of radiation is placed at one end of a laboratory bench. A detector is placed at points A, B and C in turn.

a i At which point, A, B or C, will the detector record only gamma radiation? *(1 mark)*

ii At which point, A, B or C, will the detector record alpha, beta and gamma radiation? *(1 mark)*

iii At which point, A, B or C, will the detector record only beta and gamma radiation? *(1 mark)*

b i When alpha or beta particles pass through air they collide with the air molecules, causing them to become charged. What is the name of this process? *(1 mark)*

ii How do the air molecules become charged? *(1 mark)*

c The half-life of a radioactive source is a measure of how quickly it decays. What do we mean by 'half-life'? *(2 marks)*

CCEA Science: Double Award, Unit 3, Higher Tier, November 2012, Q1 (part)

20 The Earth in space

LEARNING OBJECTIVES

By the end of this chapter you should know and understand:

- the structure of our Solar System
- the heliocentric and geocentric models of our Solar System
- how gravitational force varies on different planets and how this can affect weight
- the evidence that asteroids have collided with Earth in the past
- the processes that lead to star formation
- the evidence that the galaxies are moving away from each other
- the difficulties of inter-stellar space travel
- that the further away the galaxies are, the faster they are moving apart
- what is meant by red-shift and its significance
- that the Universe is expanding
- what scientists mean by Big Bang Theory and Steady State Theory.

Our **Solar System** is made up of one **star** called the Sun, and eight **planets** called Mercury, Venus, Earth, Mars, Jupiter, Saturn, Uranus, and Neptune. It also includes comets, asteroids, many moons and smaller objects called meteoroids.

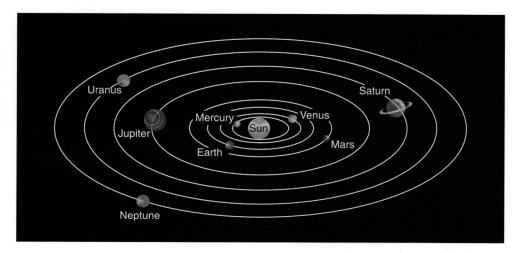

Figure 20.1 Our Solar System (not to scale)

The Sun is at the centre of our Solar System. Planets travel around the Sun in paths called **orbits**. The four inner planets (Mercury, Venus, Earth and Mars) orbit the Sun in almost circular paths. The outer planets have elliptical orbits, shaped roughly like the side view of a rugby ball. All the planets travel around the Sun in the same direction and in the same plane.

Table 20.1 summarises information about the planets in our Solar System.

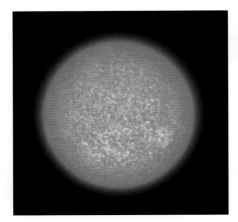

Figure 20.2 The Sun is a star

Table 20.1 The planets in our Solar System

Planet	Diameter compared to Earth	Average distance from Sun compared to Earth	Time to orbit Sun compared to Earth year
Mercury	0.4	0.4	0.2
Venus	0.9	0.7	0.6
Earth	1.0	1.0	1.0
Mars	0.5	1.5	1.9
Jupiter	11.2	5.2	12.0
Saturn	9.4	9.5	29.0
Uranus	4.1	20.1	84.0
Neptune	3.9	30.1	165.0

The Sun, as shown in Figure 20.2, is a star. It is continually producing heat and light, through the **nuclear fusion** of hydrogen to form helium. Only stars produce their own light. All other bodies reflect light.

Planets orbit the Sun. They are kept in orbit by the **gravitational attraction** of the Sun. **Gravity** is the force of attraction that exists between all objects. The bigger the mass of the objects, the greater the gravitational force between them.

Some of the planets have moons that orbit them (Figure 20.3). Moons are held in orbit by gravity.

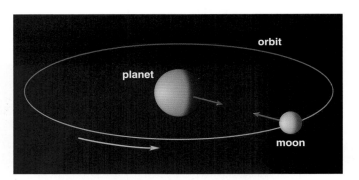

Figure 20.3 A moon orbiting a planet

Figure 20.4 A comet

Comets are large chunks of frozen rock covered by huge quantities of frozen water and gases. They orbit the Sun, just like planets, but have orbits that are much more elliptical than that of a planet. They can only be seen when they pass close to the Sun and its energy causes some of the frozen gases and water to vaporise, creating the comet's tail, as shown in Figure 20.4.

Asteroids are large chunks of rock that orbit the Sun. Most are found in the asteroid belt between Mars and Jupiter. Occasionally an asteroid is knocked out of its orbit and comes close to Earth, bringing the chance of a collision.

Large craters on the Earth's surface provide evidence that these collisions have happened in the past. Some scientists think that an Earth–asteroid collision was responsible for the extinction of the dinosaurs 65 million years ago.

▶ Gravity and weight

Gravity is the force responsible for keeping:

- planets, comets and asteroids orbiting the Sun
- moons orbiting the planets
- us stuck on the ground, as it stops us floating away.

Gravity is the force of attraction that exists between all objects. It depends on the mass of the two objects and the distance between them. The bigger an object is, the larger the force of gravity it exerts.

The force of gravity on any object is called its **weight**. Therefore, although our bodies would stay the same, if we could go to other planets our weight would change. Table 20.2 shows that the bigger the planet, the more we would weigh. This effect can be noticed very clearly in any pictures of the Moon-landing astronauts. The Moon is about six times smaller than Earth and so the astronauts weighed six times less on the Moon. This allowed them to bounce around on the Moon even though they had extremely heavy suits and packs.

Table 20.2 Weights on different planets

Planet	Weight of a kilogram mass/newtons
Mercury	3.8
Venus	9.0
Earth	9.8
Mars	3.7
Jupiter	26
Saturn	12
Uranus	9.1
Neptune	12

Figure 20.5 An astronaut in space

The effect of gravity decreases as distance between objects increases. The further we are from a planet, the less the force of gravity. This is why astronauts can experience weightlessness when they get far enough away from Earth (Figure 20.5).

▶ Geocentric and heliocentric models of the Solar System

Early humans saw the Sun, the moon and some stars appear to move across the sky. Therefore it was widely believed that Earth was at the centre of the Universe and that all the other planets, moons and even the stars orbited the Earth. This was called the **geocentric model**. It was the common view until the mid-sixteenth century.

The geocentric model had three major problems. It could not explain:

- the apparent 'looping' (retrograde motion) of some planets like Jupiter (see Figure 20.6)
- why at some times Venus is closer to Earth than Mars, so it appears brighter, but at other times Venus is further away than Mars and appears less bright
- why Venus and Mercury show phases (appear as crescent shapes), just as our moon does.

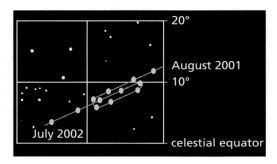

Figure 20.6 This simulation shows Jupiter's retrograde loop during 2001 and 2002. The position of Jupiter is marked at one-month intervals

Based on observations of the planets, Nicolaus Copernicus put forward the **heliocentric model**. This placed the Sun at the centre of the Solar System and put the planets in the same order that we know today to be correct. Figure 20.7 shows a diagram of this model.

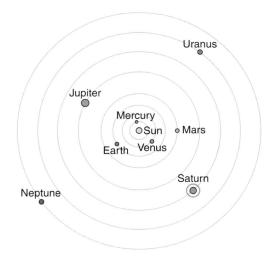

Figure 20.7 The heliocentric model of the Solar System (not to scale)

▶ Star formation

Stars form when a cloud of hydrogen, called a **stellar nebula**, comes together because of gravity. As these clouds become more and more dense, they start to spiral inwards and the temperature rises enormously. Gravity eventually compresses the hydrogen so much that the temperature reaches about 15 million °C. At this temperature, **nuclear fusion** reactions start and a star is born. The energy from the nuclear fusion is emitted as light and other radiation.

At the same time, other clouds of gas and dust come together that do not have enough material for the temperature to reach 15 million °C. Such gas and dust clouds are called **planetary nebulas**. They eventually become planets as a result of gravitational attraction. This clumping together of gas and dust is called **accretion**. The presence of a massive star may cause the new planets to become trapped in orbit. Since the gas and dust clouds originally spiralled in the same direction, so the planets all orbit the star in same way. They all go clockwise around the star or they all go anti-clockwise.

▶ Red-shift and the expanding Universe

Each colour has a wavelength associated with it. Colours at the red end of the spectrum have wavelengths around 700 nm. Colours in the violet region have wavelengths around 450 nm. (1 nm = 1×10^{-9} m = 1 billionth of a metre.) So, the visible spectrum consists of all those electromagnetic waves with a wavelength between about 450 nm and about 700 nm.

Our Sun contains hydrogen. We know this because there are black lines in the spectrum of the light from the Sun where the hydrogen atoms have absorbed light. The pattern of black lines is called the **absorption spectrum** for hydrogen. Physicists have identified over 50 different elements in it, but hydrogen and helium are by far the most common.

What happens when we look at the light from the stars in distant galaxies? Do we get the same pattern as we do from the Sun? The answer is that the pattern is the same, but it is shifted towards the red end of the spectrum. This is called **red-shift**.

If there is a red-shift in the light from another galaxy, this tells us that the source is moving away from us. The fact that we always get red-shift from distant galaxies tells us that the galaxies are all moving away from us. This is what we mean when we say the Universe is expanding.

Figure 20.8 The Sagittarius nebula

Figure 20.9 shows the calcium absorption spectra for the Sun and the galaxies Nubecula and Leo. The red-shift tells us that these galaxies are moving away from us. Leo has the greater red-shift, so it is moving away from us faster than Nubecula.

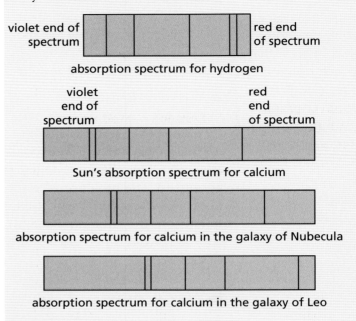

Figure 20.9 Red-shift

In 1929 an American physicist called Edwin Hubble made an important discovery. He found that the bigger the red-shift, the further away the galaxy is from Earth. This means that the most distant galaxies are also moving away from our galaxy, the Milky Way, at the greatest speed (Figure 20.10).

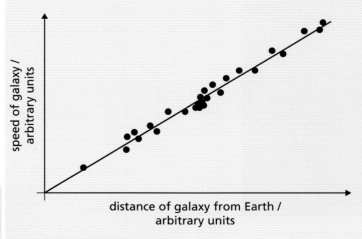

Figure 20.10 Graph showing Hubble's Law

Test yourself

What would you conclude if the light from a star in a distant galaxy was violet-shifted?

How far away are these other galaxies?

There are about 30 galaxies in the group that contains the Milky Way. The nearest is about 2.6 million light years away. The furthest galaxy from the Milky Way is over 13 billion light years away.

▶ *EXAMPLE 1*

It takes light 500 seconds to travel from the Sun to the Earth. Estimate the distance between the Sun and the Earth. Give your answer in km.

Distance = speed × time

$$= 300\,000\,000\,\text{m/s} \times 500\,\text{s}$$

$$= 150\,000\,000\,000\,\text{m} = 150\,000\,000\,\text{km}$$

▶ Origin of the Universe

There are two major scientific theories that try to explain the origin of the Universe. One is called the **Steady State Theory** and the other is the **Big Bang Theory**.

According to the Steady State Theory, new matter is continuously created as the Universe expands. It claims that the Universe had no beginning and will have no end. It also says that the Universe we see today is very much the same as it has always been. Most physicists are unhappy about accepting Steady State Theory because it suggests that the Law of Conservation of Energy is not always true. As a result, very few scientists support Steady State Theory today.

The Big Bang Theory is the generally accepted scientific theory about the origin of the Universe. The idea was first put forward by Georges Lemaitre to explain why distant galaxies are travelling away from us at great speeds (first discovered by Hubble using red-shift). It states that the Universe was created around 14 billion years ago from a tiny point, which physicists call a '**singularity**'. From this singularity there was a cosmic explosion that hurled matter and energy in all directions. This explosion was the birth of time, energy and matter.

Note

Physicists today believe that space itself is expanding. In other words, the distance between galaxies is getting bigger and bigger. If this was to continue forever, the Universe would finish in a Big Freeze as it grew colder and colder.

Although the Big Bang Theory is widely accepted today, it leaves some questions unanswered. What will happen to the Universe in the future? Whether or not the Universe keeps on expanding depends on the amount of matter it contains. This is one reason why astronomers get excited at the prospect of discovering '**dark matter**'. Dark matter is material that we cannot observe directly, but whose presence would confirm the Big Bang Theory and tell us whether the Universe will keep expanding forever or eventually begin to get smaller.

<u>Note</u>

A star may have its own solar system. This will include the star and the planets, asteroids and comets that orbit it.

Figure 20.11 The Milky Way

▶ Galaxies

Galaxies contain millions of stars and therefore millions of solar systems. Figure 20.11 shows an artist's impression of the Milky Way. It is just one of millions of galaxies in the Universe.

▶ Travel to distant planets

The next nearest star to Earth (other than the Sun) is Proxima Centauri. It is 4.2 light years away. This huge distance makes travel to planets outside our Solar System very unlikely. The main problems are:

- the journey would last many generations, so people leaving Earth would die in space
- it would be difficult to carry enough fuel, food, water and oxygen to get there.

Exam questions

1 a The diagram below shows the model of the Solar System used by the ancient Greeks.

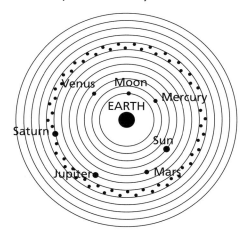

Name this model of the Solar System and give **two** differences between this model and the current model. *(3 marks)*

b The table gives the speeds of galaxies in our Universe at different distances from Earth.

Galaxy	Distance from Earth/tens of millions of light years	Speed away from Earth/ thousands of km/s
A	5	1
B	65	15
C	95	22
D	170	39
E	260	61

i Explain fully how the information in the table provides evidence for the Big Bang theory. *(3 marks)*

ii Give **one** other piece of evidence that supports the Big Bang theory. *(1 mark)*

iii How many years ago did the Big Bang occur? *(1 mark)*

iv Explain the meaning of the term 'light year'. *(2 marks)*

CCEA Science: Single Award, Unit 3, Higher Tier, February 2013, Q7

2 a The diagram below shows the Sun and its eight planets.

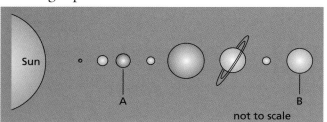

i Name the planets labelled A and B. *(2 marks)*

ii Copy and complete the following sentence. The Sun and its planets are known as the _____ *(1 mark)*

b Copy and complete the following sentences. Choose from:

moon	star	galaxy	planet

A _____ is a huge collection of stars.
A _____ is an object that orbits a planet.
A _____ is an object that orbits a star. *(3 marks)*

c Copy the following sentences and place a tick next to the statement to describe the movement, if any, of the galaxies.
They are not moving.
Staying the same distance apart.
Moving away from each other. *(1 mark)*

CCEA Science: Single Award, Unit 3 Physics Foundation, May 2013, Q7

3 a The picture shows an impact crater in Arizona.

i Name the type of object which collided with the Earth to make craters like this. *(1 mark)*

ii The object which made this crater was believed to be 46 m wide. Choose two statements which would be **true** if a much larger object collided with the Earth.
A The amount of sunlight reaching the Earth's surface would be reduced.
B The Earth's temperature would stay the same.
C Food crops will not be affected.
D Animal and plant species could become extinct.
E The amount of sunlight reaching the Earth's surface would be increased. *(2 marks)*

b Use the pictures to help explain how a star is formed. *(3 marks)*

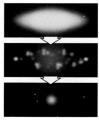

CCEA Science: Single Award, Module 6, Foundation Tier, November 2007, Q1

Index